Rainforest Warriors

PENNSYLVANIA STUDIES IN HUMAN RIGHTS

Bert B. Lockwood, Jr., *Series Editor*

A complete list of books in the
series is available from the publisher.

Rainforest Warriors

Human Rights on Trial

Richard Price

UNIVERSITY OF PENNSYLVANIA PRESS

PHILADELPHIA · OXFORD

Published by
University of Pennsylvania Press
Philadelphia, Pennsylvania 19104-4112

www.upenn.edu/pennpress

Printed in the United States of America
on acid-free paper

10 9 8 7 6 5 4 3 2 1

Library of Congress Cataloging-in-Publication Data

Price, Richard, 1941–
  Rainforest warriors : human rights on trial / Richard Price.
    p. cm. — (Pennsylvania studies in human rights)
  Includes bibliographical references.
  ISBN 978-0-8122-4300-0 (hardcover : acid-free paper)
  1. Saramacca (Surinamese people)—Civil rights. 2. Saramacca (Surinamese people)—Legal status, laws, etc. 3. Human rights—Suriname. I. Title.
  F2431.S27P728 2011
  323.1196—dc22 2010022420

Contents

Preface

This book is about a people, their threatened rainforest, and their successful attempt to harness international human rights legislation in their fight to protect their way of life. It is part of a larger story that is unfolding all over the globe. It is meant to put on record a signal example, in the hope that it may help those engaged in similar battles elsewhere. It is also intended to help readers appreciate some of the often-hidden forces, and possibilities, shaping today's world.

A 2009 news article outlines the situation in Latin America:

> In Ecuador, the Shuar are blocking highways to defend their hunting grounds. In Chile, the Mapuche are occupying ranches to pressure for land, schools and clinics. In Bolivia, a new constitution gives the country's 36 indigenous peoples the right to self-rule.... The threats to Indian land have grown in recent years. With shrinking global oil reserves and growing demands for minerals and timber, oil and mining concerns are joining loggers in encroaching on traditional Indian lands.

The Indian "revolt," continues the writer, is "rippling up and down the Andes."[1] But that revolt—the insistence on long-ignored human rights—is also ongoing among non-Indians facing similar threats.

Saramaka Maroons, the descendants of self-liberated African slaves who live in the rainforest of the Republic of Suriname, have been leading their own campaign for many years.[2] In 2008, when the Inter-American Court of Human Rights delivered a landmark judgment in their favor, their efforts were thrust into the international spotlight. Two leaders of their struggle, Saramaka Headcaptain Wazen Eduards and Saramaka law student Hugo Jabini, were awarded the Goldman Environmental Prize (often referred to as the environmental Nobel Prize), under the banner of "A New Precedent for Indigenous and Tribal Peoples." They were cited for "having guaranteed territorial rights not just for the Saramaka, but for all of the Maroons and indigenous people.... In addition, because the case was settled by the binding Inter-American Court, Eduards and Jabini changed international jurisprudence so that free, prior and informed consent will be required for major development projects throughout the Americas. They saved not only their communities' 9,000 square kilometers of forest, but strengthened the possibility of saving countless more."[3]

Suriname has the highest proportion of rainforest within its national territory, and the most forest per person, of any country in the world.[4] This book tells the story of the Saramakas' battle to retain control of their own piece of that forest.

Africans Discover America

Land, Spirits, Power

There are no useless plants, only uninformed people.
Tooy Alexander, Saramaka healer

In the middle of the seventeenth century, Suriname, in northeastern South America, formed part of a vast forested area that stretched from the Atlantic to the Andes, the home of countless indigenous peoples who lived by hunting, fishing, and gardening.[1] The first European colonists, Englishmen from Barbados who sailed over with their African slaves in 1651, soon ceded the area to the Dutch (in the famous 1667 swap in which the Dutch traded Manhattan to the English in return for Suriname), and the colony became one of the most profitable of all slave plantation societies in the Americas. By the end of the century, some 8,000 African slaves were laboring for 800 Europeans—most of the indigenous population had simply retreated into the hinterlands.

Before the end of the seventeenth century, as more and more enslaved Africans were landed in the colony, significant numbers began to escape into the surrounding rainforest. The colonists fought back, sending countless militias in pursuit of the runaways and handing out gruesome punishments for recaptured slaves—hamstringing, amputation of limbs, and a variety of deaths by torture. In 1730, for example, after two military expeditions against the nascent group of Saramakas captured a number of villagers, the criminal court meted out the following sentences:

The Negro Joosie shall be hanged from the gibbet by an Iron Hook through his ribs, until dead; his head shall then be severed and displayed on a stake by the riverbank, remaining to be picked over by birds of prey. As for the Negroes Wierrie and Manbote, they shall be bound to a stake and roasted alive over a slow fire, while being

"A Negro hung alive by the Ribs to a Gallows." Engraving by William Blake after a drawing by John Gabriel Stedman, based on an eyewitness account from 1773.

tortured with glowing Tongs. The Negro girls, Lucretia, Ambira, Aga, Gomba, Marie, and Victoria will be tied to a Cross, to be broken alive, and then their heads severed, to be exposed by the riverbank on stakes. The Negro girls Diana and Christina shall be beheaded with an axe, and their heads exposed on poles by the riverbank.[2]

But the planters' expeditions rarely met with success, for the Saramakas had established and protected their settlements with great ingenuity and had become expert at all aspects of guerrilla warfare. By the late 1740s, the colonists were finding the expense overwhelming, with typical expeditions costing more than 100,000 guilders and having to traverse (as one document put it) "forty mountains and sixty creeks" before reaching the Saramakas' hidden villages, deep in the rainforest. It had also become clear to the colonists that

"March thro' a swamp or, Marsh in Terra firma." Engraving by William Blake after a drawing by John Gabriel Stedman.

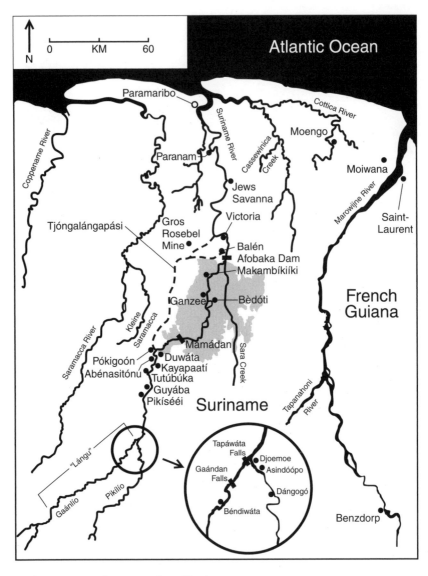

Suriname: some places mentioned in the text.

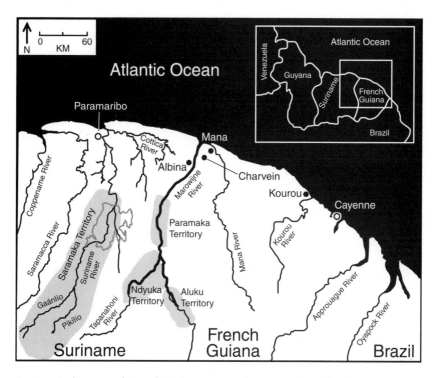

Eastern Suriname and French Guiana: some places mentioned in the text.

the expeditions themselves (which included slaves) were contributing to further marronage, by making known to the slaves both the escape routes from the plantations and the locations of Saramaka villages.

By this time, Suriname had developed into a flourishing plantation colony and had earned a solid reputation, even among such rivals as Jamaica and Saint-Domingue, for its heights of planter opulence and depths of slave misery. Indeed, one eighteenth-century historian called it "the envy of all the others in the Americas."[3] In the mid-eighteenth century, Suriname was said to be producing more revenue and consuming more imported manufactured goods, per capita, than any other Caribbean colony.[4] Planters were routinely served at table by nearly nude house slaves, who also fanned them during their naps (and sometimes all night long), dressed and undressed them each morning and evening, bathed their children in imported wine, and performed other similar tasks.[5]

Under these circumstances, the colonists decided that the increasingly costly warfare made little sense, and they came to a decision, during the late 1740s, to sue their former slaves for permanent peace. After several great battles between Saramakas and colonial armies during the 1750s, a peace treaty was at last negotiated.

On September 19, 1762, in the presence of several hundred Saramaka men, including their headmen, and representatives of the Dutch colonial government, the peace agreement was finally sealed.[6] The Dutch negotiator wrote, "They took earth and water, and each chief placed a child or youth from his own family in front of him, calling on God Above and the Earth as witnesses. Then they swore, with considerable ceremony, that anyone who violated any of the articles would perish with his people, giving a little of the mixture to the youths to consume."[7]

Saramakas remember how their ancestors cut their wrists and had the whites do the same, mixing their blood in a calabash with rum and sacred white clay, and each drinking a draft, while swearing that the treaty would hold forevermore. The whites, too, were pleased with the outcome. After the negotiators had returned to the capital, a day of public thanksgiving was proclaimed in all the churches for 5 December, to celebrate the signing of the Saramaka peace and "to ask Him to assure that the Peace be permanent and prosperous."[8]

From the perspective of Saramakas, the treaty of 1762 is a sacred foundational document that crowns their victory after nearly a century of war.[9] It granted them their freedom (while slavery on the coast would continue for another hundred years), recognized their territory, recognized their political leaders, permitted large groups of their men to come to the coast with timber and other goods for trade, and granted them annual or biannual tribute from the whites—everything from precisely specified quantities of guns and gunpowder to tools, cloth, pots, salt, and needles.[10]

Since the treaty, the Saramakas have had a paramount chief (*gaamá*), recognized by the city government, as well as a series of recognized headmen or captains (*kabitêni*) and assistant headmen. Traditionally, the role of these officials in political and social control was exercised in a context replete with oracles, spirit possession, and other forms of divination. Since the 1960s, the national government of Suriname has been attempting to intervene more frequently in Saramaka affairs—it also pays political officials nominal salaries—and the sacred base of these officials' power is very gradually being eroded. All these political offices remain the property of matrilineal clans (*lôs*), as they have been since runaway days.

Council meetings (*kuútus*) and divination sessions provide the arena for the resolution of social problems. *Kuútus* may involve the men of a clan, a lineage, a village, or all of Saramaka, and they treat problems ranging from conflicts concerning marriage or child fosterage to land disputes, political succession, or serious crimes. These same problems, in addition to illness and other kinds of misfortune, are routinely interpreted through various kinds of divination as well. In all cases, consensus is found through negotiation, often with gods and ancestors playing a major role. Saramaka law is well developed. Guilty parties are usually required to pay for their misdeeds with material offerings to the lineage of the offended person. In the eighteenth century, people found guilty of witchcraft were sometimes burned at the stake. Today, men caught *in flagrante delicto* with the wife of another man are either beaten by the husband's kinsmen or made to pay them a fine. Aside from adultery disputes—which sometimes mobilize a full canoe-load of men seeking revenge in a public fistfight—intra-Saramaka conflict rarely surpasses the level of personal relations.

*   *   *

The ancestors of today's Saramaka Maroons hailed from a large number of West and Central African societies, situated primarily in the Bight of Benin (also known as the Slave Coast), in West-Central Africa, and, to a lesser extent, in the Gold Coast.[11] They spoke a large number of languages and came from scores of different states and polities that, in many cases, were at war with one another. Once landed in Suriname, each shipload of captives was further dispersed by the planters, who chose their purchases with the intent to separate people who might have known each other or spoken the same language. Combined with a firm policy not to separate slave families when plantations were sold—the slaves in Suriname were considered to belong to the soil—the primary identity of enslaved Africans rapidly shifted from their African origins to their plantation community, where they now had family and comrades, and where they had already begun to bury their dead. On the plantations (as among Saramakas today), the term for "best friend" was *máti*, which derived from "shipmate." And the Africans who lived together on a particular plantation soon began calling one another *síbi*, which had originated as a term of address for those who had shared passage on the same ship.

Within the earliest decades of the African presence in Suriname, the slaves had developed a new creole language (Sranan-tongo and, on the largely Jewish Suriname River plantations, the closely related Dju-tongo), the core of a new religion, and much else. The striking "non-Europeanness" of this early cultural synthesis, when compared to developments in other parts of the Americas, can be explained in part by the unusually high ratio of Africans to Europeans in the colony—more than 25:1 for much of the eighteenth century, with figures ranging up to 65:1 in the plantation districts. On Suriname plantations, it was in large part recently arrived Africans (rather than Europeans) who effected the process of creolization, of building a new culture and society. In Suriname, creolization was built on a diversity of African heritages, with far less input from European and Amerindian sources. By the time the ancestors of the Saramakas escaped into the forest during the late seventeenth and early eighteenth centuries, they carried with them the seeds of a new cultural system.

The early bands of runaways confronted complex challenges. Seeking refuge in a harsh and hostile environment, they were faced with the task of creating a society and culture even as they were being pursued by colonial troops bent on the destruction of their communities. Originally organized as groups that had their origins on a single plantation, they expanded, picking up new runaways over time. Most such groups retained the name of their plantation as a collective identity—Matjáu people from the plantation of Imanuël Machado on the Cassewinica Creek, Nasí people from the Nassy family plantations at Jews Savanna, Dómbi people from the Suriname River plantations owned by Dominee Basseliers, and so forth. These groups passed on membership through the female line, becoming the matrilineal clans (lôs) that remain the primary identitarian and landholding groups within the Saramaka nation today. Each Saramaka is a member of only one lô, and each lô owns its distinctive territory along the river—originally staked out as the groups moved upstream in runaway days—and has other, usually ritual, possessions that are unique and powerful.

In the beginning, local indigenous people taught the ancestors of the Saramakas a good deal about gardening, hunting, and fishing, both while they served as slaves together on plantations and after the Africans escaped. Much of Saramaka material culture and horticultural techniques—everything connected with the growing and complex processing of cassava, many local fishing and hunting methods, the now-obsolete art of hammock-weaving, the fabrication of calabash containers, and certain kinds of basketry and pottery-making—was learned from indigenous people during the early years of cohabitation. Yet few religious, artistic, or ideological traces of Suriname's Amerindian cultures can be found among Saramakas. The indigenous people who came to live with them—mainly women kidnapped by Saramaka men and integrated into the group—shared their environmental and technical knowledge, which early Saramakas appropriated gratefully.

The adaptation that the early Maroons made to their new environment was rapid and wide-ranging. In the 1770s, John Gabriel Stedman, a Scottish mercenary engaged by the planters to fight against the Cottica rebels (the ancestors of today's Aluku Maroons) expressed his admiration for the environmental knowledge possessed by his Maroon adversaries:

> In a State of *Tranquility* they Seemed as they had Said to us [to] Want for Nothing—Being Plump and Fat at Least Such we found those that had been Shot—For instance *Game* and *fish* they Catch in Great Abundance by Artificial Traps and Springs, And Which they Preserve by Barbacuing, While with *Rice, Cassava, Yams, Plantains,* and so on, theyr fields are ever over Stoked—*Salt* they make with the Ashes of the Palm trees like the *Gentoos* in the East indies—Or Use Red Pepper. We even Discovered Concealed near the Trunk of an Old Tree a Case *Bottle* With Excellent *Butter* Which they the Rangers told me they Made by melting and Clarifying the fat of the Palm-tree Worms And Which fully Supplied the Above ingredient While I absolutely found it more Delicious—The *Pistachio* or pinda nuts they Also Convert in Butter, by their Oily Substance & Frequently use them in their Broths—The *Palm tree Wine* they are never in Want of, And which they make by Cutting Deep insitions of a Foot Over Square in the fallen trunk, where the Joice being Gathered it soon ferments by the Heat of the Sun, When it is not only a Cool and Agreeable Beveridge but Strong Sufficient to intoxicate—and Soap they have from the dwarf aloes. To Build their *Houses* the Manicole or Pinda Tree Answers the Purpose, theyr *Pots* they Fabricate with Clay found near their Dwellings While the *Gourd* or Calebas tree gives them Cups &c the Silk Grass Plant and Maureecee tree Provides them in *Hammocks* And even a kind of *Caps* Grow Natural upon the Palm trees as Well as *Brooms*—The Various kinds of Nebees Supply the Want of *Ropes, fuel* for fire they have for the Cutting, While a Wood call'd *Bee Bee* Serves for Tinder to Light it by Rubbing two Pieces on each Other,

And Which by its Elasticity Makes *Excellent* Corks—Neyther Do they
Want *Candles*, being well Provided with Fat and Oil While the Bees
Also Afford them *Wax*, And a Great Deal of Excellent *Honey*.[12]

Since the beginning, the Saramaka economy has been based on the full
and imaginative exploitation of this same forest environment—supplemented,
at first, by men's wartime raids on coastal plantations to bring back selected
Western goods; then, after the peace treaty, by trading trips to the coast and,
especially after general emancipation in 1863, by periodic work trips to earn
money to buy such goods. But for subsistence, Saramakas continue to depend
on shifting (swidden) horticulture, hunting, and fishing, supplemented by
wild forest products such as palm nuts and a few key imports such as salt.

* * *

The great bulk of the people who, once in the forest, became known as
Saramakas, escaped from Suriname's plantations between 1690 and 1712.
With very rare exceptions, they had been born in Africa. Most were men and
most were young, still in their teens or twenties. Most had spent little time in
slavery, more often months than years. By the time of their escapes, however,
most spoke Dju-tongo (or Sranan-tongo), which they then quickly developed
into their own distinctive language, Saramaccan. As they faced the challenge
of building institutions—political, family, religious—while waging war and
trying to survive in an unfamiliar and hostile environment, they drew on
the immense riches of their African pasts, though their relative youth meant
that much of the esoteric and specialized knowledge of their homelands was
not available to them. Leadership drew authority not only from personal
charisma and knowledge but also from divination, which encouraged the
communal negotiation of developing institutions. The runaways, fighting
for their individual and collective survival, had strong incentives for rapid
nation-building.

When twentieth-century Saramakas narrate their people's history, they
embed it in their understandings about interactions between the worlds of
humans, nature, and spiritual forces. For modern Saramakas, the key process
was one of discovery. They recount, for example, how, as their early ancestors
prepared their fields for planting, they encountered for the first time local
forest spirits and snake spirits and had to learn, by trial and error, to befriend
and pacify them and integrate them into their understanding of the spiritual

landscape of their new home. And they tell how newfound gods of war joined those remembered from across the waters in protecting and spurring on Saramaka raiders when they attacked plantations to obtain guns, pots, and axes, and to liberate their brothers and, particularly, sisters still in bondage. Each of these many incidents is highly localized by Saramakas. Each took place in a particular piece of the forest, which is marked forevermore, for their descendants, by what happened there on that day. The forest thus becomes personalized over time. The once-unfamiliar rainforest gradually became an intimate part of Saramaka life and a central repository of their collective history.

As one example among thousands that knowledgeable Saramakas could give, I cite a powerful "First-Time" story[13] in which an Amerindian kills a Saramaka—a Lángu-clan ancestor named Makambí, who fought the whites in a fierce battle near Victoria that I can date to 1753. This version was told to me in 2003 by Tooy Alexander, a Lángu-clan descendant of the protagonists. Note the specificity of the geographical markers, and the relationship of history and the forest.

> Antamá's brother Makambí went off to fight at Victoria. He and Bákisipámbo [another Lángu leader], Kwakú, and Kwadjaní [two leaders of the Nasí clan]. They had made a camp at Gaán Paatí. (It was near the railhead at Kabel. You pass Makambíkiíki landing, before you get to Wátjibásu, on the east side, that's where Makambí and Bákisi and Kwakú lived. That's where they left to walk on the footpath to go fight at Victoria.) After they had fought for a time, Kwakú and Bákisi called Makambí and said "Let's go, we're tuckered out." Makambí said "It's not time to be tuckered out yet." Three times they called him to leave. Three times he said no. So, they left him there to continue fighting. That's when the Indian hidden up in a tree shot him with an arrow! So, he took the arrow and yanked it out but his guts poured out too. He bent over and shoved his guts back in with his fingers. He left Victoria and went up Company Creek and across to Makambí Creek and went up it until he got to a stone called Tósu-gbéne-gbéne. When he got there, Kwakú and Bákisi were already resting at their camp at Gaán Paatí. Makambí couldn't go on, so he lay down on the stone. He began snoring there. The others heard him and went all the way to him. He died just as they arrived. They buried him there in a cave. That place had been Nasí-clan territory but it became Lángu's. And that's why it's called Makambíkiíki [Makambí Creek].

This kind of precise encoding of history in the Saramaka landscape—the knowledge that the land around this creek belongs to the Lángu clan because of the heroic death of one of its forefathers on a particular, named boulder there—is typical of the way Saramaka history is tied in with the territory granted them in the treaty of 1762.

*   *   *

One day in 2005, Tooy reflected on what his ancestors had brought over on the slave ships from Africa: "When the Old Ones came out from Africa, they couldn't bring their *óbia* [magical] pots and stools—but they knew how to summon their gods and have them make new ones on this side. They no longer had the original pots or stools but they carried the knowledge in their hearts."

What Tooy's ancestors were in most cases *not* able to bring with them on the ships seems clear enough: in addition to "*óbia* pots and stools" (and other material objects), what couldn't cross the ocean were most of the traditional African institutions themselves.[14] Members of kingdoms and villages of differing status came, but different status systems could not. Priests and priestesses arrived, but priesthoods and temples had to be left behind. Princes and princesses crossed the ocean, but courts and monarchies could not. Commanders and foot soldiers came, but armies could not.

Yet immense quantities of knowledge, information, and belief were transported in the hearts and minds of the captive Africans. Moreover, even though they came from different ethnic and linguistic groups and were rarely in a position to carry on specific cultural traditions from their home societies, these people shared a number of cultural orientations that, from a broad comparative perspective, characterized most West and Central African societies. And these shared cultural orientations further encouraged the building of new Saramaka institutions. Common orientations to reality would have focused the attention of individuals from West and Central African societies upon similar *kinds* of events, even though the culturally prescribed ways of handling them might be quite diverse from one society to another in terms of their specific form. To cite a simple example: historically, the Yoruba "deified" their twins at birth, enveloping their lives and deaths in complex rituals, while the neighboring Igbo summarily killed twins at birth—but both peoples could be said to be responding to the same set of underlying principles having to do with the supernatural significance of unusual births, an idea widespread in West and Central Africa.

Once in the forest, Saramakas created rituals of an enormous variety, based largely and loosely on African models, to assist them in coping with their new environment. As they moved farther from the plantations, they discovered kinds of gods previously unknown to them, who inhabited the trees and boulders and streams of their new surroundings. And each new kind of god, as well as each individual deity, taught these pioneers how to worship them, how to lay out their gardens safely and successfully, how to hunt in their territory, and much else. From the perspective of Saramaka Maroons, their ancestors literally discovered America, revealing all sorts of usually invisible powers that continue to make their world what it is today.

As they confronted their new environment, these early Saramakas learned about local gods through a process of trial and error, drawing on a tightly interwoven complex of pan sub-Saharan African ideas and practices regarding illness, divination, and causality. A misfortune (whether an illness or other affliction) automatically signaled the need for divination, which in turn revealed a cause. Often this cause turned out to be a local deity previously unknown to them (since they had never before lived in this particular environment). The idea that local deities could cause illness when they were offended (for example, when a field was cut too close to their abode in a large tree or boulder) was widespread in rural West and Central Africa. But the classification of local deities, as well as the identities of individual deities in Africa, varied significantly from one society to another.

These early Saramakas frequently engaged in communal divination, with people from a diversity of African origins asking questions together (through a spirit medium or other divinatory agent) of a god or ancestor in order to grasp the nature of the kinds of gods that now surrounded them. The detailed pictures that emerged of the personality, family connections, abode, whims, and foibles of each local deity permitted the codification by the nascent community of new religious institutions—classes of gods such as Vodús (boa constrictor deities) and their close cousins Wátawenús (anaconda deities) or Apúkus (forest spirits), each with a complex and distinctive cult, including shrines, drum/dance/song "plays," languages, and priests and priestesses. Indeed, such public divination, an arena for the communal creation of new cultural forms, worked as effectively as it did in part because of the widespread African preference for additivity rather than exclusivity in most religious contexts.

Saramaka accounts of the origin of their twin rituals provides one example of how they envision the process of discovery that they see as having so marked their early years in the forest. Here, the metaphor is not divination but a different kind of divine intervention. It nevertheless represents a precise Saramaka way of speaking about the process of legitimizing a newly created institution that took place nearly three centuries earlier. The story, as recounted in 1978 by my late Saramaka friend Peléki, runs as follows:

> Ma Zoé was an early Wátambíi-clan runaway. Once in the forest, she gave birth to twins. One day she went to her garden, leaving the infants in a nearby open shed. But when she returned for them, she saw a large monkey sitting right next to them. So she hid to watch what would happen. She was afraid that if she startled the animal, it might grab the children and carry them into the trees. She was beside herself and didn't know what to do. So she just kept watch. She saw that the monkey had amassed a large pile of selected leaves. It was breaking them into pieces. Then it put them into an earthenware pot and placed it on the fire. When the leaves had boiled a while, it removed them and poured the leaves into a calabash. With this it washed the child. Exactly the way a mother washes a child! Then it shook the water off the child and put it down. Then it did the same with the other child. Finally, it took the calabash of leaf water and gave some to each child to drink. The woman saw all this. Then, when it was finished, the monkey set out on the path. It didn't take the twins with it! And the mother came running to her children. She examined the leaves—which ones it had given them to drink, which had been used for washing. And those are the very leaves that remain with us today for the great Wátambíi twin *óbia*.

Today, this Wátambíi cult services all twins born in Saramaka, involving their parents and siblings in a complex set of rituals that draws on ideas and practices from a variety of West and Central African societies (such as the widespread African association of twins with monkeys). From an anthropological perspective, Peléki, who was himself a twin and therefore a frequent witness to the Wátambíi rites, is describing—through this metaphorical historical fragment relating a Saramaka discovery—a particularly pure example of the process of inter-African syncretism.

Such processes and events, multiplied a thousandfold, created a society and culture that was at once new and dynamic. African in overall tone and feeling, it was nonetheless unlike any particular African society. The

Tree-felling for a garden site, mid-twentieth century.

governing process had been a rapid and pervasive inter-African syncretism, carried out in the new environment of the South American rainforest.

*   *   *

Permission to clear a garden in a particular stretch of forest must be given by the captain of the *lô* that owns that territory. A woman then has the right to use the area during her lifetime—but no rights to pass it along to her offspring. But getting permission from one's captain is only the beginning. There are spiritual forces in the forest that must accord permission as well.

When men go into a stretch of forest to choose a garden space for a wife or sister, they consider such physical variables as slope and exposure and soil, but also look to see whether there are nearby boulders or silk-cotton trees, which may be the abode of forest spirits, or termite hills that are the abode of redoubtable spirits called Akataási. Once they find a potentially appropriate site, they ask the "god-who-has-the-place" for permission, using any of several divinatory techniques—they might, for example, leave a calabash with an offering on a forked stick for a week to see if the god accepts it, or suspend a palm-frond on poles overnight for the same purpose. Sometimes, the domestication of a piece of forest in preparation for making gardens is more complex, as evidenced by a story told by Captain Gomé of Tutúbúka in 1978 about how his own ancestors were able, in the mid-nineteenth century, to gain permission from a particularly fierce local Apúku (forest spirit) to cut gardens in its domain.

> Father Waimau Amosu, his wife Pelamma, and his brother Uwii came into the creek to cut gardens. But the creek didn't want people to come inside it; the Apúku who lived there, called Masikweke, fought with them, surrounded them with a hundred evil things. Well, they made a shed.... [Waimau went hunting and returned.] He said, "I went hunting and killed only one bird!" His wife said, "Go to the Afoompisi people. They have Baimbo *óbia* [magic]. Go to them. Beg them for help." So he went.... They told him what to prepare. He assembled... [a combination of various raw foods used in certain sacrifices], cane drink, parrot feathers, cowry shells, a white-cloth hammock sheet, a white cock. Then they "killed the chicken" [a form of divination] to ask whether the place would accept them now. And they were able to come on over.... That Apúku had been so baad! If you tried to

Entrance to a Saramaka garden marked by palm-frond guard and offerings (in calabash) to the "god-who-has-the-place."

cross the creek in a canoe, it would sink you! So, they did it all [the ceremony]. Killed the chicken. Its testicles were pure white! [Indicating that the god was pleased.] They raised the flag. They poured the sugar-cane libations at its foot. The Apúku had said they could work the land there.

Often, however, despite the good intentions of Saramakas, a forest spirit is offended—by having a field cut too close to its abode or by being seared when a field is burned too close. Eventually, it possesses a person and becomes an avenging spirit for that person's lineage, for time immemorial. In spirit possession, it announces its name, reveals its kinship relations, and elaborates its likes and its dislikes, and whenever Apúku rites are held it will come to dance and, often, speak through its new medium.

The second moment of discovery in the standard gardening process is the burning of the field, after the brush and trees have been cut and left to dry for some weeks. The day after the raging fire has consumed all but the large, still-smoking trunks, men and women walk gingerly through the ashes looking for the skeletons of boa constrictors that may have been caught in the fire. If

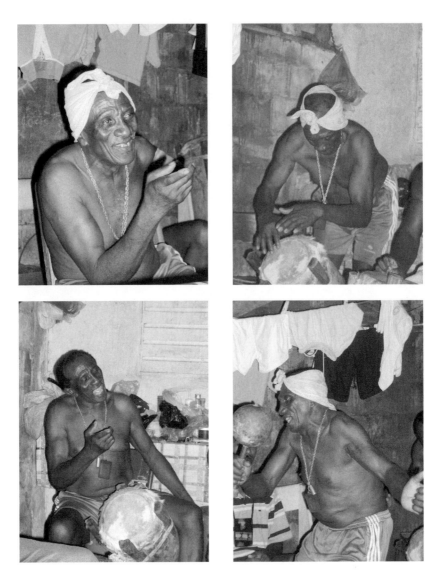

Tooy singing and drumming for the Apúkus, Cayenne, 2003.

A snake-god rite among the Ndyuka Maroons.

found, the remains are placed in a tiny, specially built coffin and buried ceremonially. And before many weeks pass, the spirit of the Vodú god who lived in the snake will possess someone, usually a woman, in the matrilineage of the woman who owns the garden. The god, once domesticated by a long and complex series of rites, will speak intelligibly, tell its name, disclose details of its family and residence, and reveal its special likes and dislikes. That woman's lineage will thenceforth remain in a special relationship with that god, now an avenging spirit.

These two examples show how Saramakas interacting with their environment in the process of making gardens discover normally invisible spiritual beings who enter into long-term relations with them and, through spirit possession and other forms of divination, become active agents in the ritual life of the village. Through such gods, Saramakas discovered, and continue to discover, the workings of the spiritual world. And with the advice of these gods, they make, remake, and come to understand, in ever-expanding detail, the specifics of the rainforest environment in which they live.

Once a garden is cleared and burned, a woman plants her major crop, dry (hillside) rice, the Saramaka staple food, but she cultivates a variety of other crops as well, such as cassava, taro, okra, maize, plantains, bananas,

Saramaka garden.

pumpkins, sugarcane, and peanuts. When her menfolk come and visit, since women stay in their garden camps for a week or two at a time, they spend most of their days hunting and fishing. The right to hunt in a part of the forest, like gardening there, belongs to the *lô*.

Domesticated trees such as coconut, orange, breadnut, papaya, and calabash are mainly grown in the villages. And the forest provides a plethora of products for daily use: the fruits of the various palms from which women make cooking oil, the leaves of the several kinds of palms that men use for the roofing and siding of houses, a variety of trees that yield wood for the items that men carve for domestic use, and hundreds if not thousands of medicinal plants.

Saramakas have also always produced the great bulk of their material culture, much of it embellished with decorative detail.[15] Exploiting their knowledge of the rainforest and highly developed artistic prowess, men build and decorate houses and canoes and carve a wide range of wooden objects for domestic use, such as stools, paddles, winnowing trays, cooking utensils, and combs. But Saramaka men also continue the tradition of emigrating for years at a time to coastal Suriname or French Guiana to earn money to buy

Saramaka garden.

the Western goods considered essential to life in their home villages, such as shotguns and powder, tools, outboard motors, chainsaws, cooking pots, cloth, hammocks, soap, kerosene, and (for ritual use) rum and beer. Meanwhile, since the nineteenth century, women have sewn imported cloth into patchwork and embroidered clothing, and carved decorative motifs into calabash bowls.

*   *   *

Shrine at Túlíobúka, at the confluence of the Pikílío and Gaánlío, just below the mighty Tápawáta falls. In moments of catastrophic drought, it is here that the *gaamá* prays to the Mother of the Waters, Gánsa, the Tonê god.

Our first outsiders' view of what Saramaka life looked like dates from the middle of the eighteenth century, thanks to the detailed diaries of the German Moravian missionaries who were sent out to live in Saramaka villages right after the 1762 peace treaty. What we learn is that in its main lines Saramaka life, including religion, was already very similar to its present form, with frequent spirit possession and other forms of divination, a strong ancestor cult, institutionalized cults for the Apúku and Vodú gods encountered in the forest, and a variety of gods of war. But even the great Saramaka war *óbias* (magical powers), including those with names that point to a particular African people or place such as Komantí, were in fact radical blends of several African traditions, forged in processes very similar to that of the Wátambíi twin cult. They, too, were largely developed in Suriname via processes of communal divination. By the time the Saramakas had signed their peace treaty with the Dutch crown after nearly a century of guerrilla warfare, there were few African-born Saramakas still alive, and their culture already represented an integrated, highly developed African-American synthesis whose main processual motor had been inter-African syncretism, viewed from a Saramaka perspective as an ongoing process of discovery.

The process of ritualization of the rainforest did not stop with the pioneer generations. Gods (speaking in possession or through other means of divination) have continued to instruct Saramakas about landscapes and gardens—their layout, the use and misuse of particular plants, and much else—ever since. Indeed, some of the most important deities and *óbia*s of Dángogó, where we lived in the 1960s and 1970s, were discovered by Saramakas only at the beginning of the twentieth century. For example, the highly developed cult of Wénti sea-gods (who travel upriver and live near rapids), Mamá-Gádu (the second most-important carry-oracle in the village), and Dúnguláli-Óbia (Dángogó's most powerful *gaán-óbia* ["great magical power"], a highly complex cult involving curing, protection, songs in an esoteric language, and a multitude of leaves and vines), were all discovered at the turn of the twentieth century. Each is imbricated in multiple ways in the forest and river and involves the whole region in relationships with the local environment.[16]

* * *

Throughout Saramaka territory, the forest, gardens, streams, and rivers remain highly ritualized—and historicized—places, as particular trees, bushes, boulders, and streams continue to hold enormous powers. "There are no useless plants," said Tooy to Sally Price recently, "only uninformed people." From the varied and complex ritual "guards" hung in fruit trees to prevent theft to the disposition of protective and curative plants around houses, from the snake gods and forest spirits who share garden spaces with Saramaka men and women to the river and sea gods who share their village landing-places (and who form an intimate part of daily life), the relationship of people and their territory is rich, ongoing, systematic, and ever-developing. For Saramakas, their forest-and-riverine territory is their life—historically, spiritually, and materially. This why they have reacted so strongly whenever their territory—from their perspective, guaranteed in the treaty of 1762—has been threatened by outsiders.

Earth, Water, Sky

The Dam at Afobaka

Salamaka toónbe-oo, Salamaka toónbe, lúku,
Salamaka toónbe-ee, Salamaka toónbe-ee, gádu!
(Lêndema-ee, Lêndema-ee, Salamaka toónbe.)

Saramaka's fallen, Saramaka's fallen, look,
Saramaka's fallen, Saramaka's fallen, gods!
(Lindeman [the construction manager of the dam],
Lindeman, Saramaka's fallen.)

Saramaka popular song,
composed by Wáifoló, a woman from the village of
Pempe, mid-1960s[1]

We first came near the great dam at Afobaka in August 1966, as we ended our sweaty, bumpy several-hour journey in the back of a truck from Paramaribo and transferred our gear, covered with red-brown bauxite dust, to a waiting Suriname government motor canoe for the several-day trip upriver.[2] But it was only as the two Saramaka boatmen pointed the slim craft out into the artificial lake that we saw, looking back, the immensity of the construction, the broad sweep of concrete in between hundreds of meters of high-packed red earth, looming out of the fetid water.[3]

At last we were on what Saramakas were still calling "the river," and for the next few hours our winding, tortuous path was lined on either side with the bare grey tops of forest giants (what one observer has called "the river-bones"), standing as skeletal sentinels in a vast space of death. As we followed the course of the twisting, ancient riverbed far below us, the Saramaka steersman would point and call out to us the name of each submerged village, buried forever beneath the muddy waters, with its houses, shrines, cemetery, gardens, and hunting grounds, places where great battles had been fought and famous miracles effected.

The Moravian church at Ganzee, ca. 1965, as it sank forever beneath the waters of the lake.

After four or five hours of surreal travel, winding our way though the flat, unnatural, brown, and eerie silence of the lake, amidst the walls of dead tree-tops, we heard a low roar, growing louder as we approached, and suddenly broke into the exuberance of the bright green forest and plunging waters of the most famous rapids on the Suriname River, Mamádan, "Mother of all Waters."

The river rushed at us from all sides, the foaming water coursing through numerous channels divided by giant boulders. After libations on shore at the shrine for the gods of the rapids, and a fitful night's sleep on an island in the midst of this liquid plenitude, we continued upstream toward the first of the Saramaka villages that had not yet been sunk by the dam.

The lake, 2005.

Wénti shrine at Mamádan, ca. 1955.

Handwritten notebooks from our stay in the Saramaka *gaamá*'s village, far upriver, attest that during our first days there the one subject that I tried obsessively to record—and that Saramaka men were intent on teaching me—was the names (and clan affiliations) of the forty-three villages that, during the course of the previous months, had been literally wiped off the map.[4] (The colonial government's permission for our fieldwork had specified that we neither write about, nor study, nor visit those Saramaka villages displaced by the hydroelectric project, in part for our own safety—the forced "transmigration" of villagers was not yet complete on our arrival in 1966, and the threat of violence was real.) When we accompanied the *gaamá* to the city several weeks later, having achieved our goal of arranging tentative permission to return to upper river Saramaka for a two-year stay in several months, the canoe slid down a final rapids to meet the flat waters of the lake—though the surrounding forest was still at that point as green and vibrant as ever—a couple of kilometers above what had been Mamádan. The greatest of all rapids had, since our upriver journey, disappeared beneath Alcoa's lake.[5]

*   *   *

Saramakas whom I spoke with in the 1960s and 1970s tended to trace the initial plan to dam the river back to Queen Juliana's 1957 visit to Suriname, when she expressed her personal enthusiasm for the colony's modernization. But as early as 1948 the idea of building this remarkable "dam in the middle of the jungle" had been floated by Prof. ir. W. J. van Blommestein (after whom the lake is officially named), and various detailed economic and engineering studies had been underway since at least 1950, with reports and publications appearing throughout the decade (for example, a 1952 preliminary report by the Société Anonyme des Grands Travaux de Marseille, a 1952 feasibility study by an engineering firm from the Hague, and a 1954 report from the Harza Engineering Company of Chicago, all of which supported the project).[6] In 1956, Alcoa—which had been mining bauxite in Suriname since 1916—and the Suriname government began final negotiations, leading to the Agreement of 1958 ("De Brokopondo-overeenkomst," which called for the immediate implementation of the nearly US$200 million project), in which Alcoa agreed to finance, build, and maintain the massive dam and its six giant hydroelectric generators, keeping 90 percent of the electricity for its new alumina refinery and aluminum smelter at Paranam and providing the remaining 10 percent to provide electricity for Paramaribo. (The Agreement also called for Alcoa to build a road to the capital and provided various long-term tax advantages to Alcoa as well as a two million hectare concession to exploit for future bauxite mining.) Suriname would be responsible for the costs and implementation of the "transmigratie" of the people whose lands were to be flooded by the lake (which the CEO of Alcoa described during a cocktail party as "a hell of a job"), though in the end the State spent more to support Operation Gwamba—the organized rescue of animals trapped by the rising waters—than they did for the whole transmigration of Maroons.[7]

From the perspective of the Dutch government, and Suriname's politicians, this largest of all development projects seemed a natural stride into modernity. From the Saramaka perspective, the project was unthinkable, almost impossible to grasp. The government's initial messenger, District Commissioner drs. Jan Michels, was already a seasoned colonial hand with a long-standing relationship with Saramaka Gaamá Agbagó Abóikóni and his village captains.[8] (Saramakas would soon begin to refer to him as Tú-búka-góni—"double-barreled shotgun"—because he spoke of the transmigration out of both sides of his mouth.) In 1959, a year after the Agreement had been signed to build the dam, he decided he had to go to Gaamá Agbagó to inform him of what was about to happen, and some months later he persuaded the government to organize a large delegation to the *gaamá*'s village where the minister-president of Suriname officially informed the Saramaka people of the plan to build the dam and sink their villages. Michels (who once told me he had the unenviable task of "selling the idea of cheap electricity for the city" to jungle-dwelling Saramakas) reported that the *gaamá*'s bitter, resigned, but astute reaction was: "This plan holds nothing for us and everything for the city folk."[9] "Old-time chattel slavery," said the *gaamá*, "is now being replaced by economic slavery."[10]

According to Michels' recollections about that official meeting, what truly enraged the Saramakas was that they were being presented with a *fait accompli*—a sentiment I often heard from Saramakas in the later 1960s as well. Remarkably, from the perspectives of today's notion of human rights, there had been no prior consultation of any kind with Saramakas. District Commissioner Michels reminisced in his flat, understated manner that "Gaamá Agbagó and his advisors were very angry about the fact that a decision had been taken in Paramaribo to build a dam and hydroelectric generating station smack in the middle of Saramaka territory without our having consulted a single Saramaka representative."[11]

Gaamá Agbagó, in the middle of a discussion about other matters, spontaneously told me his version in 1978:

> The treaty says "from Mawási to Atjámina [the source of the Saramacca River] and on up to the headwaters of this river [the Gaánlío], that's for us Saramakas. But when they decided to close off the river, they didn't tell us. They never said "There's this thing we're going to do." When they began to work [around Afobaka], I went to the government office in the city and said, "What are you doing up there?" They replied, "Well, it has to do with the bauxite we dig at Paranam. We're going to make a machine up there [at Afobaka]. The water from the river is going to make the machine spin around." I said, "Well, that's *our* territory you're using to make your machine turn around! How much are you going to pay us?" They answered, "Well, as for that, we're not going to pay anything at all."
>
> Now, we'd already made the treaty with them where they said this land would be ours forever more. How can they take it back? Let's say I buy a plot of land in Paramaribo. Then they say they want it back. Well, they would have to pay for it! So, we argued until they said they understood. "We'll discuss this later," they said.

Well, by the time "later" came, the Americans had already arrived. With all their heavy equipment! What could we do? They'd simply taken it away from us—our own land![12]

Other accounts of the presidential delegation's visit to the *gaamá*, which I took down from eyewitnesses in the late 1960s, emphasize the promises that Suriname's government lavished on the Saramaka leaders—they immediately upped the salaries of captains and assistant captains, they promised a bonanza of new jobs, they promised that the river would become full of fish, they promised significant compensation for the material losses suffered by the residents of the flooded villages, and they brought for the *gaamá* 20 fancy chairs (which still graced the *gaamá's* "office" in the 1980s) and four shotguns as presents. Michels later complained to me that during this whole period, he was simply unable to persuade Saramakas of the reality of what was to come. They were, he insisted, too much like children. (Carlo Hoop generalizes about that meeting: "The government treated the forest dwellers... as primitive and childlike. Sweet promises were made—a child's hand is easily filled."[13])

District Commissioner Michels also played a key role in supporting the several-year-long operation to save the animals. It was a 1964 letter from Michels, then secretary of the Society for the Protection of Animals in Suriname, asking for money and ending with the phrase "Time is short and the water rises," that led to the largest single operation ever undertaken by the International Society for the Protection of Animals.[14] That Michels spearheaded both the badly botched and underfunded transmigration of Saramakas and the successful international animal rescue project suggests something of the priorities of the movers and shakers in Suriname at the time.

In February 1964, Minister-President Johan A. Pengel, Saramaka Gaamá Agbagó, and numerous other dignitaries attended the ceremonial closing of the dam. "Every person ate a half a chicken!" I was told. The dam was festooned with celebratory firecrackers. A siren screamed. Drums were beaten. Many people—from the city as well as Saramakas—openly wept as giant cranes lowered the sluice doors, closing off the river. Three months later, the first rapids were covered. After six months, the first villages—Watjíbásu and Makambíkiíki—went under. As the waters approached, some people fled into the forest, others screamed and cried. When the water reached the houses and people ran to the riverside with belongings, they often couldn't return to

Interior door of a house, carved about 1930 by Captain Heintje Schmidt, Ganzee. In 1968, District Commissioner Michels told me that he rescued the door as the old captain was throwing it into the forest, in preparation for leaving his beloved village for the last time. The door hung for years in Michels' office and is now owned by the Surinaams Museum.

their house to get the rest. Guns sank. All sorts of possessions—pots, stools, clothes, *óbia*s, tools, and more—were lost. No one left until the last minute. There were tremendous fights over land as flooded-out villagers arrived to establish new village sites above the lake.[15]

Most Saramakas absolutely did not believe that the waters would flood them out until it actually happened. District Commissioner Michels held meeting after meeting in the to-be-affected villages, but with little success at convincing people they had to plan to move. "Village captains would tell me they weren't going anywhere—this was their land. They wouldn't leave their houses. They would refuse to budge. It was less violence than passive resistance," he told me in 1968.[16] Government officials pleaded with people to leave their villages in an orderly fashion in advance of the floodwaters, bringing all the belongings that they could. But Saramakas waited until the last minute, believing that the waters would never arrive. Many insisted that the whitefolks simply wanted to take over their villages.

Not knowing whom else to blame, many of the flooded villagers became convinced that Gaamá Agbagó had sold them out in some kind of monetary deal with the government. During the first half of the 1960s, when he traveled to the city, he went by plane rather than motor canoe, fearing the wrath of the lower-river villagers. And when he was in Paramaribo during that period, the government provided him with an armed bodyguard.

From the government's perspective, aluminum was the country's life-blood. By 1967, Suriname was exporting nearly four million tons of aluminum and ore each year—about 80 percent of all its exports—and Suriname was the source of two-thirds of all the aluminum ore used by the United States.[17]

My fieldnotes from 1967–1968 contain snippets of the chaos that still reigned in the flooded regions four years after the dam had closed. Several men told me disparagingly about responses to the water rising along the Sara Creek, where some Ndyukas had their villages. In Lebidoti, the carry-oracle Gaan Tata had made a big *óbia*, an elaborate wicker screen designed to stop the water in its tracks. One week later the whole village was submerged. Or, there was the *óbiama* who shot a magical arrow at the water to halt it—but it just came faster. One whole group of people from the village of Kiikipan-dasi were still moving up the Sara Creek little by little. They'd moved themselves three times so far, directed by their Gaan Tata oracle. Their new village was now surrounded by rising waters and everyone had gone to the captain's house at the top of the hill, the only dry place left, where Gaan Tata was still insisting that they should not move. People from another nearby village, Pisiang, who had moved further up the creek, had now sent desperate messages to the government that they wished to be moved down below the lake.[18]

More recently, a Western-educated Saramaka woman suggested longer-standing effects.

> The forced relocation . . . has led to a crisis in the beliefs of the Maroon society. The gods and the ancestors, who are expected to protect the community, were unable to prevent these disasters. Traditional leaders who had assured their people that the water would not swallow their villages were proven wrong. Traditional medicine men and women stood helpless against forces from outside.[19]

And an expert on forced resettlement projects, with considerable experience in Suriname, recently wrote of the transmigration villages below the lake,

> As most of the ... new villages are located away from the river and away from their traditional forest, the two mainstays of the ... society have been lost. Fish and forest resources were not replaced by other means of livelihood, so unemployment is very high, and quality of life very low. Displacement by the reservoir converted once dynamic and independent Maroon communities into traumatized and dysfunctional communities. The new villages have been abandoned by those youths able to obtain work in Paramaribo or elsewhere, leaving mainly elderly people in the villages. We saw a demoralized people during our visit in 2005, forty years after they had been displaced. The society is dysfunctional even today after such a long time; the society has not healed.[20]

* * *

For Saramakas, the culminating moment of their history as a people had come in 1762, when after nearly a century of warfare with the colonists, their ancestors accepted Dutch overtures for peace and signed a definitive treaty (sealed by drinking each other's blood). The Saramakas agreed to desist from raiding coastal plantations or accepting new runaways, and in return the Dutch declared the Saramakas and their descendants free in their forest domain, far up the Suriname River. For nearly 200 years, that peaceful entente endured. Then came the government announcement: the dam, at the very northern edge of traditional Saramaka territory as defined in the treaty, would create an artificial lake flooding half of Saramaka lands, including some forty-three villages—home to 6,000 inhabitants. The flooded-out people would have to choose between moving below the dam into newly constructed, treeless, grid-pattern towns specially built for them (4,000 people made this choice) or moving upriver, above the new lake, to squeeze their new villages in between already existing ones, creating considerable extra pressure on already scarce agricultural land. The government also held out the carrot of a job bonanza in construction work on the dam, akin, their representatives boasted, to the boom days during World War II when the Americans, with the help of Saramaka laborers, constructed what later became Suriname's international airport. Saramakas, though not believing that the great river could actually be dammed, certainly welcomed the promise of jobs. In fact, however, between 1960, when construction started, and 1964, when the sluices were finally closed, an average of only 2,100 men worked on the project, most of them Saramakas from the very villages that would be flooded.[21]

One of the men who worked at the dam was my friend Tooy, a great healer and drummer, at the time in his late twenties. From 1960 to 1962, he told me, he was right in the thick of it. The end came suddenly, when a steel beam dropped seven meters and he was unconscious from Saturday until Tuesday. So many men were dying in accidents—"People drowning, machinery killing them, every sort of death you can imagine!"—that he decided just to quit and went to live in the nearby Saramaka village of Balén, just below the dam.

While he was there, Gaamá Agbagó came down from the Saramaka capital and lived in Balén for several months. There were repeated council meetings about damming the river—one lasting several days—that included the paramount chiefs of all the other Maroon peoples. They concluded that it wasn't Agbagó's fault; he couldn't be held responsible for the dam. And the day they poured libations for Agbagó, to ask the ancestors to exonerate him for the dam-building, it was Tooy who played the *apínti* drum. Every morning, Tooy told me, he woke up the *gaamá* with the appropriate drum rhythms, playing his drum name *Naná-u-Kêlempé Kílintínboto-fu-Lámbote*.

As for the promised compensation for the flooded-out villagers' losses (which the government later decreed would be only for houses and fruit trees, not for land, which the government said it owned), in the end it averaged less than US$3 per person.[22]

The year after the dam was closed, a group of despairing village leaders wrote a letter to the Dutch queen, which captures some of their suffering:

To Her Majesty the Queen, from Brokopondo [District].
Let it be known:
We, Maroons of the Saramaka tribe, who have lived since the eighteenth century in the interior of Suriname ... in various villages, are true-born Netherlanders under the law and, since the peace treaty signed with our forefathers on 18 September 1762, have been known as Free Bush Negroes, as free people who have their own territory etc.,
— that we have left our old villages and lands in the interest of the development of the land and people of our beloved Suriname;

— that we, some 5,000 Maroons who have been flooded out by the waters of the Brokopondo lake, have had to seek shelter elsewhere;
— that we have now been forcibly moved to places that we have not consented to;
— that we have come to the conclusion that we have suffered significant degradation in our spiritual/mental, physical, and communal lives;
— that we have suffered great losses when our houses, villages with fruit trees, churches, gardens and territory, etc., were destroyed;
— that we wish to continue to live as free people knowing we have the right to a financial settlement for the loss of our former villages and lands;
Faithful to the House of Orange Nassau, we seek rightful compensation for all these losses, and in the hope that our precious freedom shall not be lost.

[signed by five captains of destroyed villages,
now living in transmigration villages, with a copy
to the colonial governor of Suriname][23]

During the subsequent years, the social and economic problems of the squalid transmigration villages only increased. In the first decade after the construction of the twelve new villages below the lake, the population of the larger ones declined by some 40 percent.[24] One scholar concluded, "The great unhappiness among the people and the limited perspectives for the future offered by the transmigration villages have transformed them into mere half-way houses to the coast, French Guiana, and the Netherlands."[25] A Saramaka schoolteacher compared the villages to "concentration camps."[26] And an American visitor, who had previously admired traditional villages upriver, commented on seeing the largest transmigration village: "Your reaction is shock. You know you're looking at the nation's poor. You have the same feeling as when you drive through rows of weathered sharecropper shacks in Mississippi's piney woods."[27] Or, as an elderly Saramaka woman told a researcher in 1995, "We suffer here like dogs."[28]

The woman from the upper-river village of Pempe who composed the very popular song used as this chapter's epigraph was not wrong. Saramaka had indeed fallen, more than anything else in terms of the sovereignty that its proud and dignified people believed their ancestors had definitively won in the Treaty of 1762.

Rockets at Kourou

Mi bái helú, déé sèmbè,
Mi bái helú dá de,
Mi bái helú dá déé Amíngo.

I'm washing my hands of them, everyone,
I'm washing my hands of them,
I'm washing my hands of those "Amigos."

Saramaka popular song, composed
by a man working in Kourou
in the mid-1960s, expressing his concerns
about being knifed by Colombian fellow-laborers[1]

The several-billion-dollar French rocket project in French Guiana dwarfed the nearly contemporary Dutch dam-building in Suriname. In the late 1960s, when we were living far up the Suriname River, fully half of the men from the surrounding villages were off in Kourou, at the site of the future space center, earning money to buy goods to bring back home after a couple of years of wage-labor. During an official visit to French Guiana in 1964, President De Gaulle had announced that "a great French project, which will be known worldwide"[2] would soon begin there, and in the months that followed, an international labor force from several neighboring countries—with Saramakas providing the single largest contingent—cleared the rainforest; built bridges, roads, and a power plant; expanded the seaports and international airport; created a state-of-the-art rocket launching facility; and constructed the second largest city in French Guiana almost from scratch. This new city, created for the workers at the Space Center, was built on the site of a sleepy Creole village of something over 100 farmers and shopkeepers. A French sociologist described the place soon after its completion.

Let's look at how the world of Kourou was organized in 1971:
— The *Quartier des Roches*, separated neatly from the rest of the town, this is the finest residential neighborhood. It includes a sea-side *grand luxe* hotel with 100 rooms, a restaurant, bar, and swimming pool [as well as tennis courts]. Right next door is a private club. A bit farther, facing the sea, are the villas of the two directors as well as six others reserved for senior staff of the Space Center.
— The white-collar quarter. To the west, but still along the seashore, are 100 identical villas, set in rows, which house the engineers and administrative personnel of the base.
— The "downtown" area. Italianate in style, ... this includes an interior shopping plaza where cars are banned, decorated with flower beds and ornamental pools and surrounded by arcades giving access to the shops and the Prisunic-chain supermarket. Just outside this space there is the town's second hotel, with about forty rooms, a café, and a large self-service restaurant designed to serve 600 meals a day. The residential buildings, two to three stories high, include more than 200 apartments, occupied by technicians, staff, and shopkeepers.
— The "Calypso" quarter. This consists of 300 prefabricated chalets (imported from France), on the eastern side of the shopping plaza. These were the first lodgings built, originally to house the people who set up the Space Center and later for people involved in construction. This quarter, like those mentioned above, is inhabited almost exclusively by *métropolitains* [white French people].
— The low-income district. These are low-rise multiple-family dwellings that stretch west and south of the center. In these 250 or so apartments, there is a mixture of *métropolitains* and Creoles [Afro-Guyanais], mainly semi-skilled workers, but also some schoolteachers.
— The quarter of very low-income housing. High-rise blocks built last, at the entrance to town. Some 200 apartments for the Creole work force.
— Housing for the relocated. At the edge of town, these absolutely minimal, low-rise concrete structures house the sixty or so families of cultivators whose land was expropriated for the missile base—the people who lived in Kourou before it was taken over for the Space Center. By 1971, the area already had a decidedly dilapidated look to it.

— The Maroon village. Well hidden behind the stadium and the empty lots that separate the housing for the relocated from the old town center, this village was built around a water standpipe by Saramakas and Bonis, with the help of recycled materials (old planks, beams) that were "generously" provided for them. In fact, there are two distinct sections; the Saramakas and Bonis do not mix. It is rows of rudimentary shacks, which, far from resembling the charming villages along the Maroni, form nothing but a sad shantytown, despite the clear efforts of the inhabitants to make the place nice.

— The Amerindian village . . . is at the entrance to town, next to the sea, and far back from the road.

— The old town . . . is on the old highway, which is now a dead-end street. With its old wooden houses, quaint town hall, and little church, the old town retains its flavor as a rural Guyanais Creole settlement.

This, then, is the conception of the new town of Kourou! Could one have dreamed up a more striking demonstration of the expertise of Whites to orchestrate the countless hierarchical encounters that allow them to maintain the ideological bases of their domination?[3]

In fact, the so-called "Village Saramaka" was far more squalid than this scholar suggests—several thousand men squeezed into tiny jerry-built shacks on stilts with no sanitation or other amenities. Over the years, the Village expanded and by the 1980s housed an increasing number of Saramaka women brought along as wives for variable periods of time. Initial work in forest-clearing, carpentry, and construction eventually gave way to work on maintenance and other more menial jobs. But Saramaka men continued to come to work there for years at a time before returning to their families in Suriname.

Memorable moments visiting Saramaka friends in the Village include sharing a watermelon in a tiny wooden room whose walls were decorated with top-secret blueprints of rocket engines—because our host (who was not literate) worked as a janitor and had rescued the plans from a wastebasket. Or, sitting in another tiny shack drinking beer on the national holiday and watching, on a flickering TV, the tanks roll down the Champs Elysées in the traditional July 14 military parade. Or again, hearing the roar of a fiery Ariane rocket, with its American satellite payload, climbing into the

Village Saramaka, Kourou, 2002.

nighttime sky over the shacks—might some of the aluminum used in that rocket and communications satellite have originated in Suriname, mined by Saramakas who worked for Alcoa? Or, finally, accompanying a woman who had been our neighbor twenty years earlier in Dángogó on what she called "a little trip to her garden"—entering the small Chinese-run supermarket nearby, barefoot and bare-breasted, selecting her groceries: a frozen chicken from Brittany (with labels in French and Arabic), a tin of sardines from Nantes, and some Parisian candies for the kids. (The next day, in Cayenne, we were invited by colleagues from a French scientific research organization to a posh restaurant where, under a set-piece "tropical" thatch roof, we drank fine wines from the metropole and ate stews of howler monkey, armadillo, and tapir—the everyday foods of Saramakas back home in Suriname.) In the 1990s, we were warned by friendly gendarmes in the center of Kourou not to venture into the Village Saramaka at all, because it had become, they said, the center of drug trafficking for all of French Guiana—and indeed, we've seen fancy cars, driven by whitefolks, cruising the nighttime road that runs by the Village. In any case, since the 1960s, "working for the Man" at

Kourou, and living in the Village Saramaka, has become an integral part of many Saramakas' lives.

*   *   *

From the perspective of Saramakas, the Afobaka project was a direct assault on their property rights and sovereignty, and its wounds continue to fester—they've never fully recovered from its depredations and continue to suffer from its multiple effects. In contrast, the French rocket base (to which Saramakas, of course, go voluntarily) constituted a more subtle assault, this time on their dignity. Insofar as it can be argued that the concept of human dignity underlies human rights law, including the jurisprudence of the Inter-American Court of Human Rights, this assault on Saramaka dignity finds a legitimate place in the larger story this book tries to tell.[4] A little history, and some folklore, may help explain the Afobaka/Kourou contrast and make clear how Saramakas have managed to maintain their dignity and sense of Saramakaness despite the servile labor environment at Kourou.

Soon after the 1863 emancipation of slaves in coastal Suriname, which made travel to the coast more comfortable for Saramaka men, they came to prefer French Guiana to Suriname as a site to earn money and even to settle down. When conducting logging or trading trips to the coast of Suriname, they felt themselves embedded in a rigid colonial system and they were aware that other ethnic groups saw them as low men on the totem pole. Coastal Suriname continued to represent the very world from which their ancestors had extricated themselves by force of arms, but French Guiana was perceived as a looser system, as a "homier" place with a more relaxed environment—and as providing opportunities for earning good money far more freely, in occupations that left them considerable independence. Elderly Saramaka men like to say that although Suriname is their *mamá kônde* (their matrilineal [home] village), French Guiana is their *tatá kônde* (their "father's village," their sentimentally favored place to be).

During the French Guiana gold rush of the 1860s, Saramaka men became the mainstays of the colony's river transport, using their extraordinary skills in building canoes and maneuvering them through the fierce rapids, carrying merchandise and men upriver and gold back down. They took their pay from Antillean prospectors in bags of gold dust and lived high off the hog with what their descendants still remember as gorgeous Creole women who were always available, they say, for men with gold in their pockets. The relative

Saramaka canoemen in French Guiana, late nineteenth/early twentieth century.

welcome felt by Saramakas in French Guiana, as opposed to the coldness they have always sensed in coastal Suriname, was clearly expressed during the late 1970s, when the situation of Maroons in newly independent Suriname was already beginning to deteriorate, by nonagenarian Gaamá Agbagó Abóikóni: "If only I were a few years younger," he joked. "I would simply pull up stakes and lead my whole [Saramaka] people across the Marowijne [the border river between Suriname and French Guiana]."

When river transport slowed with the waning of the gold rush, Saramakas switched to other forest endeavors, but they continued to earn their money in occupations that left them largely free to set their own schedules and pace of work. Depending on the place and time, many worked in the balata (rubber)-bleeding industry and even more in cutting rosewood, especially during the early decades of the twentieth century. (During the 1920s and 1930s—until the trees were depleted and the industry moved to the Brazilian Amazon— French Guiana was the world's largest producer of rosewood oil, the essential ingredient of Chanel No. 5.) From the nineteenth century to the present, a number of Saramaka men have also worked mining gold. At any time during the first half of the twentieth century, somewhere between 1,500 and 2,500 Saramaka men (depending on the date) resided in French Guiana—between one-third and one-half of all adult men. During Suriname's recent civil war (1986–1992), thousands of new Saramaka migrants—men and women and children—joined those who had long been in French Guiana, so that today nearly one-third of Saramakas live in this little piece of France in South America, the majority illegally (that is, without French residence papers).

Saramakas at Kourou, though working for outsiders to earn money, spend the great bulk of their social lives with other Saramakas. Meanwhile, their *imaginaire*—their thoughts, their dreams, their hopes—is forever grounded in their homeland in the neighboring country of Suriname. In French Guiana, even though they've come there voluntarily, they're always in exile. Their central point of reference is their home village and its spiritual possessions, the stretch of river and forest that surrounds it, the places they've hunted and gardened in, the world that their heroic ancestors first carved out in the Suriname rainforest more than 300 years ago.

From the beginning, men took their preadolescent sons and sisters' sons to French Guiana for several years to be socialized into this "other half" of the world in which they would some day have to function as men. And men continued these trips well past middle age, until ill health finally forced them into the undesirable position of economic dependence. Economic necessity put practical limits on variations in the rhythm of coastal trips. No married man could afford an unbroken stay of more than three years in Saramaka, unless, because of chronic illness or other personal misfortune, special arrangements had been made. After two years, his supplies of such items as cloth, kerosene, ammunition, and rum were seriously depleted, and his wives had passed the half-way point in expending their salt, soap, cloth, and so forth. In spite of fluctuations in wages and consumption patterns over the past century, there has been a fairly stable ideal that a man, having gone to work on the coast, should bring back supplies to last his wives four to five years, until his next return. Since the beginning of the twentieth century, most Saramaka men have spent nearly half of their lives in French Guiana. (It is only during the past decade that these patterns have begun to change, as gold mining and other new opportunities—including sex work in the gold fields for women—have opened up for young Saramakas in Suriname.)

Some Saramaka men never came home, founding large families with Creole women—many of their daughters, and daughters' daughters, married later Saramaka immigrants. But the very great majority of Saramaka men in French Guiana returned to their villages in Suriname, often going back and forth at several-year intervals during their whole adult lives, until they came home to die.

*   *   *

In the mid-1960s, Saramaka labor opportunities took a new turn. The space center at Kourou brought with it a new way of life. Saramakas lived on the outskirts of a company town (with government-run bordellos, featuring sex workers from the metropole), wore western clothes, cut their braids, and made genuine attempts to speak French Guiana Creole. Nevertheless, labor trips remained as much as ever a thoroughly institutionalized aspect of Saramaka life, and while on the coast men remained conceptually and physically close to other Saramakas and in frequent communication with their home villages (primarily by tape-recorded messages carried by men going and coming on a daily basis).

The departure for the French missile base, which we witnessed many times in Saramaka, is—even today—preceded by a complicated series of rituals performed over many days (and often in several different villages) to protect the man from the various kinds of supernatural dangers and pollution still associated with the world outside. A man departing from the village of Dángogó, for example, is escorted by Gaán Táta (the village's head-carried oracle-deity) and its "priest" and attendants when he leaves the village to board the waiting outboard-powered canoe. At the missile base, in off-duty hours he is largely with other Saramakas, concerned with Saramaka gossip, and using imported Saramaka oracles and other forms of divination whenever he has a personal problem. And on his triumphant return, soon after the other villagers finish trekking back and forth to the loaded canoe, carrying supplies intended to last several years, he begins rituals to be purified from the various kinds of pollution to which he has been exposed on the coast.

Since the construction of the space center, the kinds of jobs available to Saramakas in French Guiana have shifted away from the formerly predominant forest and river occupations, which offered considerable freedom and independence. Servile wage labor has now become the norm—most of the Saramakas at Kourou, who are considered by their bosses to be unusually conscientious workers (compared to other Maroons or to Creoles), sweep the offices and clean out the toilets of French engineers, and do other low-paid local construction and maintenance or gardening work. No matter how personally demeaning these jobs seem, the men who hold them consider themselves lucky. Given the political and economic situation in Suriname, such jobs have become almost the only game in town—they put food on the table and allow some savings for a hoped-for better tomorrow back home. Yet the men who labor at Kourou remain concerned about their compromised dignity. Engaged in servile labor, they keep their equilibrium by referring frequently to "First-Time" (antiwhite, anti-Western) ideology, and by reminding themselves that they must never forget who they really are. As I have written elsewhere:

> For all those respected Saramaka historians or ritual specialists, for all those renowned woodcarvers or dancers who are forced by economic necessity (and lack of Western schooling) to clean out toilet bowls in the French missile-launching base at Kourou, First-Time ideology cannot help but remain a powerful, relevant force.... Continuities of oppression, from original enslavement and torture to modern political paternalism and economic exploitation, have been more than sufficient to keep First-Time ideology a living force.[5]

But First-Time ideology is only half the story. A related aspect of this struggle to maintain dignity involves Saramaka insistence on their own definition of present-day reality, their refusal to accept the white man's definition of the labor situation. In Saramaka terms, a man can maintain his dignity even when doing degrading and servile labor *as long as he never accepts the Other's definition of the situation*. Indeed, for Saramakas, this is the only successful way—barring violence—to deal with the alienation of labor that their forefathers encountered on the slave plantations of Suriname and that they now face each day at the missile base. Having for some years moved back and forth between servile wage labor in French Guiana and work in their own fields and forest back home, Saramaka men are acutely aware of the contrasts between controlling their own activities and selling their labor as a commodity. Emblematic of these concerns is a Saramaka folktale, in which plantation slavery and wage slavery are poetically merged, and the secret to survival in these contexts is clearly spelled out—Never let the white man impose his definition of the situation.[6]

> It used to be there was plenty of wage-labor work. You'd go off to look for work, and there would always be some job available. There was one guy and you'd just go ask him for work, a white man. He was the

one in charge of it. Now when you went to ask him for work, you'd say, "Well, Brother, I've come to ask you for a job." Then he'd say to you, "Well, look. I've got some." He has a big tremendous rice field. He's got a cacao field. He's got all kinds of fields spread out all around. He's got pigs. He's got cows. He's got chickens. He's got ducks. So you just appear out of nowhere, and ask him for a job, and he says to you, "Well, Brother, I've got some cacao over there. You could go gather the pods and bring them back to me. I'll give you a bag." So off you'd go. But when you went to touch it, one of the cacao pods would break off, and all the beans would fall down and run all over the place. The plant would be absolutely stripped. So you walk back to the king. (That's the white man who has the jobs. He's just like a king.⁷) You'd talk to him and say, "Well, king. Here I am. I went and touched one of the cacao plants to harvest it, and all the beans fell on the ground." So you told him about how everything fell down to the ground. The man says, "Really? Well, my boy, when the cacao fell like that, did it hurt you?" He said, "Yes, my king, it hurt me." King says, "OK, bring your butt over here." He'd slice off a kilo of butt. One kilo of flesh that he just cut right off and took. When the time came, you'd just go off to your house and die.

Then the next person would come along asking for work. He'd say, "My king, I've come to ask you for a job." He'd say, "Well, no problem. In the morning, just go let out those cows I've got over there, let them out of the pen and bring them outside." In the morning, the man went and opened the pen right up. The cows fell down, *gúlúlúlú*, fell down, all over the ground, dead. He went back and said, "My king, I went like you said and opened the cows' pen over there. All of them fell down on the ground, dead." He said, "My boy, did it hurt you?" He said, "Yes, my king." The king said, "Bring your butt over here." He turned his butt toward the king and went over. The king sliced off one kilo and took it. The guy went off and died.

So that's the way it went. He just kept killing people. But the name of the king—I forgot to mention that. The king was "King Nothing-hurts-him" (or "King Nothing-can-get-him-angry").

But there was a young guy who decided to go ask for work. His mother didn't want him to. She said, "Child, don't go. The place where you're going to go ask for work—Well, not a single person has gone to ask for work there and returned. If you go ask for work there, you're as good as dead and gone. Don't go." He said he was determined to go. He arrived. He said, "My king, I've come to ask you for a job." "All right," he said. He said, "My boy, do you know who I am?" The boy said, "No." He said, "I am King Nothing-hurts-him." He said, "OK, no problem." And he went off to the work he had. He went off to pick the cacao. As he reached up to touch it, all the beans fell down and ran *gúlúlúlú* all over the ground. He went back to the king. He said, "King, I went to touch the cacao over there to harvest it, and it fell off all over the ground, it all broke off and fell down before I even touched it." He said, "My boy, did it hurt?" The boy said, "No. My king, it didn't hurt me." King said, "OK. No problem. It's all right." He said, "Let's go to sleep for the night."

In the morning he said, "Well, my boy, I'd like you to go harvest a field of rice I've got over there. Just go on and cut the rice." He went off, reached out to cut a stalk of rice, and they all fell and covered the whole area, *gúlúlúlú*. He went back, and he said, "My king, I went to cut the rice over there and all the stalks fell over to the ground." He said, "My boy, didn't it hurt?" He said, "No. How could it have hurt me?" He said, "OK." So nothing happened.

The next morning, he said, "I'd like you to let out some chickens I've got over there." He went to let them out. But as he opened the door, all the chickens fell down on the ground, dead. As things fell, he would take something and just kill them right off. It didn't bother him if things fell. This was a kid who wasn't hurt by anything. He'd just cut things down. He'd just cut it down and kill it. The king said, "Well, my boy. In the morning you'll go and open a duck pen I've got over there." He opened it. Whoosh Flap! They just kept on coming out and falling down. He finished every one of them off, just cut them up, dead! He went back and said, "My king, those ducks I went to let out, well, such-and-such a thing happened." He said, "Well, my boy, did it hurt you?" The boy said, "My king, it didn't hurt me." "Oh," he said. Well, this kept going on and on until there was nothing left in that place. I don't need to list all that was gone. There was absolutely nothing left. He'd killed everything. All that was left was some pigs he had.

So he said, "Well, my boy, go open up the pig pen over there." So he went to let out the pigs. The pigs all fell down. So he jumped out and he clubbed them all to death. Cut them all up. Cut off their tails and took them. Then he buried those tails. He took the rest of the pigs' bodies and hid them off in the underbrush. He just buried those tails until all that was left above ground was a teeny tiny bit, the tips were barely sticking up.

He did it just to make a problem with the king. He killed absolutely all of them. Then he came out and he ran to him. He went straight to his king. "My king, my king!" he said. "I went to go let out the pigs, and all of them burrowed down under the ground! So I ran back to tell you!" The king said [very agitated], "Where?" He said, "Over there!" The king said, "Let's go!" He ran off and when he arrived he looked around. Now, the way they were buried, the pigs' tails went deep into the ground, and only a little piece was sticking up. You couldn't grab it to pull it out. They grabbed them as tight as they could. The king said, "This won't work. You know what we'll do?" "What?" said the boy. "Run back to my wife, in the house over there. Go have her give you a shovel. Quick! Bring it back."

The kid ran back there. He really ran fast to get there, and he said, "Quick! Hurry up, as fast as you can. My king says to!" "All right," she said. So then he told her "My king says to tell you—Well, what he says is that I should 'live' with you." "What did you say?" she asked. "Yes," he said. "Quick! Quick! Quick! That's what he said!" She said, "No way!" The king turned and shouted back to her, "Quick! Give it to him quick! Give it to him quick! Give it to him right away!" She said, "OK, I understand." The king said "Give it to him! Give it to him! Give it to him! Fast! Fast!" That's what he said. "Give him! Give him! Give him! Give him! Give him!" The boy took the wife and threw her right down on the bed. And then he went to work. Well, that shovel that the king sent the boy back for, in a rush, so they could dig up the pigs—Well, the boy didn't bring it back so quickly. He was gone for quite a while, and finally the king said, "Something's wrong." He ran on back to the house, looked in, and the boy was on top of his lady. He fell over backwards and just lay there. The boy said, "My king, did this hurt you?" He said, "Yes, this hurt me." The boy said, "Bring your butt over here!" The king turned his butt toward the boy and approached him. He brought his butt over. The boy lopped off a kilo. And then the king died. That's why things are the way they are for us. Otherwise, it would have been that whenever you asked for work from a white man, a king, he'd kill you. The boy took care of all that for us.[8] That's as far as my story goes.

Refusing to accept the white man's definition of the situation, the boy triumphed in the end. And however hard it is for Saramaka men to retain their inner strength and dignity while submitting to humiliating work in Kourou, tales like this help them keep going. None of the other versions of this folktale known to me from non-Maroon sources—from the Cape Verde Islands, Puerto Rico, the Dominican Republic, coastal Suriname, and Haiti—contain the same, prototypically Maroon, central message. These others focus on explicit contests or wagers between a boy and a king (sometimes a boy and a devil) to see who can keep from getting angry the longest. In this comparative context, what is striking about the Saramaka version of the tale is that it describes an ongoing, long-term labor situation—indeed, alienated labor itself—and that, rather than a particular, explicit "contract" about not getting angry, the story hinges on the hero figuring out (after many of his fellows have already been killed in the attempt) that the only way to triumph is to question the very nature of the system itself, not to accept the boss's definition of the labor situation, be it slavery or servile wage labor.

*   *   *

Saramaka men (like many Caribbean folk) are quintessential transnationals. Descended from Africans who three centuries ago participated in the greatest international migration in human history, they have been moving back and forth across the border with French Guiana for more than a century and a half. Their movements are driven by the mysterious workings of far-off markets—in gold, aluminum, rubber, perfume, and timber—as well as by the geopolitics of space travel. Yet despite their mobility, and their penchant for long-term stays in French Guiana, they remain strongly grounded in their forest domain far up the Suriname River. My friend Tooy, who has been living and working in Cayenne for fifty years, is not unusual in the strength of his mental groundings back in Suriname. *Travels with Tooy*, an account of his life and wisdom, makes clear on every page his attachments to the history, the ritual knowledge, and the territory owned by his (Lángu) clan, all of which he has spent a lifetime learning and teaching about and celebrating. Speak with any Saramaka man—whether in Asindóópo, Paramaribo, Kourou, or Rotterdam—and he'll display his pride in, and knowledge of, his clan's history and achievements. Their bodies may be elsewhere, but their minds and spirits are anchored in those riverine villages deep in the Suriname rainforest.

Sovereignty and Territory

The Aloeboetoe Incursion

Questions of how a treaty came about and was
concluded, in particular from the indigenous viewpoint,
cannot be answered without—sometimes extensive—
reference to historical and cultural circumstances. No
treaty is self-explanatory.

U.N. Special Rapporteur on Treaties, 1992

On our first trip to Saramaka in 1966, after we had slept on that island near
Mamádan rapids, our canoemen (lent by the district commissioner) stopped
at Abénasitónu, one of the first villages above the lake. We were made to
wait there for three days, based in the schoolteacher's house—it was summer
vacation and he was absent—while the Saramaka boatmen went upriver to
the village of Asindóópo to ask Gaamá Agbagó formal permission to bring
whitefolks into Saramaka territory. Only on the fourth day, when the boatmen had returned with permission to proceed, were we able to continue
upriver toward the Saramaka capital.

This procedure was standard at the time. Outsiders, whether from the
government or elsewhere, did not venture into Saramaka territory without
this nod to the principle that the *gaamá*, on behalf of his people, maintained
full territorial control. The government's unilateral decision to build the
Afobaka dam had, of course, cut a deep wound into this ancient idea of territorial sovereignty. But in 1966, asking permission before entering what was
left of Saramaka country remained very much the proper thing to do. Any
non-Saramaka setting foot in Saramaka territory did so as a guest of the Saramaka people.

Saramakas trace this directly to the Treaty of 1762. They believe that three
main principles were forever inscribed in that sacred document: freedom

(from slavery), independence (from the colonial society and including the right to govern their own society as they wish), and control of their own territory, stretching from Mawási Creek (some 15 kilometers downstream from the dam, near present-day Victoria) to the headwaters of the Suriname River. Gaamá Agbagó was fond of repeating the litany, "From Mawási on up, the forest belongs to us."

As far as Saramakas who lived above the lake were concerned, once the dam had been completed and the people from the flooded villages moved to new locations, things returned more or less to that status quo. At the time, Saramaka men often expressed to me a fear (or prophesy?) that they'd learned from their fathers, mothers' brothers, and other elders, which continues to form a centerpiece of their people's ideology: "Those times"—the days of slavery and the struggle for freedom—they would say, "shall come again." Indeed, there are specific continuities of "othering" by the city people who control the government that reproduce the conditions that make such a fear well grounded.

For present purposes we need not rehearse the litany of oppression visited upon Saramakas since the early colonial period that they refer to as "First-Time." Suffice it to say that during the initial century of Dutch rule in Suriname, the planter class came to refer to Maroons—the collective enemy of the slaveocracy—by such terms as "vermin," "pernicious scum," "a crowd of monsters," and "a Hydra." Maroons recaptured by the colonists were routinely punished by hamstringing, amputation of limbs, and a variety of deaths by torture. Indeed, until the late eighteenth century, theatrical public tortures and executions of recaptured maroons continued to be commonplace in Paramaribo. Today the attitudes motivating such acts are far from being dead letters.

First-Time ideology lives in the minds of twenty-first-century Saramaka men because it is relevant to their own life experience—it helps them make sense, on a daily basis, of the wider world in which they live. For more than a century and a half, every Saramaka man has spent many years of his life on the coast earning money. There he meets bakáas—"outsiders," white and black—who treat him in ways that he fits comfortably into a First-Time ideological framework. Asipéi, a dignified man in his sixties, described an incident that may appropriately stand here for dozens of similar ones I heard recounted. When he was a boy, visiting the city with his mother's brother, an urban Afro-Surinamer derisively called him a "monkey," to which his uncle replied angrily but with pride: "Where you live, you pay to drink water, you pay to have a place to shit. But in the forest where I live, I drink the finest water in the world whenever I like and I defecate at my leisure."[1]

Saramakas insist that the city folks who continue to hold the strings of power in Paramaribo—despite most of them being, like themselves, the descendants of enslaved Africans—cannot under any circumstances be trusted, as history has taught them time and time again. When the subject is seriously discussed, Saramakas often hark back to the tale of Kwasímukámba, their great eighteenth-century triumph over the cleverest of all Afro-Surinamer wolves-in-sheep's-clothing.[2] As a Saramaka explained in 1976, apropos of this tale:

> And that's why, Friend, Maroons do not trust Creoles [non-Maroon Afro-Surinamers]. Which is why it is so hard for us to get ahead in the modern world. We don't believe them. Because of what happened to our ancestors. If you take one of them as a friend, that's what they'll do with you. You must not trust them with a single thing about our life. City people! They fought against us along with the whites. . . Maroons still believe that outsiders are always trying to learn our secrets so they can someday come kill us.[3]

Modern city people (with some notable exceptions, including a few poets and intellectuals) have done very little to change the picture. Even among lower class Creoles, who have the most contact with Maroons (and occasionally engage them as curers), there is widespread denigration: as one scholar wrote, "Deprecating stereotypes are widely foisted on Bush Negroes [Maroons] by urban Creoles."[4] Or as another put it, "indigenous peoples and maroons . . . still are perceived by urban residents as a kind of remnants of the stone age who need to be 'developed' or brought into the modern era."[5] Among the elite of Paramaribo, including government officials, the downward-tilted continuum seems to run from a highly paternalistic (br)othering (there but for the grace of education and bourgeois upbringing go I, your dark-skinned city brother) to a deep disdain (for the brutish, dirty, and uncivilized). Ethnic jokes about Maroons are common coin among educated Creole nationalists: "Have you heard the one about the two hunters who'd bagged nothing all day? Well, they sat down under a tree to rest, and by accident one of their guns went off. Luckily it was pointing straight up. Guess what fell out of the tree? A 'Djuka'!"

In the 1970s, a development project was drawn up that would have forcibly compressed all Maroons into several centrally planned new towns in the interior. It died on the drawing boards only for lack of funding. One Creole parliamentarian, responding to a question about whether the plan might not endanger Maroon culture, said: "Culture? Their culture in danger? Let me tell you something. They have no culture as such. Everyone's always going on about culture but that's a lot of horseshit. These folks are runaway slaves and all they've got in the interior is their little thatched roofs. But now they too will be able to benefit from the new Suriname!"[6] And in summer 1992, the head physician at the French hospital of St. Laurent (just over the border with Suriname), who has treated sick Maroons routinely for years there, described to me his shock, during a medical inspection he and a team of specialists had made to monitor the medical situation in Paramaribo, at the "utter disdain" shown by urban, educated Surinamers—including physicians and public health officials—for Maroons. "They see them," he said, "as the lowest of the low, as hardly human, and they firmly believe the French have been 'spoiling' the Maroons on their side of the river."

*   *   *

Within a short time of the coup d'état of 1980, in which the military supplanted the democratically elected government that had been in place since independence in 1975, Commander-in-Chief Desi Bouterse declared a state of emergency, suspended the constitution, dissolved the parliament, stripped the civilian police of its power, and blanketed neighborhoods with revolutionary "people's committees" and a "people's militia." Anti-Dutch (and anti-imperialist) rhetoric was the order of the day, as the regime set up close ties with Castro's Cuba and Bishop's Grenada. As early as the beginning of 1981, the International Commission of Jurists "visited Suriname and reported widespread illegal arrests and detention, maltreatment of detainees, and curbs on the freedom of the press."[7] The arrest, torture, and summary execution of fifteen prominent citizens—the president of the Suriname Bar Association, three former government ministers, the dean of the Faculty of Economics at the university, the president of the most important trade union federation, four journalists, and others—during the night of 8 December 1982 (the notorious "December Murders"), carried out by Bouterse and his closest associates, led to the suspension of Dutch development aid (something over $100 million per year) and to Suriname's international isolation.[8] Money from the cocaine trade and control of the booming black market began to replace Dutch aid as far as the military was concerned but the country as a whole went into an economic tailspin.

By the end of 1985, in the hope of pleasing its potential creditors (the I.M.F., the Dutch, and the Americans), Suriname lifted the ban on the activities of political parties and Bouterse began talking of a return to democracy. Although Captain Etienne Boerenveen, a close friend and member of Bouterse's ruling junta, was arrested a few months later by agents of the U.S. Drug Enforcement Administration in Miami and convicted of drug smuggling, implicating the Suriname military in a broad scheme of narcotrafficking, Bouterse decided to visit New York and address the U.N. General Assembly. In order to promote Suriname's image internationally, the government hired a Washington, D.C., public relations firm (Van Kloberg & Associates)— "one of more than a score of consulting firms in Washington that work on improving the image and access of foreign governments and companies"[9]— which brought Bouterse to Barney's in New York to fit him out with a properly sober blue suit and conservative tie (instead of the fatigues he'd been sporting), arranged ceremonial meetings with Mayor Koch and John Cardinal O'Connor, and wrote the stirring speech about democracy that he then delivered to the U.N. General Assembly.[10] At the same time, Suriname made other internationalist gestures, including ratification of the American Convention on Human Rights (on 12 November 1987). This strategy bore fruit: by mid-1988, after the ratification of a new constitution and elections, the Dutch agreed in principle to the resumption of development aid to their former colony.

A number of observers questioned whether these changes were more than skin-deep. In 1989, Dutch anthropologist H. U. E. Thoden van Velzen concluded that "After more than a year of civilian 'rule,' the position of the military is stronger than ever. The new government is little more than a convenient facade for Bouterse's dictatorship."[11] And looking back two years later, Dutch historian Gert Oostindie stated that

> The 1987–1990 period may be characterized as a persistence of all that some in 1980 had hoped would be suppressed forever (political incompetence, corruption), and of what others had expected to change for the better in 1987 (economic distress, civil disorder, the omnipresent military). Sadly, Suriname continued on a downward slope.[12]

Drug trafficking also continued apace. By 1990, 60 percent of all cocaine confiscated in the Netherlands (which served as the major European entrepot for the Colombian drug cartels) was being shipped there via Suriname.[13] In

1991, it was reported, Suriname was home to "laboratories for the refinement of coca paste, stockpiles of cocaine-producing chemicals and supplies of refined cocaine awaiting shipment to the European market. Several airstrips... have been carved out of the jungle and accept several flights per week from Colombia. Simply put, then, the entire area to the southwest of Paramaribo is... Surinamese military-controlled and devoted to narcotics processing and transshipping."[14]

This period was also marked by continued and repeated human rights abuses, largely against Maroons but also against other innocent civilians. The military did its best to intimidate human rights activists. In 1988, while Stanley Rensch—the director of Suriname's principal human rights organization, Moiwana'86, and himself a Western-educated Saramaka—was in Washington at the invitation of the U.S. State Department to participate in the fortieth anniversary celebration of the Universal Declaration of Human Rights, the government of Suriname issued a warrant for his arrest for subversive activities. After holding a press conference in Miami to alert international opinion, and arranging to be met at the airport by the Venezuelan ambassador to Suriname and the French chargé d'affaires, he returned, only to be arrested and jailed. A sustained barrage of international outcries from governments and human rights groups succeeded in getting him liberated, but only after eleven days of detention.[15] Likewise in 1989, Reverend Rudy Polanen, chairman of the Organization for Justice and Peace, another Suriname human rights group, was pulled from an airplane by the Military Police while on his way to a meeting of the Caribbean Council of Churches, accused of being a threat to national security, and detained in Fort Zeelandia; his successor, Ilse Labadie, was repeatedly threatened.[16] And in 1990, after four Amerindian men "disappeared" while in military custody, a group of their wives and mothers carrying out a campaign for a government investigation were seriously threatened; two of the women fled with their families to the Netherlands, where they were granted political asylum.[17]

On Christmas Eve 1990, Suriname's military once again assumed official power in a (this time) bloodless coup. After considerable international protest, however, they arranged new elections in May 1991.

These events took place against the background of a civil war that ebbed and flowed between May 1986 and August 1992, pitting the national army of Suriname against a small guerrilla force known as the Jungle Commando, under the leadership of Ronnie Brunswijk, a Ndyuka who had served as bodyguard for Bouterse. (Most of the Jungles were young Ndyukas, but it included a number of Saramakas as well.) In August 1992 a "Peace Agreement" was reached between the government and the Jungles, officially ending the war. According to many observers, its main effect was to carve up the country into two major zones for the drug trade, with former Jungle leader Brunswijk getting the eastern part of the country and former dictator Bouterse the rest.[18]

*   *   *

August 1992, Village Saramaka, Kourou. Sally and I sat squeezed among a group of teenagers in the tiny front room of our old friend Amoida as they leafed through the dog-eared pages of a copy of *Afro-American Arts of the Suriname Rain Forest*.[19] When they came to page 52, Amoida pointed to one of the two toddlers in a 1968 photo: "There's Asipéi. He was shot by the soldiers at Pókigoón!"

Flashback to New Year's Eve 1987. Two months after the people of Suriname had ratified a new "democratic" constitution and one month after they

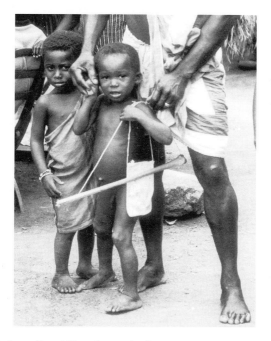

Two boys with "guns" and "hunting sacks."

had voted (under the watchful eyes of the military) in general elections, an "incident" occurred in the first large Saramaka village above the lake, Pókigoón.[20] The initial report, written by the Suriname human rights group Moiwana'86 and dated 15 January 1988, includes the following testimony:[21]

> More than twenty Maroons were severely beaten and tortured—all men and all unarmed.... The victims were hit with rifle-butts, and some were seriously wounded with bayonets and knives. They were made to lie flat on the ground. Soldiers stomped on their backs and urinated on them. All this took place in the presence of some fifty people including old and young, men and women. Almost all of the victims and bystanders had just arrived [in Saramaka territory] from Paramaribo, where some had gone to collect old-age [social security] pensions [for relatives] and all had taken advantage of the post-election cease-fire to purchase food supplies in the capital. On the way back to their villages, they had to travel via Atjóni [at Pókigoón] since that is the end point of bus and truck transportation to the interior, and the journey from there upriver is possible only by canoe.
>
> The victims came from various [Saramaka] villages.... The captain of Guyába [the highest Saramaka official present], as well as victims and bystanders, explicitly told Captain Leeflang of the army that he was dealing with civilians and not with members of the Jungle Commando. The commander [Leeflang] dismissed this information from the village captain.
>
> After their mistreatment and torture at Atjóni, some of the victims were allowed to proceed on their way. However, seven were blind-folded and dragged into a military vehicle. Before they left, a soldier announced they were going off to celebrate New Year's with them. So they drove down the Tjóngalángapási [the road] toward Paramaribo. Among the seven was a fifteen-year-old boy.
>
> At Kilometer 30 the vehicle stopped. The soldiers ordered or dragged the victims from the truck. They were given shovels, and a short distance from the road they were ordered to start digging. When one of the victims asked why they were digging, a soldier said they were going to plant sugarcane. Another soldier repeated that they were going to celebrate New Year's together. Aside [one of the young men] did not wait to be killed and tried to escape. They shot at him and hit him but did not go after him, thinking he was wounded and

would die. Soon, he heard the volleys and screaming. The remaining six, including the fifteen-year-old boy, were killed.

Those victims and witnesses at Atjóni who continued their upriver journey spread the word. Men from the villages of Guyába and Gaántatái left on Saturday, 2 January 1988, for Paramaribo, to demand information about the seven victims from the authorities. As they passed Kilometer 30 they noticed many vultures and an unbearable stench. In Paramaribo, no one was able to inform them about the whereabouts of the victims. They visited Mr. Orna Albitrouw (Coordinator for the Interior, at Volksmobilisatie) and the Military Police headquarters at Fort Zeelandia. At the latter place they tried to see Ensign Achong, Head of S-2.

On Monday morning, 4 January, they returned to begin their own search along the road. Maroons from the Brownsweg area joined the search party. They arrived at Kilometer 30 at 7 P.M., searching the environs with flashlights until they made the horrible discovery: one man, Aside, was found alive, seriously injured and in critical condition. The search party also discovered the corpses of the others, already partially devoured by vultures. They took Aside away and hid him. He told them he was the only survivor of the massacre. He had been shot in the thigh above the right knee and the large wound was filled with maggots. A large X had been carved into his right shoulder blade. He said that a soldier at Atjóni had used his own pocketknife for that.

The group, now headed by Captain Tóntobúka Kadósu of the village of Makambíkiíki, returned to Paramaribo where members of the search party reported their experiences to me [Stanley Rensch], and asked me to establish communication with the International Red Cross. After twenty-four hours of negotiations with the [government/military] authorities, the representative of the I.R.C. received permission to bring Aside to the city, where he was admitted to University Hospital on the night of 6 January. Beginning on 8 January, Military Police stood guard outside the hospital room of Aside and refused permission to relatives who wished to visit him. . . . Since the discovery of the bodies, members of the search party, including relatives of the victims and village leaders, have been requesting permission to bury those killed. Until now, no such permission has been granted.

As Aside lay slowly dying of his wounds in his Paramaribo hospital bed ("a cast on each of his legs and a bandage on his right shoulder, [with] a fever and evidently in great pain"), he was interviewed by David Padilla, assistant executive secretary of the Inter-American Commission on Human Rights (IACHR), who had been invited to Suriname on other business—to attend the inauguration of the newly elected civilian government.[22] His notes add some details.[23]

> Aside and several other riverboatmen . . . were taken from their boats by the soldiers. He and a number of men were forced to lie face down on the ground. There were many soldiers, more than thirty. The soldiers beat him and the other Maroons with their belts. The soldiers also kicked them and hit them with their rifle butts. The victims . . . were blindfolded with their own tee-shirts and placed in an army truck. They were taken away and told that they "would be planted like sugarcane," that is, upside down. In other words, they would be partially buried. When the truck stopped near Kilometer 30, Aside, who was not tied, took off his blindfold and tried to run away, but was shot by the soldiers and then fell on the ground. He was shot in both legs as well as the right shoulder. . . . When Aside fell, he played dead. . . . Later, he heard a salvo of shots. He heard one of the other prisoners named Beri scream. He heard the soldiers cheer and then another shot. . . Aside said that I was the first person to interview him officially. He had not been questioned as of this date by any lawyer or military or police investigator. . . . He stated further that the soldiers had stolen all his money and possessions.[24]

In other words, a group of Suriname government soldiers had entered Saramaka territory, publicly beaten and tortured more than twenty Saramaka civilians, and selected seven whom they took back toward Paramaribo by truck, before executing six and seriously wounding one by the roadside.

Within five weeks of the event, the IACHR transmitted to the government of Suriname relevant portions of Rensch's report on the incident, along with a series of questions about its handling of the affair.

Some six months later, after a second request had been made, the Permanent Representative of Suriname replied that

> Mr. Aside was interrogated by the Military Police and an official report has been filed. While hospitalized, the aforementioned Aside

passed away. According to the post-mortem examination, Aside died of a shortage of oxygen in the blood.

The Permanent Representative wishes to state furthermore that the initial investigation into the death of the alleged six victims at Pokigron was performed by the Military Police. As a consequence of that investigation seven soldiers were taken into custody for interrogation. Since the outcome of that interrogation provided no grounds for further detention, the soldiers were released.

At that stage the investigation of case 10.150 was declared closed by the Military Prosecutor.

In December 1988, members of the IACHR made an on-site visit to Suriname and interviewed at length the president of the Republic, the vice president, the president of the National Assembly, and the minister of foreign affairs, as well as the minister of justice, the acting attorney general, and the president of the Supreme Court. They asked the authorities why they had released the soldiers who had been detained after simply interrogating them, but received no response. There were also no answers to other troubling questions about the case—why, for example, the bodies had not been released to the families and why Officer Leeflang, allegedly in charge of the military unit responsible, had never been questioned. After some further bureaucratic back-and-forths, the Commission informed the government of Suriname in February 1989 that it was placing itself at the service of the parties concerned "with a view to reaching a friendly settlement of the matter in terms of possible reparations" and proposed a meeting during its April sessions in Washington. The government did not send a representative but did send a fax proposing that an amnesty act concerning actions occurring during the civil war, then under consideration by the National Assembly, would make these issues moot. At its September sessions, the Commission heard formal arguments that the government had violated various articles of the American Convention and that the proposed amnesty act would not relieve the government of its obligations under international law.[25] The representative of the government of Suriname asked for a reasonable time to consult with officials in Paramaribo about their position.

In November 1989, Professor Claudio Grossman, attorney for the Saramaka complainants, and Dr. David Padilla, on behalf of the Commission, met with Dr. E. J. Sedoc, Suriname's minister of foreign affairs, to discuss a friendly settlement of the case. Dr. Sedoc promised a prompt response from his government. Six months later, having received no response, the Commission summoned the parties to a hearing. The government of Suriname did not attend, instead submitting a long rambling note to the Commission, arguing (among other things) that "The Government which took office on 26 January 1988 is not to be blamed for the occurrences at issue."

With this highly equivocal response in hand, and citing violations of a number of articles of the American Convention and a pattern of non-compliance with the Commission's previous requests for information and investigation of the events, Professor Grossman submitted a request that the case be sent to the Inter-American Court of Human Rights as a contentious case for purposes of litigation.[26] The government of Suriname was given one final chance to investigate the violations, punish those responsible, and pay just compensation to the victims' next of kin within the subsequent ninety days. This period expired without response on 27 August 1990, and the Commission then referred the case (*Aloeboetoe et al. v. Suriname*) to the Inter-American Court of Human Rights.

On 2 December 1991, the Court scheduled a public hearing in Costa Rica for the presentation of oral arguments on the preliminary objections. But Suriname—represented by its attorney general, a government pathologist, and a member of the foreign ministry—used the occasion, instead, to make an abrupt reversal, laconically accepting responsibility for the events leading to the trial. Suriname's lawyer announced:

> The Republic of Suriname... accepts responsibility for the consequences of the Pokigron case, better known as *Aloeboetoe et al.*... I simply wish to reiterate that Suriname accepts its responsibility in the instant case.

The Court concluded, unanimously, that the Republic of Suriname had now admitted responsibility and that the dispute relating to the facts of the case had been concluded, but that the case should rest on its docket in order to fix reparations and costs. The final and most revealing round of legal wrangling was about to begin.[27]

*   *   *

The Commission's memorial regarding reparations weighs in at nearly 200 pages and presents detailed arguments for the payment of specified amounts of material damages to the victims' dependents (compensation for financial losses suffered), moral damages to the dependents (compensation for the psychological impact of the murders and their aftermath, including the denial of rights to bury the bodies), moral damages to the Saramaka people as a whole (for the army's incursion into Saramaka territory, for the public torture and execution of unarmed men), and various legal costs, as well as certain non-pecuniary measures (public recognition of the government's guilt, identification and prosecution of those responsible).

The identification of dependents was carried out with great care, as Stanley Rensch and a team of human rights workers journeyed three times to the war-torn interior to take sworn depositions from the families and participate in lengthy deliberations about just compensation in each case. The Commission was able to present, for each victim, a detailed list of dependents, estimates of annual income, and other pertinent data. I was brought in at this stage to help ensure that Saramaka notions of legal dependency— which differ from Western practice (including that of urban Surinamers)— were properly represented in the Commission's procedures, and to establish a case for moral damages suffered by the Saramaka people as a whole.

My fax of March 1992, written at the request of the Commission to outline the reasoning behind demands for reparations for the Saramaka people as a whole, was submitted as Annex 15 of the Commission's memorial. It argued, among other things, that

The treaty signed in blood on 19 September 1762... recognizes the Saramakas' freedom (though slavery remained in effect in coastal Suriname for another 100 years) and recognizes that they have a right to sovereignty in their villages and territory. Tacitly in this document, and explicitly in subsequent Saramaka-government negotiations, Saramaka territory was considered to begin... near present-day Brokopondo [below the dam] and continue southward. Thus, the military incursion into Saramaka territory in December 1987 (all the way to Pokigron) was, in terms of 200 years of agreements between Saramakas and the government, an illegal invasion of Saramaka territory.... The [paramount] chief has traditionally had absolute control over who enters Saramaka territory and what goes on within it. Saramaka identity—their very existence as a people—is centered on their war of liberation from slavery, which culminated in the Treaty of 1762. The inviolability of their territory and their sense of sovereignty and internal political control has always been very strong. The idea that outsiders—the national army of Suriname—could simply invade their villages and wreak havoc there runs against more than 200 years of Saramaka history and pride.[28]

The government of Suriname replied to the Commission's memorial with a counter-memorial. Couched in a triumphalist rhetoric trumpeting the human rights successes of the most recently elected administration and announcing a "new" stance toward Maroons, the ten-page text argued that while there may have been disdain and abuses under previous administrations, this was no longer the case. Maroons, it claimed, now benefitted from every privilege of full Suriname citizenship and were considered by people in the ruling party as their brothers.

The climactic public hearing took place in San José on 7 July 1992, and lasted from 10 A.M. until 8 P.M.[29] I was the first witness and testified for four hours. Much of this time was spent providing straightforward responses to a range of carefully prepared questions about Saramaka realities, posed by the

The Inter-American Court of Human Rights, San José, Costa Rica.

Commission's lawyer: "Would you find it strange or normal that a Saramaka was married to three women?" "Is being a construction worker in Paramaribo something that Saramaka men do?" "Are there telephones in Saramaka villages?"[30] "What is the level of illiteracy in Saramaka villages?" Other questions called for mini-lectures about Maroon history, ideology, and daily life: "In the context of Saramaka culture, what would be the impact of the manner in which the victims were killed... assaulted, abducted, and forced to dig their own graves?" "Would this be compounded if the government refused to give an explanation, investigate, or punish those responsible?" "Can you comment on the statement that Maroons do not feel themselves treated with dignity in Suriname, that they are subject to racial insults, and that these values are expressed in their treatment in political, financial, and socioeconomic matters and in matters concerning education and medical care?" A number of questions concerned the reasonableness of compensation proposed by the Commission and whether Saramakas were sufficiently "responsible" to handle the sums requested. In my testimony, I stressed not only my long-term acquaintance with Saramaka life and culture, but also the fact that I had just spent two weeks in the company of a group of Saramakas, including Gaamá Songó Abóikóni (Agbagó's successor), in Washington, D.C., where they had come to participate in the Festival of American Folklife, and had discussed my upcoming testimony with them at length.[31]

Ironically, much of the cross-examination by Suriname's lawyer helped me make the Commission's case stronger, by giving me openings to stress Saramakas' cultural distinctiveness and isolation from the coast: "Doctor, how would anyone know the actual number of wives a member of the Saramaka tribe has?" or "Doctor, aren't there government registries in the interior of the country where Saramaka marriages are registered?"

Other questions from Suriname's lawyer gave me the opportunity to expound on more fundamental issues: "Doctor, you said that the incursion of the Suriname army into Saramaka territory constituted an illegal invasion. Does this mean that Saramaka territory is sovereign and independent of Suriname? Do Saramakas have laws and a government that are independent of the central government of Suriname?" My first response, according to the transcript, was: "In Saramaka terms, from the Saramakas' point of view, the answer to those questions is 'Yes.'" But I then asked permission to expand my answer and during the next few minutes discussed the sense in which Saramakas formed a nation, in the same way that many Native North American peoples were using that term, and that they had long been considered by

anthropologists to be a "state-within-a-state." "As far as Saramakas are concerned," I argued, "their treaty signed in the eighteenth century does give
them sovereignty within their territory, including authority to handle judicial cases that take place within their territory, including murder and other
serious violations, which they have always handled themselves." The following pages of the transcript contain considerable further discussion between
Suriname's lawyer, expressing incredulity that the eighteenth-century treaty
might still hold force, and me (as well as the Saramakas' lawyer), restating the
sacredness and importance of that treaty to Saramakas.

The judges' subsequent questions were careful—they also requested a
full set of Sally's and my published books and articles about Saramakas. They
seemed particularly interested in the nature of traditional Saramaka territorial
and judicial rights and the ways that Saramakas conceptualized sovereignty, as
well as the way family structure worked and how that might affect the distri-
bution of reparations. Much of my subsequent testimony concerned the ways
that Saramakas, since the eighteenth century, have used their own judicial system, including the meting out of capital punishment. But territoriality—who
owns the land—also repeatedly came up in the questioning. At one point, one
of the judges asked me, "Is it customary for members of the Suriname military
to ask permission before entering Saramaka territory? "To my knowledge," I
answered, "everyone, including the district commissioner and other officials
of the Suriname government who want to come into Saramaka territory,
always ask permission and always... treat the captains and the *gaamá* with
considerable respect." I further explained that a radio-telephone had recently
been installed in the *gaamá*'s village and that the district commissioner, or
other government officials, could now speak to the chief and discuss visits
without sending an emissary—but that the principle still held.

By the end of my testimony, I—and the Commission's lawyers—felt that
the winds were blowing in a favorable direction.[32]

*   *   *

The testimony of Suriname's star witness was officially "disregarded" in
the Court's final judgment on the grounds that "the Court formed an [unfa-
vorable] impression of the witness because of the manner in which he gave
his testimony, his attitude during the hearing, and the personality he displayed during it."[33] Nonetheless I found it the most interesting testimony of
the trial, as it came from one of Bouterse's close associates, Ramón de Freitas,

who had held the position of judge advocate general under every political administration since the 1980 coup d'état. Suriname's lawyer began his friendly questioning by asking de Freitas about the investigation of the seven deaths, which took place under his authority.

> de Freitas: Certain suspects were arrested and held in detention, but they were later freed since the corpses presented were not those of the people alleged to have been killed.
>
> Lawyer: Was there further investigation?
>
> de Freitas: Yes, it's still continuing. [With a smirk.] These cases go on for years.

The lawyer then began delving into more interesting territory.

> Lawyer: Tell us about the current human rights situation in Suriname.
>
> de Freitas: There've been great advances. In the constitution, the power of the military has been eliminated.[34]
>
> Lawyer: What is the government's attitude toward the present case?
>
> de Freitas: The government of Suriname sees it as part of its turn to democracy.
>
> Lawyer: What do you think of the idea that the president of Suriname ought to make some public recognition of the incidents in this case?
>
> de Freitas: I have read this proposal and must be very careful what I say, not to speak personally. So I shall state only that this requirement [for an apology] is not necessary because the president and his political party consider the Maroons to be their brothers. In fact, the president and his political party received a large number of votes in the interior of the country, exactly where these people were killed. . . . Furthermore, the president has recently made a visit to the interior.

And then the lawyer got to the crux of the matter, producing a telling response.

> Lawyer: Mr. de Freitas, what is the current validity of the Treaty of 1762 in Suriname?

de Freitas: It's a long story. In 1760 and 1762, the Dutch colonizers signed treaties with the Negroes—with the Aukaners [Ndyukas] and Saramakas. These treaties established a kind of *apartheid* between these Negroes and the Dutch. *Apartheid* because the Negroes were given a separate jurisdiction in the country. They were permitted to punish their own people and to deal with civil problems, but not to travel to Paramaribo. There was a separation between the interior and the coast. These treaties established states-within-a-state and therefore the Negroes controlled their own territory. What they had were "homelands." It was in this context that the title of Granman or Governor of the Negroes came into practice. But these treaties were not respected because the Negroes were very aggressive and, in order to end slavery, conducted guerrilla operations. I would stress that it was the descendants of those same Dutchmen who later went to South Africa and created an *apartheid* regime there. These two [Saramaka and Ndyuka] treaties were actually experiments or tests of *apartheid*. I wish to stress this point because it is the idea of *apartheid* that established whatever rights these Negroes claim to possess.... In 1975, when Suriname became independent, a final end was put to all of this. In other words, the laws of Suriname, including laws of inheritance, are the only ones currently applicable to all Surinamers.

The tale that de Freitas spun is part of a long history of attempts by the colonial, and then the national, elite in Paramaribo to abrogate *unilaterally* the understandings in the eighteenth-century treaties between the Dutch crown and the Maroons. Learned interpretations of various Suriname constitutions and the status of the treaties—all offered, of course, by non-Maroons—have consistently minimized Maroon rights.[35] The issue arose in most pointed form during the constitutional debates at the moment of independence in 1975. Minister of Justice E. Hoost declared that the eighteenth-century treaties would henceforth lose their validity "as they restricted both the Bush Negroes' and other Surinamers' movements." And he proclaimed that since "the government had long ago ceased to restrict the movement of Bush Negroes *out* of their protected areas, it would not be in the Bush Negroes' interests to have the treaties enforced." In any case, he concluded, "most of their traditional rights would be protected under the more general terms of the new constitution's fundamental rights."[36] Maroons have never been consulted. As legal scholar H. F. Munneke has written, "The antipathy of Suriname politicians to legal diversity makes them insensitive to the problems of Maroons and Indians wishing to preserve their own legal cultures in their traditional home territories."[37] Legal commentators Ellen-Rose Kambel and Fergus MacKay sum up the situation with regard to the continued validity of the treaties:

> We have found no evidence that the treaties with the Maroons have ever been legally terminated. Moreover, the Independence Treaty between the Netherlands and Suriname in 1975 did not affect the validity of the treaties as prior legislation was saved... [that is, it] would not be affected by the decolonization process.[38]

The more general status of treaties signed between indigenous peoples (or Maroons) and European settlers during the colonial era has had its ups and downs during the past several centuries around the world. Between the sixteenth and eighteenth centuries, "indigenous peoples were clearly considered to be sovereign entities capable of holding and enforcing rights in international law.... Wars and treaties evidenced European recognition of the political personality and territorial sovereignty of Indian nations."[39] In the late nineteenth and twentieth centuries, international law questioned whether indigenous peoples had the legal capacity to enter into international agreements but, more recently, understandings have again shifted. In 1998, the special rapporteur for the U.N. Commission on Human Rights concluded, after a detailed ten-year study, that such treaties "were and remain international instruments."[40]

Until there is jurisprudence from the Court on the question of whether the Saramaka treaty qualifies as "international," the jury remains out. Kambel and MacKay argue that "extensive research" will be required before it is possible to fully support that claim, though they offer a good deal of supporting evidence. But "while the treaties may or may not be international in character, they certainly are enforceable domestic contractual arrangements that the Maroons can rely upon to support their rights to, among others, territory and the autonomous administration thereof.... They are public law contracts."[41] Meanwhile, Kenneth Bilby, who has studied Maroon treaties throughout the Americas, states that

> In concluding treaties with European colonial powers in their own manner, Maroons were both swearing by the past—drawing on the legitimating powers of their African gods and ancestors—and swearing to the future, by endorsing a new life of peace and prosperity that

these pacts promised. From the Maroons' perspective, the sacred basis of the treaties has remained unchanged, partly because oath-taking procedures similar to those used during the eighteenth century remain embedded in Maroon religion and social practice.[42]

Or, as Kambel and MacKay write, "The Maroons undoubtedly understood the treaties to be binding and by swearing a blood oath expressly declared both themselves and the Dutch bound for all time."[43] We are a long way from the story told by Judge Advocate General de Freitas.

The Court's judges, however, continued questioning de Freitas, picking away at his testimony.

Judge Barberis: If, as you said, the law now applies to Saramakas, how were they made aware of it? Is there a Saramaccan translation of the civil code?

de Freitas: The official language of Suriname is . . .

Judge Barberis: That's the reason for my question! Answer me yes or no. Is there a Saramaccan translation of the civil code?

de Freitas: No.

Judge Barberis: Right. Well then how can the Saramaka population be acquainted with the laws of Suriname?

de Freitas: By means of Dutch, which they learn in school.

Judge Barberis: Most Saramakas speak Dutch?

de Freitas: They speak Dutch as far as I know, but especially since 1986.[44]

Judge Barberis: You said that the laws of Suriname hold all over the nation's territory, but are they really effective in the interior or is there instead customary law there?

de Freitas: All Surinamers are subject to the same law, including in the interior. And Saramakas are Surinamers.

Judge Barberis: I want to make an observation. The Court has now listened to three witnesses [Price, Rensch, and de Freitas] who have given two completely different images of reality. According to the first two, there exist customary laws and a very particular situation [in Saramaka]. According to the last witness, the laws of Suriname apply there as if it were on the outskirts of Geneva or Neuchâtel.

These somewhat bizarre proceedings were concluded with closing arguments by each side. The Commission's arguments were brief, relying largely on its detailed memorandum. The lawyer for Suriname concluded simply that, in the opinion of the president of Suriname, "indemnization in the present case should be in-kind, not financial, and include such things as proper housing, agricultural land, social security, and medical and educational facilities [for the Saramakas]." Since the time for rebuttals had passed, no one had a chance to ask why such things were not already the rights of Saramakas, according to their status as citizens of Suriname.

The Court adjourned, and everyone stood as the black-robed justices slowly filed out. Judge Advocate General de Freitas strolled over to me and extended his hand. "You know," he said in Dutch with a smile, "since the Revolution [coup d'état, 1980], Maroons no longer live as separate peoples. Since you were last in Suriname [1986], they've all moved to the city, they all go to school, they all read and write, and there's no more polygamy. In fact, President Venetiaan considers them his brothers." And then he added a more personal message: "My colleagues and I [in the army] are well aware of your many writings and we hope you will come back to Suriname soon. Indeed, we will be preparing a very special welcome for you, whenever you arrive."

In addition to this thinly veiled threat, I was upset by the militant, revisionist ideology of the government toward its Maroon populations as expressed by de Freitas, which seemed to pose a new and dangerous menace. In his version of reality, the ownership of Maroon territory would shift to the State, Maroon law would lose its force, children of polygynous marriages would become bastards, and a host of other aspects of Maroon rights to exist as distinct peoples would simply be erased. This attempt to extinguish ethnicity by fiat, or by the unilateral wishful thinking of an urban elite, seemed even more potentially devastating than direct aggression.[45] But though, in certain contexts, it might well have suited the government of Suriname—for military and other venal reasons—to erase most cultural difference, it seemed clear to me that their attempts would not go uncontested.

Not long after the Aloeboetoe trial, the paramount chiefs of the Maroon groups were pressed by the government to lend their names to the Peace Agreement of August 1992 (*Akkoord voor Nationale Verzoening en Ontwikkeling*), officially ending the six-year-long civil war. The 20-page document is largely devoted to issues of rights to land, minerals, and natural resources—all of which are claimed unambiguously by the State. The document left no doubt that the government was embarking on a rigorous program, in regard to its Maroon and Amerindian minorities, of legal unification, uniformization, and ultimately appropriation. And the paramount chiefs, sacred rulers from the perspective of their subjects, were being redefined by the State as mere civil servants. District Commissioner Libretto—in charge of Maroon affairs—declared, in no uncertain terms, that "the government's intent is to relegate the [Maroon chiefs] to a purely ceremonial function. No longer, as in past times, will they be able to say 'Yes' and that means yes, or 'No' and that means no. . . . Their wishes are no longer law."[46]

The paramount chiefs complied by signing, but during a subsequent official visit to the Netherlands, they asked for clarification about the "land rights and titles" mentioned in that document, and they reiterated their claims to traditional authority over their territories in the interior of Suriname. "Incidentally," anthropologist H. U. E. Thoden van Velzen wrote me after attending these meetings, "Gaamá Songó Abóikóni was [the] most outspoken about land rights: 'from Mawási Creek on up, all of the forest is ours. Do we have to fight our ancestors' war all over again?' he asked—at which point District Commissioner Libretto left for a cup of coffee."

*   *   *

The forty-page judgment in the Aloeboetoe case (dated 10 September 1993 [CIDH 1993]) directed Suriname to pay some four dozen Saramaka individuals compensatory damages totaling US$453,102. The Spanish-language document gives cause for both pride and disappointment. That the government of Suriname was officially found guilty of murdering seven Maroon civilians, that it was ordered to pay their dependents nearly half a million dollars (in hard currency), and that the definition of these dependents takes account of some of the specificities of Saramaka social structure is a victory for the Moiwana'86 activists and the Commission. That it proved so difficult to effectively communicate certain other key arguments about cultural difference, ethnic autonomy, and territorial integrity to the Court was a frustration, leaving key issues to be resolved in future litigation.

Sprinkled throughout the Court's decision were statements endorsing the importance of cultural difference and ethnic autonomy.

The only question that interests us here is to determine whether Suriname family law applies to the Saramaka tribe. In this regard the evidence shows that the laws of Suriname on this subject have no force with respect to that tribe; the members of the tribe do not know them and are governed instead by their own norms. For its part, the State does not maintain in the tribal area the structures needed to register marriages, births, and deaths.... Moreover, disputes that arise on these subjects are not submitted by Saramakas to the Government courts, and the intervention of the courts in such matters with respect to the Saramakas is virtually nonexistent.[47]

And at several points the document tried to spell out local custom in some detail, based largely on my testimony and publications. Yet despite these ethnographic excursions, the Court repeatedly failed to make full use of its newly acquired knowledge of cultural difference, almost as if it enjoyed acknowledging the existence of, say, "matriliny" or "polygyny" but was unable to come to grips with their implications in those situations where they contradicted what the judges took to be "natural" Western family norms—or, as they phrased it, raw "human nature."

The Court, for example, repeatedly held that it was not necessary for the Commission to demonstrate what "we" consider "natural" sentiments or relations of kinship solidarity. They wrote, for example, that "The parents are presumed to have suffered psychologically for the cruel death of their sons, because it is human nature for any person to feel grief because of his son's suffering under torture."[48] Yet the Court did not consider persuasive the Commission's arguments, put forth largely through my testimony, that in Saramaka society, a person might feel equal grief for the sufferings of a sister's son, stating that they would have needed specific evidence to show that such dependents suffered psychological injury—apparently testimony of a psychologist/psychiatrist who had interviewed the parties in question. Nor did the Court accept that certain kin named as dependents by the Commission—people such as a sister or a mother's sister of a victim—should receive compensation for loss of support (despite their acceptance of polygynous wives and their children). "The Court," they wrote, "is aware of the difficulties in the present case: it involves a community that lives in the jungle, whose members are virtually illiterate and use no written documentation. Nonetheless, other [unspecified] means of proof could have been used."[49] In this aspect of the case, where matrilineal, extended-family kinship relations that ran against Western norms were involved, general ethnographic testimony about domestic organization combined with case-by-case sworn statements by Saramaka relatives were summarily deemed insufficient. And in this same vein, for people the Court designated "heirs" (an unproblematic, universal category for the Court) rather than "dependents" (considered to be a culturally charged category), special proofs were considered unnecessary in the determination of either material or psychological damages. Here is how they managed the triage between these categories of kin, at once paying lip service to local custom and overriding it in practice (through the application of universalist antisexist principles):

> It is common rule in most bodies of law that a person's heirs are his children. It is also generally accepted that a spouse shares in the goods acquired during the marriage. . . . If there are neither children nor spouse, common private law recognizes the ascendants as heirs. . . . These terms—"children," "spouse," and "ascendant"—should be interpreted in accordance with local law . . . [which] in the present case is not Surinamese law, because that law is not in force in the region, with respect to family law. Consequently, Saramaka customs must be taken into account . . . insofar as they are not in conflict with the American Convention. Hence, in referring to "ascendants," the Court will not make any distinction because of sex, even if that should be contrary to Saramaka custom.[50]

So much, as they say, for matriliny.

For reasons one can only imagine, the Court in this case chose to sidestep the key issue of Saramaka territorial integrity. Although in the relatively "safe" area of family law, the Court for the first time took "customary law" clearly into account, it turned its back on addressing the thorny issue of ethnic autonomy or sovereignty within nation-states. The Court noted that

> The Commission's brief maintains that the Saramakas enjoy internal autonomy under a treaty of September 19, 1762, which allowed them to be governed by their own laws. The brief states that this people *"acquired their rights on the basis of a treaty concluded with the Netherlands, recognizing, among other things, the Saramakas' local authority over their own territory."* The brief is accompanied by the text of the treaty mentioned, and it adds that the *"obligations under the treaty are applicable by succession to the State of Suriname."*[51] [italics in original]

But then it concluded, with no explanation, that

> The Court does not consider it necessary to investigate whether the agreement is an international treaty. It confines its comments to observing that if it were an international treaty it would be invalid today because it would be contrary to the rules of *jus cogens superveniens* [where a new peremptory norm of international law voids any conflicting provisions of an older international treaty][52]

What the Court was arguing here is that because the 1762 treaty includes several articles specifying the return of fugitive slaves, and since slavery and the slave trade are prohibited by non-derogable norms of general international law (*jus cogens*), "an agreement of this kind cannot be invoked before an international court of human rights,"[53] and that all claims based on this document are moot before the Court. The Court further stated that it "does not deem it necessary to determine whether the Saramakas enjoy legislative and jurisdictional autonomy in the region they occupy,"[54] since for purposes of the present case, "the only question that interests us here is to determine whether Saramaka family law [as opposed to Suriname family law] applies to the Saramaka tribe" (and they rule that it does).[55]

The Court, then, summarily dismissed the Commission's argument that the Suriname military had violated Saramaka territory (which could have opened a Pandora's box for countries like Brazil, Colombia, or Peru), on a legal technicality—choosing not to examine the broader legal issues. Similarly, the Court rejected the payment of compensation to the Saramaka people as a whole for moral damages, arguing that the Commission's case that the killings were in part motivated by ethnic hatred remained unproven.[56] As David Padilla commented, "On this issue [of moral damages to the Saramaka people as a whole] the Court appears to have missed the relevant issue entirely."[57]

But there is more to this story. Was it simple political expediency for the judges not to address the central legal issue of "tribal" peoples within nation-states, or did something darker occur? The judgment (pages 12–13) refers to Court decisions, taken after the final hearing in Costa Rica, "to employ the expert services" of two Surinamers "to obtain more complete information," only some of which was ever shown to the Commission, and to send the assistant secretary of the Court on a week-long visit to Suriname for similar purposes. There is reason to believe that information gathered by these means, which the Commission did not have a chance to rebut and some of which seems to have come, unbeknownst to the Court, from sources close to the military, played an important role in tilting the balance against the Court's accepting the Commission's arguments about the nature of Maroon autonomy in Suriname. A person heavily involved in the making of the Peace Accord of August 1992, which confirmed the State's ownership of lands and resources in the interior, was one of the Suriname "experts" consulted by the Court. Any ruling by the Court that recognized Saramaka territorial rights, or their corporate rights "as a people," could have risked overriding that just-concluded Peace Accord and the judges may have decided, for this reason, to leave the relevant legal issues unexamined. Or, the Court may simply not have been ready to address such issues at the time, especially since they were not indispensible to the specific issue before the Court.

The Aloeboetoe judgment—the first case brought before the Court by Suriname Maroons—set the stage for the cases of *Moiwana Village v. Suriname* (which the Court heard in 2004) and *Saramaka People v. Suriname* (which they heard in 2007). Building upon one another, these cases bring us a long way toward defining the issues of autonomy and territorial control that were raised but partly dodged in *Aloeboetoe v. Suriname*.

The Moiwana Massacre

In the settlement of Moiwana, not far from Albina, a
soldier had torn an infant from its mother's arms, placed
the barrel of his gun in its mouth, and pulled the trigger.

Kenneth Bilby

The civil war that lasted from 1986 to 1992 provided city folks with a splendid opportunity to act on their long-standing prejudices against Maroons. In 1987 a U.S. human rights investigator reported that "several sources allege that the Surinamese Government is not merely seeking to crush the rebels, but that it is committing genocide against the Maroons," and that military strongman Desi Bouterse, in radio broadcasts, "shamed all Maroons... threatened to 'kill all of you' and to 'find your planting grounds and bomb them.'"[1] "Ultimate responsibility for the civil war lies squarely with the national army led by Commander Bouterse," wrote a distinguished Dutch scholar in 1988.

It was this army that, beginning in May 1986, adopted the policy of collective reprisals against Maroon communities.... Fueled by their open disdain for Maroons and their culture, the military was content to let the conflagration spread over most of the interior of the country.... Maroon religious shrines became special targets. In Mungo Tapu, the shrine of Gaan Gadu, one of the high gods of the Ndjuka, was destroyed. Maroons who earned money in the timber industry had been using that shrine as a savings bank. The soldiers took 96,000 guilders from the holy place.[2]

Anthropologist Kenneth Bilby, a near-eyewitness to these events, wrote that

The turning point... came in November and December 1986, when a military campaign in eastern Suriname resulted in more than

150 civilian deaths; in a number of Cottica River Ndjuka villages,
unarmed Maroons—including pregnant women and children—were
rounded up and massacred. . . . Within a few weeks, more than 10,000
of these Maroon refugees had arrived in French Guiana. Witnesses
narrated horrific accounts of defenseless villagers being lined up and
mowed down with automatic weapons while they pleaded for their
lives. I was there when the refugees began to pour into Saint-Laurent,
and I spoke to several of these eyewitnesses, only days after the mas-
sacres took place. Of the many atrocities related, one in particular
seemed to stand out for its brutality. In the settlement of Moiwana, not
far from Albina, a soldier had torn an infant from its mother's arms,
placed the barrel of his gun in its mouth, and pulled the trigger.[3]

A seventy-man-strong military unit (about half Amerindians, including
a number that were chosen because they were personally acquainted with
the village inhabitants) was sent by the army with orders to level Moiwana,
alleged to be a stronghold of the Jungle Commando leader, on 29 November 1986.[4] Using automatic weapons, hand grenades, and dynamite, they
carried out their task methodically. First, they sealed off each end of the
two-kilometer string of hamlets that constituted Moiwana, and then, for
the next four-plus hours, proceeded from one to the next. It was no ran-
dom act of violence. "Everyone was shot—the unarmed, women, pregnant
women, a baby barely seven months old. . . . No distinctions were made."[5] At
least thirty-nine unarmed Ndyuka civilians—mostly small children (four of
them infants) and girls, but also several young pregnant women and elderly
people—were killed in cold blood, some hacked to pieces with machetes,
many others were wounded, all the houses were burned to the ground, and
large numbers of other villagers escaped into the bush.[6] In December alone,
according to a U.S. State Department report, 244 Maroons were killed by
the national army and "military death squads [were widely] operating on
government instruction against Bush Negroes."[7] Soon the Ndyuka villages
of Wanhati, Sabana, Mungo Tapu, Morakondee, Abaadukondee, and others
in eastern Suriname were leveled, often with the aid of light planes and helicopter gunships, sometimes with bulldozers. When a United Nations investigator was driven through the area some months later, he reported that,
other than military personnel, "no human being or living creature was seen
apart from starving dogs in Albina. The jungle vegetation had taken over the
destroyed buildings."[8]

Four years after the Moiwana killings, one of the survivors—eight years old and living in a refugee camp in French Guiana—was given felt-tip pens by a nurse and asked to draw a picture of anything he wished. His response: a Suriname army helicopter raining down bombs on three women and, under the ground, dead, two small children, an older girl, and a woman with a baby in her belly. For decoration he used the ink stamp of the establishment in which he had been parked for half of his lifetime, "CAMP RÉFUGIÉS ST-LAURENT."[9]

Within days of the Moiwana massacre, after the appearance of numerous articles in the Dutch press (including photos of women's and children's bodies that had been thrown into the back of a truck), the official Suriname News Agency ran a story of its own.

Over recent days the question has been raised, in the Netherlands but also in Suriname, to what extent the government, in its fight against Brunswijk's terrorists, has violated human rights. The question has come up especially because various sources have claimed that during military maneuvers in eastern Suriname civilians have also been killed.

The deaths of civilians occurred during an attempt to put an end
to terrorism. The deaths of civilians must therefore be understood in
the context of the fact that the terrorists themselves opened fire from
their villages on the patrols of the national army.
— Who is really responsible for the deaths of civilians in this war?
— Can the responsibility for this be dumped in the lap of the military?
— Did the army go into east Suriname without any provocation to
    carry out a senseless military action?
— Has not the Dutch press, in its lust for sensationalism, transformed
    Brunswijk from a terrorist into a freedom fighter?
— Who has taken refuge with civilians and used them as shields
    against the national army?
— Who are the real violators of human rights and by whom are they
    supported?

The answer to these questions is simple. No one appointed Brunswijk.
He is controlled from and created by the Netherlands. Without him
and his bosses Suriname would have suffered much less damage,
fewer deaths, and less grief.
— Who then is responsible for this?
— Are human rights in Suriname violated by the government or
    by ... ?[10]

Two and a half years after the Moiwana killings, in the wake of considerable international pressure (as well as ongoing rivalry between military
and civilian police), the civilian police took one of the participants, Orlando
Swedo, into custody for questioning and placed the investigation under the
direction of Police Inspector Herman Eddy Gooding (who was also working
on a number of other cases in which the military was implicated). Stanley
Rensch reports that Swedo,

who had been in civil police custody, was physically pulled out of the
jail by thirty-five heavily armed members of the military police and
brought, amidst loud applause, into a gathering being addressed by
Commander Desi Bouterse, where he was feted with military honors.
At this same gathering, Bouterse declared that Inspector Gooding
should have talked to *him*, instead of arresting Swedo, because Swedo
was simply following orders. Openly, he dared the [civilian] police

henceforth to bring their complaints directly to him, the commander, if they wanted to discuss Moiwana.[11]

Despite this warning, Inspector Gooding decided to continue his investigation. Then, on the night of 4–5 August 1990, shortly after he left a meeting with the deputy commander of the Military Police, he was found shot to death, thirty meters from the office of Commander Bouterse.[12]

From the perspective of Suriname's government, Gooding's death signaled the end of the investigation of the bloodbath at Moiwana. In 1993 a mass grave was discovered near the site of the destroyed village and some corpses were disinterred and identified, but despite international pressure the minister of justice and police concluded that "Suriname's social and economic problems must take precedence over the investigation of a shooting spree" and nothing more was done.[13]

*   *   *

Most of the survivors of the 1986 Moiwana massacre managed to reach French Guiana, where they spent six years with thousands of other Maroon refugees from the civil war in Suriname in sordid camps surrounded by barbed wire and guarded by French Legionnaires and other military. The French State provided the funds (allegedly US$10 million per year) to contain and keep alive these desperate people, many of whose relatives had been massacred and whose homes had been destroyed. The State did little else.

No one wanted them—not Suriname, which saw them as enemies; not French Guiana, which was being overrun by illegal immigrants from Haiti, Brazil, and Guyana, as well as Suriname; and certainly not France. In 1989, the Parisian daily *Libération* reported in a shocked tone, under the headline "Condemned Without Rights," that

> For more than two years, in a French *département*, Guyane, many thousands of Surinamers have been "parked" in camps under the control of the French army, without rights of residence, the right to work, the right to attend school, any guarantees that they won't be sent back to the land they fled because of persecution, the right of free speech, and so forth. . . . These Maroons have been placed outside the law . . . without the official status of refugees to which both normal French law and international law entitle them.[14]

Another French observer explained that

> France has never wanted to grant the status of "refugee" to the
> Surinamers whom they consider simply as "people who have been
> temporarily displaced"—because the status of refugee brings with
> it almost all the rights of citizenship; for example the right to work
> and the right to receive various welfare benefits. A second reason is
> to discourage the flood of new arrivals in order to assure the calm
> and security so important to the smooth functioning of the space
> center at Kourou. And finally, there would be a violent political
> reaction in French Guiana were France suddenly to grant the sta-
> tus of refugee to 10,000 immigrants. This refusal to grant refugee
> status, linked to a wish to remain master of its own territory, has
> led France to bar the U.N. High Commissioner for Refugees from
> taking over the camps and allowing the H.C.R. only to act as one
> of three parties in an ongoing and difficult dialogue with Suriname
> and France.[15]

When Sally and I first visited the camps in the early 1990s, the women and
children who made up the majority of the several thousand persons incarcerated there had settled into a deadening routine. They received enough food
to live on and adequate health care but they were cut off from both their past
and any foreseeable future. A visit that we described in our 1991 diary may
give something of the flavor:

> Then off to a meeting with the [French] psychiatrist, who has asked
> our assistance in communicating with a fourteen-year-old Sara-
> maka patient currently incarcerated in a Ndyuka refugee camp.
> The background, according to the psychiatrist: Young "Baala" was
> brought to the hospital by an older brother a few months ago, after
> having suffered a nervous crisis one night. The doctor tranquilized
> him and, after several days, interviewed him, eliciting a story about
> a broken calabash that had been made by his mother. The doctor
> told us that the boy's condition was due to his relationship with his
> mother, symbolized by the broken calabash, and he spun out for us
> various Freudian implications. ("What's it like to conduct a psychi-
> atric interview when you don't speak the patient's language?" we
> queried. "Thank goodness for the universal language of symbols,"

the good doctor replied.) After several days of chemical treatment, Baala was placed in Camp A (no literary abbreviation; the official name is "Camp A")—the refugee camp next to the St. Laurent airstrip. The psychiatrist ended his summary of Baala's pathology by recounting how the boy stopped speaking as soon as he arrived in the camp. RP remarks to SP, under his breath, that this case makes him think of the incident described by Stedman in which a fourteen-year-old Suriname slave had been deliberately deprived of speech and driven mad by a sadistic overseer. SP: "Ou malin! [Martiniquan creole, roughly: Don't be such a smartass!] The psychiatrist is just trying to pull Baala out of what he sees as a psychotic episode. How can you compare torturing a slave with the practice of modern psychiatry?"

Since Baala had been abandoned by his relatives, who never came to see him, the psychiatrist hoped that we would be able to give an opinion and help him figure out what to do with the boy. (The immediate concern was that the psychiatrist was about to leave St. Laurent for several weeks and he needed to be able to give some kind of instructions to the people who would be holding down the fort during his absence.) With the psychiatrist at the wheel, the car was

Entrance to Camp A.

waved through the military checkpoint at the entrance to Camp A, which, like the other Ndyuka refugee camps, is run by the French army. At our approach, Baala's behavior confirmed the doctor's summary—he was silent, and he seemed disturbed. We asked the doctor, in French, to leave us alone with him, and greeted him in Saramaccan. Suddenly, a broad grin, a normal fourteen-year-old. We introduced ourselves and said we were interested in what had happened to him.

He'd been held there against his will, he said, for many weeks, surrounded by Ndyukas who spoke a language he could barely understand. The words came tumbling out. The white doctor scared him, the white nurses scared him, the soldiers scared him. His brother, he said, had been visiting him every three or four days, sneaking in across the back fence because *he* was scared of the soldiers and the nurses and the doctors—he had no French papers and, like many Saramakas in French Guiana, lived in constant fear of discovery and deportation back to Suriname. And the broken calabash? Baala explained that he'd had an argument with his brother, who then went off to wash the dinner dishes at a creek and, on purpose, broke Baala's drinking calabash. He was furious. That night some sort of "god" had come into his head and made him cry out violently. His brother delivered him to the hospital the next morning. Since then, he'd been fine and simply wanted to get out of this awful place. Did his brother and the rest of the family want him back, we asked? Of course! he said. We told Baala we'd see what we could do and went off with the psychiatrist, who agreed that we should visit the family to confirm that they were prepared to receive him back.

Off we drove to a Saramaka settlement 10 kilometers out on the road to Mana, just past the largest of the Ndyuka refugee camps. Baala's friends and relatives were delighted that he could be released, and confirmed the story he'd told us. Nothing would please them more, they said, than to be able to have him back, but they'd been too frightened of the soldiers and the doctor to try to arrange his release themselves. We took one of Baala's brothers with us and drove down the road to the giant refugee camp where the psychiatrist was consulting. A menacing aspect to this place, where white crew-cut soldiers live on a central hill surrounded by a heavy barbed wire barrier hung with a large skull-and-crossbones warning sign. We persuaded the psychiatrist to release Baala into his brother's custody that very day, and he wrote a note for us to take, along with Baala's brother, back to Camp A.

Before leaving, we couldn't resist a comment or two on why Baala had been silent—no one spoke his language, he was terribly frightened of the soldiers and the doctor, he was incarcerated in a squalid camp—and we tried to explain what French colonialism, backed by automatic weapons, looked like from the perspective of a fourteen-year-old boy who'd grown up in a Saramaka village in the interior. The psychiatrist appeared not to comprehend, protesting that he'd never been anything but kind toward the boy (which was certainly true). We drove back to Camp A, and Baala was soon on his way home.[16]

By 1992, when the peace accords were signed in Suriname and when France announced the imminent closing of the camps and repatriation of their inhabitants, many women and children (and some men), including those from Moiwana, had lived in the camps for six years. The French— under considerable pressure from local politicians—devised a carrot-and-stick strategy to get rid of the refugees, who still feared for their lives in Suriname. They first managed to persuade nearly half of the people in the camps to cross the river, by offering monetary inducements (4,000 F per adult, 2,000 F per child, roughly US$ 700 and $350, respectively). And they then subjected the remaining camp population to policy changes designed to discourage their continued presence. While carefully holding the camp diet at the internationally mandated number of calories for each refugee, the Foreign Legion (which had taken over the administration of the camps from the regular army more than a year before) discontinued rice, a Maroon staple, and substituted lentils, a food that Maroons find distinctly unappetizing. At the same time, Legionnaires—again acting on the authority of local politicians—blanketed with herbicide the manioc gardens where many Ndyuka refugees had been growing some of their own food near the camps. By November 1992, all but two large camps had been closed. But traffic back and forth across the border river remained brisk and certainly included "repatriated refugees," who had taken the French money and simply returned to the area outside the camps.

In 1993, as a humanitarian gesture, the French government permitted several hundred of these holdouts from repatriation, many of them survivors of Moiwana, to settle at Charvein in the commune of Mana. During the first part of the twentieth century, Charvein had been the most notorious of the penal colony's forced labor camps, where "incorrigible" prisoners worked stark naked cutting trees and hauling logs through the jungle. During the Suriname civil war, when Camp A and Camp B near St. Laurent became overcrowded with refugees, the abandoned penal colony camp was transformed into Camp C, controlled from the first by the French Foreign Legion. At its height in 1988, some 3,000 Ndyukas were housed there, including most of the survivors of the Moiwana massacre.

In 2001 we visited the Ndyuka captain of Charvein, Eddy Pinas, now living in freedom, not far from the site of Camp C. Sitting under a large mango tree, he and his family painted a grim picture of life in exile. As many as 2,000 Ndyukas were living in the area, many illegally. Large numbers of youths—he pointed to several speeding by on motorcycles—were involved in the drug trade. Ronnie Brunswijk, he told us—now a parliamentarian in Suriname—controlled the cocaine and marijuana trade in eastern Suriname. (The drug trade in the rest of the country, as was widely known, was controlled by former dictator Bouterse, who, in 1999, had been convicted of international drug trafficking *in absentia* by a Dutch court and sentenced to sixteen years in prison—reduced to eleven on appeal—and a fine of $2.3 million.)[17]

Brunswijk was giving Ndyuka youths who came over from French Guiana motorcycles as well as the drugs, which they then distributed in French Guiana on his behalf. In the Cottica River area, where Moiwana once stood, drug gangs were now shooting it out on a weekly basis, sometimes with the military taking part, according to Captain Eddy. It's hard, he told us, to say who has it worse—those refugees who returned to Suriname, where they no longer had their land or houses, or those who have tried to make a new life in French Guiana, where young people no longer pay heed to their elders. The youths who have stands by the roadside in Charvein, selling tourists the crude woodcarvings that for the most part they buy in Suriname, actually do their main business in imported drugs, said the captain. He told us the story of an elderly Ndyuka, who had served as a mule by swallowing cocaine-filled condoms and transporting them to Amsterdam—on his third trip he was caught and is now awaiting trial. The women from Eddy's compound joined us and expressed their fears about returning to Suriname—stories about how the Paramaribo hospital was selling Ndyuka babies abroad when mothers couldn't pay their bills, and how the police were shooting young Ndyukas accused of stealing in the

Moiwana Memorial erected by the survivors in Charvein.

street without a trial. Clearly, these Moiwana exiles were still traumatized and quite loath to return.

*   *   *

Among those Moiwana refugees who did return to Suriname were some who began to organize for justice. But two sets of dates complicated their efforts to get their case heard. First, Suriname had ratified the American Convention on Human Rights (and accepted the authority of the Inter-American Court) only in November 1987, a year after the killings at Moiwana. Second, Suriname's retroactive amnesty law, promulgated in 1992 (undoubtedly in part with the perpetrators of the Moiwana massacre and cover-up in mind), covered human rights violations between 1985 and 1991, and gave the government a further excuse for ignoring complaints about Moiwana.

In 1996, after a number of efforts to involve the Suriname justice system in investigating the case (including formal petitions to the attorney general and the president of the court of justice), the victims, assisted by the human rights organization Moiwana'86, concluded that they could get no satisfaction from the government and decided to petition the Inter-American Commission on Human Rights. In 1997, the IACHR accepted the case.[18]

As Fergus MacKay explains, the Inter-American system of human rights law is based on two foundational documents—the 1948 *American Declaration of the Rights and Duties of Man*, which holds for every member state of the OAS upon their joining the organization, and the 1969 *American Convention on Human Rights*, which holds only when the member state in question has officially ratified that document. The Commission was in the position, then, of basing its findings on the *Declaration* (since Suriname had joined the OAS at Independence, in 1975) rather than on the *Convention*.[19] After a number of unsuccessful attempts to engage the government of Suriname in pursuing the complaints of the Moiwana survivors, the IACHR issued a series of recommendations to the State: that an investigation of the circumstances of the original massacre be made, that the responsible parties be appropriately tried and punished, that appropriate reparations be given to the aggrieved families (with relations of kinship to be based on Ndyuka customary law), and that Suriname's amnesty law (which "allows for impunity for human rights violations, and crimes against humanity") be repealed.[20] When Suriname did not comply, the IACHR in December 2002 referred the case to the Court.

At this point the rules changed. It became necessary for the Court to focus on *ongoing* violations of rights—violations of justice that had occurred subsequent to Suriname's 1987 ratification of the *Convention* and acceptance of the Court's authority—but not on the original violations (the massacre itself), which occurred before Suriname ratified the *Convention*.[21] (Accepting this shift, the plaintiffs argued that "the denial of justice alleged in this case is specifically linked to Suriname's acts and omissions occurring in 1989, 1992, 1993, 1995, and 1997, and continues to the present day."[22]) A day-long public hearing was held in San José on 4 September 2004, and the Court issued its judgment on 15 June 2005.[23]

Regarding Article 5 of the *American Convention* (Right to Humane Treatment), the judgment held that

> The State's failure to fulfill this obligation has prevented the Moiwana community members from properly honoring their deceased loved ones and has implicated their forced separation from their traditional lands; both situations compromise the rights enshrined in Article 5 of the Convention. Furthermore, the personal integrity of the

community members has been undermined as a result of the obstruction of their persistent efforts to obtain justice for the attack on their village, particularly in light of the Ndyuka emphasis upon punishing offenses in a suitable manner.[24]

The judgment then expanded upon the separation of community members from their lands:

The proven facts demonstrate that a Ndyuka community's connection to its traditional land is of vital spiritual, cultural, and material importance. Indeed, as the expert witnesses Thomas Polimé and Kenneth Bilby commented, in order for the culture to preserve its very identity and integrity, the Moiwana community members must maintain a fluid and multidimensional relationship with their ancestral lands.

However, Moiwana Village and its surrounding traditional lands have been abandoned since the events of November 29, 1986. Numerous community members are internally displaced within Suriname and the rest remain to this day as refugees in French Guiana. Unable to practice their customary means of subsistence and livelihood, many, if not all, have suffered poverty and deprivation since their flight from Moiwana Village.[25]

The Court then concluded that the State had indeed violated the plaintiffs' rights under Article 5.

In addition to ruling that the State also violated Articles 22 (Freedom of Movement and Residence) and Articles 8 and 25 (Judicial Guarantees and Judicial Protection), the judgment homed in on the issue of land rights. Regarding Article 21 (Right to Property), the Court pointed out that before it could determine whether Suriname's effective expulsion of the villagers from their site comprised a violation, they needed first to "assess whether Moiwana Village belongs to the community members, bearing in mind the broad concept of property developed in the Tribunal's jurisprudence."[26] Here, in part, is the Court's discussion of the community's rights to territory:

130. The parties to the instant case are in agreement that the Moiwana community members do not possess formal legal title—neither collectively nor individually—to their traditional lands in and surrounding Moiwana Village.

131. Nevertheless, this Court has held that, in the case of indigenous communities who have occupied their ancestral lands in accordance with customary practices—yet who lack real title to the property—mere possession of the land should suffice to obtain official recognition of their communal ownership.[27] That conclusion was reached upon considering the unique and enduring ties that bind indigenous communities to their ancestral territory. The relationship of an indigenous community with its land must be recognized and understood as the fundamental basis of its culture, spiritual life, integrity, and economic survival.[28] For such peoples, their communal nexus with the ancestral territory is not merely a matter of possession and production, but rather consists in material and spiritual elements that must be fully integrated and enjoyed by the community, so that it may preserve its cultural legacy and pass it on to future generations.[29]

132. The Moiwana community members are not indigenous to the region; according to the proven facts, Moiwana Village was settled by Ndyuka clans late in the nineteenth century. Nevertheless, from that time until the 1986 attack, the community members lived in the area in strict adherence to Ndyuka custom. Expert witness Thomas Polimé described the nature of their relationship to the lands in and around Moiwana Village:

[The] Ndyuka, like other indigenous and tribal peoples, have a profound and all-encompassing relationship to their ancestral lands. They are inextricably tied to these lands and the sacred sites that are found there and their forced displacement has severed these fundamental ties. Many of the survivors and next of kin locate their point of origin in and around Moiwana Village. Their inability to maintain their relationships with their ancestral lands and their sacred sites has deprived them of a fundamental aspect of their identity and sense of well being. Without regular commune with these lands and sites, they are unable to practice and enjoy their cultural and religious traditions, further detracting from their personal and collective security and sense of well being.

133. In this way, the Moiwana community members... possess an "all-encompassing relationship" to their traditional lands, and their concept of ownership regarding that territory is not centered on the individual, but rather on the community as a whole.[30] Thus, this

Court's holding with regard to indigenous communities and their communal rights to property under Article 21 of the Convention must also apply to the tribal Moiwana community members: their traditional occupancy of Moiwana Village and its surrounding lands—which has been recognized and respected by neighboring Ndyuka clans and indigenous communities over the years—should suffice to obtain State recognition of their ownership. The precise boundaries of that territory, however, may only be determined after due consultation with said neighboring communities.

134. Based on the foregoing, the Moiwana community members may be considered the legitimate owners of their traditional lands; as a consequence, they have the right to the use and enjoyment of that territory. The facts demonstrate, nevertheless, that they have been deprived of this right to the present day as a result of the events of November 1986 and the State's subsequent failure to investigate those occurrences adequately.

135. In view of the preceding discussion, then, the Court concludes that Suriname violated the right of the Moiwana community members to the communal use and enjoyment of their traditional property. In consequence, the Tribunal holds that the State violated Article 21 of the American Convention, in relation to Article 1(1) of that treaty, to the detriment of the Moiwana community members.

At the end of its judgment, the Court ordered that various reparations for the violations committed by Suriname be effected within a set period of time, including the proper investigation of the original massacre and the prosecution of the responsible parties; the recovery and return of the remains of the community members killed in the massacre; the guarantee of the safety of those community members who wished to return to the site of the village; the establishment of a community development fund (US$1.2 million), to be directed to health, housing, and educational programs for the Moiwana community members; the holding of a public ceremony in which Suriname would recognize its international responsibility and issue an apology; the construction of a memorial in a suitable public location; the payment of an indemnity for material damages of US$3,000 to each of the victims; the payment of an indemnity for moral damages of US$10,000 to each of the victims; and the payment of certain costs of the trial.

The Court made special efforts to spell out nonpecuniary reparations related to land rights and territory. Under the heading "*Collective title to traditional territories*," the Court wrote:

209. In light of its conclusions in the chapter concerning Article 21 of the American Convention (*supra* paragraph 135), the Court holds that the State shall adopt such legislative, administrative, and other measures as are necessary to ensure the property rights of the members of the Moiwana community in relation to the traditional territories from which they were expelled, and provide for their use and enjoyment of those territories. These measures shall include the creation of an effective mechanism for the delimitation, demarcation, and titling of said traditional territories.

210. The State shall take these measures with the participation and informed consent of the victims as expressed through their representatives, the members of the other Cottica Ndyuka villages and the neighboring indigenous communities, including the community of Alfonsdorp.

*   *   *

In response to a formal request from Suriname for an interpretation of aspects of its judgment of June 2005, the Court issued an additional judgment in February 2006. Although it dismissed most of Suriname's comments as improper attempts to retry issues whose outcomes had not pleased the State, it did take the opportunity to expand briefly about land rights. In its request, the State had argued that:

Suriname is inhabited by more than fifteen different tribal communities, among which maroons and indigenous peoples. All these groups have certain traditional areas in the interior they live on. Members of these tribal communities also live in cities in the coastal area. A decision as to measures regarding demarcation and delimitation can only be taken in the light of a case regarding the particular issue of land rights in Suriname. This case did not provide enough facts and circumstances on the specific issue of land rights to satisfy the Court's conclusion and judgment in this regard. The State respectfully requests the Court's explanation on this particular matter because it is convinced that this Court adopted a decision on a matter that was not placed before this [. . .] Court and for which not enough facts and circumstances were provided to take a well accepted legally sound decision.

And, in response, the lawyers for the Ndyukas had stated their own wish for clarification on these matters, writing that:

Considering the nature of Suriname's reaction—as evidenced by its statements in the Request—to the Court's ruling on the Moiwana community's communal property rights, we believe that further elucidation of the scope and meaning of Suriname's obligations with respect to the Court's ruling on this issue is both important and necessary, particularly as it may relate to assisting the State and the Victims to understand and implement the ordered measures.

With regard to interpretation of the scope and meaning of these parts of the judgment, the Victims respectfully request that the Court clarify the following two issues:

a) The scope, meaning, and content of the "informed consent" requirement contained in paragraph 210, and in particular: (i) that the Court explain the broad principles governing the substantive and procedural requirements that apply to obtaining the "informed consent of the Moiwana community, the other Cottica Ndyuka villages and the neighboring indigenous communities;" and (ii) that the Court clarify that informed consent is required in relation to both the "legislative, administrative and other measures" the State must adopt to ensure the property rights of the Moiwana community "in relation to the traditional territories from which they were expelled," as well as to the actual delimitation, demarcation and titling carried out pursuant to those measures once adopted.

b) The scope and meaning of the term "property rights" in paragraph 209 and 233 in order to clarify that: (i) this term encompasses collective ownership rights; the area(s) to which these rights correspond shall be delimited, demarcated and titled in accordance with the community's customary laws, values, usage and mores; and, given the finding in paragraph 86(5) of the judgment, that such ownership rights must be recognized and guaranteed in law and protected in fact; and, (ii) the term "traditional territories" does not exclusively refer to the former village site as it existed prior to 29 November 1986, but also encompasses those areas which, according to Ndyuka customary law, the community and its members may by right own and control or otherwise occupy and use.

In its new judgment, the Court replied to these comments:

In this regard, the Court deems pertinent to point out that, by recognizing the right of the Moiwana community members to the use and enjoyment of their traditional lands, the Court has not made any determination as to the appropriate boundaries of the territory in question. Rather, in order to render effective "the property rights of the members of the Moiwana community in relation to the traditional territories from which they were expelled," and having acknowledged the lack of "formal legal title," the Court has directed the State, as a measure of reparation, to "adopt such legislative, administrative and other measures as are necessary to ensure" those rights, after due consultation with the neighboring communities. If said rights are to be properly ensured, the measures to be taken must naturally include "the delimitation, demarcation, and titling of said traditional territories," with the participation and informed consent of the victims as expressed through their representatives, the members of the other Cottica Ndyuka villages and the neighboring indigenous communities. In this case, the Court has simply left the designation of the territorial boundaries in question to "an effective mechanism" of the State's design.

But in a separate opinion to this new judgment, Judge A. A. Cançado Trindade suggested that the Court should in future take a more aggressive stance:

The Inter-American Court should, in my opinion, *say what the law is*, and not simply limit itself to resolving a matter in controversy. This is my ample understanding of an international tribunal of human rights,—and in this particular issue I am aware of the fact that I am in a minority position (the majority has an entirely different position that is much more restrictive)—and one which I maintain with determination. Aside from resolving the current controversy, the Court should respond to a specific portion of Suriname's request, which was adequately answered by the victims' representatives, and demonstrate—above all convince the State of—the imperious necessity to repair the *spiritual damages* suffered by the Ndyukas of the Moiwana Community, and create conditions for a speedy reconstruction of their cultural tradition.

Accordingly, I find delimitation, demarcation, titling, and the return of their traditional territories indeed essential. This is a matter of survival of the cultural identity of the Ndyukas, so that they may conserve their memory, both personally and collectively. Only then will their fundamental right to life *lato sensu* be rightfully protected, including their right to cultural identity. [his italics]

A more explicit and expansive ruling by the Court on matters of Maroon land rights would have to await the judgment in *Saramaka People v. Suriname*, two years later.

*   *   *

Suriname subsequently complied with the "easy" parts of the 2005 judgment—as it had in *Aloeboetoe v. Suriname*—in this case paying out cash indemnities as required, commissioning a memorial from the leading Ndyuka sculptor, Marcel Pinas, and making a (rather equivocal) public apology.[31] But five years after the Court's judgment, Suriname has still done nothing about the tougher core issues: identifying and punishing the perpetrators of the massacre, recovering and returning the remains of those murdered, or changing the laws of the land to recognize the rights of tribal peoples, such as Maroons and Amerindians, to collective ownership of territory.

In light of these failures to comply with the Court's judgment (and the State's consistent noncompliance to provide requested updates to the Court), on 18 December 2009, the president of the Court issued an order to "convene the Inter-American Commission, the representatives of the victims, and the State to a private hearing that will take place at the seat of the Inter-American Court on 1 February 2010 . . . in order to receive complete and updated information from the State on the actions taken in compliance with the Judgment issued in this case, as well as the observations from the Commission and the representatives."[32] So, the Moiwana legal process grinds on.

In terms of land rights, the judgment in *Moiwana v. Suriname* went beyond that in the Aloeboetoe case (despite considerable testimony on that subject there), establishing that the people of Moiwana Village, as tribal peoples, held legitimate collective rights to their lands (despite that being impossible under current Suriname law). Taken together, these two cases helped set the stage for the more far-reaching litigation brought by the Saramaka People in their own land rights case against Suriname.

It is worth noting that these issues were argued at very different moments, from the perspective of indigenous and tribal rights internationally, as well as within the inter-American system. At the time of the Aloeboetoe judgment in 1993, there was little relevant international jurisprudence—little serious discussion about self-determination, consent, and a range of related rights. But by the time of the Moiwana judgment in 2005, there had been a significant shift globally and the Court had issued its 2001 judgment in *Awas Tingni v. Nicaragua*[33]—its first binding judgment recognizing indigenous peoples' property rights as being grounded in custom.[34] And—as we shall see in what follows—by the time the Saramaka People judgment is rendered in 2007, there has been a further shift, encouraged by the adoption of the U.N. Declaration on the Rights of Indigenous Peoples, which makes it easier for

Moiwana Memorial by Marcel Pinas, unveiled in July, 2008.

the Court to talk about self-determination and consent, although these issues remain controversial within the Court. (It was only at the last minute, for example, that the Court changed the name of the case from *Wazen Eduards et al. . . .* [and before that, *Twelve Saramaka Clans . . .*] to *Saramaka People v. Suriname.*) Serious consideration of self-determination, consent, and related "peoples'" issues represent a relatively recent and psychologically difficult shift both for the Court and for nation-states.

Trees

They [the Chinese] come in and cut with machines. They
clear-cut everything. They cut down absolutely everything.
There is nothing at all left in the areas where they work.
There isn't a single tree left standing.

Saramaka Headcaptain Wazen Eduards

In 1997, in the chill of a misty morning deep in the Amazonian rainforest, Silvi Adjako was bending over her peanut plants, quietly singing to herself. Suddenly, she heard strange rumblings in the distance. Frightened, she walked back to her village and told her uncle César, the village captain. With two other men, César went to have a look, but the path to the gardens was blocked by gun-slinging soldiers from the Suriname army who told them that the land now belonged to the Chinese, whom they could barely make out through the trees behind the soldiers, riding great earth-moving machines. If they interfered with Chinese logging operations, they were told, they would be arrested and imprisoned.[1]

Since the middle of the twentieth century, shipping containers have formed the backbone of world commerce, and the vast majority of the world's containers are fitted with hardwood floors or pallets. At any moment, there are several billion hardwood pallets in use in U.S. containers and considerably more globally—at sea, in the air, on rail, and on trucks. The hardwood pallet industry consumes just under half of all the hardwood cut in the world's forests each year—more than ten million tropical hardwood trees are cut down every year for use as container floors.[2]

China's forests were the principal source of the world's hardwood until the late 1980s. But in the wake of disastrous floods in 1988, regional governments declared logging bans along the headwaters of the nation's largest

Silvi Adjako in her rice garden, 2009.

rivers, and a few years later, after floods along the Yangtze had killed thousands and left millions homeless, the national government followed suit with yet more draconian laws banning logging. The race was suddenly on to find timber outside its borders and Chinese laborers were sent out to engage in the (frequently illegal) harvesting of forests in neighboring Russia, in Indonesia, and in Papua New Guinea, as well as halfway around the world in Suriname, where Silvi Adjako and the other 55,000 Saramaka Maroons lived in one of the least disturbed rainforests on the planet.[3]

In early 1997, with the permission of the Suriname government, subsidiaries of a company called China International Marine Containers Ltd. (CIMC), which was registered on the Shenzhen Stock Exchange, began logging operations in Saramaka territory. Though little known to the general public, CIMC was the world's largest manufacturer of standard containers and the second largest manufacturer of refrigerator containers, controlling 37 percent of the global market.[4]

In Suriname, in order to get around the Forestry Management Act, a law passed by the National Assembly in 1992 that limits the concessions of any single company to 150,000 hectares (1,500 square kilometers), CIMC operated through a bewildering number of subsidiaries (front companies). By 1998, they had obtained twenty-year concessions to at least 450,000 hectares.[5] Here, in part, is how they did it: China International Shipping Containers (Hong Kong) Co., Ltd. (CIMCHK), a wholly owned subsidiary of CIMC, bought 88 percent of the shares of Highfield Development Corporation (registered in the British Virgin Islands) for US$11 million through its wholly owned subsidiary Goldbird Holding Inc. (also registered in the B.V.I.), and Highfield owned Tacoba Forestry Consultant N.V. as well as Topco Forestry N.V. through Supercrown Enterprise Inc. (Both Tacoba and Topco were corporations registered in Suriname, each holding concessions of 150,000 hectares of forest.) By this time, Goldbird had bought 75 percent of the shares of Global World Investment Limited (registered in the B.V.I.) for US$2.25 million and Global World now wholly owned LumbrexSuriname N.V., a corporation registered in Suriname, which had a concession for another 150,000 hectares of forest.

In early 1997, Tacoba became the first of these companies to begin logging above the lake in Saramaka territory,[6] followed in 1999 by another CIMC subsidiary called Jin Lin Wood Industries, and in 2002 by Ji Shen, Lumprex, and Fine Style.[7] The government of Suriname by that time had granted or was entertaining requests for logging concessions to almost the whole of Saramaka territory.

*   *   *

In terms of granting lucrative concessions to multinational companies, it didn't seem to matter which of Suriname's political parties was in power. An investigative journalist reported that during the Venetiaan administration of the early 1990s, "the forest was sold off bit by bit" with Suriname's ethnic politics greasing the gears—"the Javanese leader 'Silent Willy' Soemita paved the way for the Indonesian timber company MUSA, the Hindu politicos around Mr. Mungra invited Berjaya [at the time, the seventh largest company on the Kuala Lumpur stock exchange] to come in." (In Spring 1994, the government signed a letter of intent with MUSA granting exploitation rights for 30 million acres in exchange for more than US$1 billion, but the deal was never consummated. Nevertheless, by 1999, MUSA, through its sixty-three local subsidiaries, was negotiating logging concessions of close to 1 million acres, including most of Saramaka territory, and had applied for an additional 5 million hectares that covered all of Matawai and Ndyuka territory as well.[8]) Then, after Bouterse's party took power in 1996, there was "a fire sale" of the interior and by 1999 "at least half of the territory of Suriname—and according to some people, much more—had been doled out in concessions." The reporter claimed that "Ivan Graanoogst, governmental advisor and right-hand man of Bouterse, has been named as the contact for Barito Pacific, a new company that received a concession of 600,000 hectares following the visit of President Wijdenbosch to Indonesia in October 1997."[9] And he concluded, "A handful of top politicians and their friends are getting enormously rich from this. . . . And the inhabitants of the interior are treated as if they don't exist."[10]

One expert, speaking of large Asian logging companies more generally, explained that "these corporations prefer to operate in countries where laws regulating the exploitation of forest resources are weak, poorly enforced, or nonexistent."[11] During the 1990s, MUSA, Berjaya, and Barito Pacific had each been convicted of various crimes—from bribery in the Solomon Islands to destruction of communal forests in Sumatra—and been expelled from several countries.[12] But in Suriname, Rene Ali Somopawiro, deputy director of the Foundation for Forestry Management and Production Control (Stichting Bosbeheer en Bostoezicht), reiterated the government's priorities: "If a company wants to come in and invest and provide jobs and is willing to obey the laws, we think they ought to be given a chance."[13]

A biologist explained to a reporter in 1998 that "It is the task of the government to monitor timber production, but there are so many bribes passing over and under the table that they can do what they please." "What [the logging companies] practice is hit and run," said Roy Hilgerink, who worked for the Foundation for Forestry Management.[14] A news report claimed that "The Foundation for Forestry Management doesn't have enough inspectors to check the 245 logging concessions on 4.7 million acres."[15] Hilgerink admitted that the Foundation owned but three Land Rovers, and said of the foreign loggers, "Those guys get a chainsaw and are left alone in the forest. They level as many trees as they can, because they are paid by the cubic meter. Later, much of the wood is rejected."[16] Two economists observed that "Chinese who have recently entered the market for Suriname timber are believed to be speculating on the potential prices that can be commanded for less well-known species, without concrete financial information on the viability of harvesting

Logging road in the Ji Shen concession.

these species."[17] And by late 2001, Ji Shen had cut so many trees in the prior four months, and created such an enormous pile of logs on the site of their concession in Saramaka territory, that the Foundation for Forestry Management issued a stop-work order requiring that the harvested logs be removed prior to any further cutting. Whether or not it complied, the company was soon back at logging again.[18]

While a few individuals were getting very rich from these concessions, noted a journalist, there was hardly anything flowing into the State's coffers. Logging companies enjoyed a tax holiday of five years and the tax laws themselves dated from 1947, with no adjustment for Suriname's hyperinflation. According to this report, the government was still receiving only 5 Suriname guilders, worth about US 2 cents at the time, for each log exported from the country.[19]

*   *   *

By the late 1990s, Chinese logging was causing massive destruction in Saramaka territory. In 2001, a visiting American journalist reported that environmental degradation

was all too clear walking through the Jin Lin concession. The company had plowed large, muddy roads about 45 feet wide into the forest, churned up huge piles of earth, and created fetid pools of green and brown water. Upended and broken trees were everywhere and what were once plots of sweet potatoes, peanuts, ginger, cassava, palm, and banana crops—planted in the forest by Maroon villagers— were muddy pits.[20]

The government professed to have no answers to such problems. Between 1997 and 2001, the areas of rainforest doled out in concessions grew by 41 percent.[21] Development remained the keyword (even though the State profited little), and considerable benefits continued to flow, clandestinely, to government officials and their friends.

Surinamese officials point out that only eight million of the nation's thirty-two million acres of rainforest will be opened to logging. Unfortunately for the Saramakas, the acres being offered to foreign loggers happen to be right where they live. "This *is* a problem," conceded Rene Somopawiro, deputy director of the government's Foundation for Forest Management and Production Control. "Every time we talk about forest development, this question of indigenous people comes up," Somopawiro said. "And so far we really don't have a good solution."[22]

Suriname pressed ahead to encourage more Chinese investment. In 2002, President Venetiaan received a high-level delegation from China and sent his own trade and industry minister there. "At the moment," reported Suriname's main newspaper, "there is an imbalance in this trade, with Chinese exports to Suriname at around US$16 million and Chinese imports from Suriname at some US$4 million last year," adding that "Most exports to China consist of wood and wood products from Chinese companies based here."[23]

*   *   *

From the beginning, Saramakas had borne the brunt of this trade policy. As early as 1996, Chinese representatives from Tacoba (apparently speaking English) announced to Captain Zepêni of Duwáta, at the southernmost edge of the lake, that villagers were now forbidden to go more than 1 kilometer into the forest, since their village was part of a Tacoba concession. If he complained or tried to file a suit in the city, the captain was warned, he would lose and be put in jail. By this time, Tacoba had already constructed fifteen logging roads off the main road near Duwáta and was cutting a substantial amount of timber that was being loaded on ships at MUSA's dock at Kromenie (just upstream from Paranam).[24]

One man recounted his personal experience several years later:

I often hunt and fish in the area of the Kleine Saramacca River. Some months ago, the soldiers let me pass to go fishing, but when the Chinese from the logging company saw me, they drove me away very roughly. Later the soldiers asked the Chinese officially whether they could give me permission to hunt. The Chinese said no.

Then the soldiers advised me to go to Paramaribo to look for a license from the army commander. A captain of the National Army gave me a letter for the Chinese. In Paramaribo, I called the manager of the Chinese logging company who was in the city to supervise the loading of a boat with timber at the harbor. He said to me: "Why do you want to hunt in *my* forest? I have a concession." I don't understand this because it has always been *our* forest. Can the government give away our forest without consulting us?

The soldiers told me: "Forget about the Chinese, go hunting here (in an area where the Chinese had finished cutting already). But don't let the Chinese see you." Well, I went there. I saw destruction everywhere, the forest was destroyed. In Paramaribo, people don't know what the Chinese are doing. Shouldn't someone control the logging activities of foreign investors? The Chinese had cut hundreds of trees, dragged them to a place, and piled them up there. Then they abandoned them in the forest because they did not need them anymore. For us, people of the interior, it is terrible to see cedar trees [used for woodcarving] and silk-cotton trees [sacred to Saramakas] cut down, since they are so important for us. And all this destruction made the animals flee as well.[25]

Other Saramakas were telling similar stories. At a meeting in 2002, people from the region around Pókigoón recounted their recent experience with the logging companies. Village spokesmen complained about the destruction of the forest by Chinese concession holders who were bulldozing agricultural plots, blocking off creeks and polluting them, and keeping men from hunting and fishing—all this with the help of the National Army. They reported that enormous amounts of cedar wood, which is of special importance to Saramakas, were being cut and left behind in the forest as commercially uninteresting. They also complained that the Chinese cut first and then waited until later to see if they needed to use the wood.[26]

Around this time, the Chinese loggers also destroyed the gardens of Captain César Adjako, leader of the village of Kayapaatí. "All of a sudden, armed men were denying me access to the land I've worked for thirty years. How can that be?" Adjako said. "My ancestors have been living here for centuries." He added some details:

We have our garden camps between km 52 and km 59 of the Tjóngalángapási [the road connecting Pókigoón to Paramaribo]. . . . Normally we go hunting and fishing deep in the forest. We consider this area as our ancestral lands, since our people have lived on it and used it for centuries. Today we face a situation that is a violation of our rights. We see this whenever we meet up with Chinese loggers and workers, and with soldiers and police, while we're hunting. They prevent us from going into the forest and they harass us. They steal our game and the fruits and crops from our gardens. When we complain, the police and the soldiers, who guard the concessions of these Chinese, don't listen to us. They work hand-in-hand with the Chinese.[27]

These armed men were in fact active-duty Suriname military personnel who had established a formal military post to guard the Jin Lin concession. The ministry of defense claimed that this was both legal and necessary.

According to a press release from the National Army, these activities do not constitute illegal or unauthorised activities by the military, but rather concern the safety of government-determined economic objectives, for which protective measures appear to be required. . . . The press release further claims that the military also keeps an eye on the environmental aspects of the economic activities.[28]

Yet there may be another reason why the military had an increasing presence in the Chinese concessions. It was widely reported, though never confirmed, that many of the Chinese loggers were, in fact, prisoners from Chinese jails forced to do logging in this far-off rainforest as part of their sentence.[29]

Saramakas worried particularly about the logging roads that the Chinese had begun cutting deep into their territory.[30] By 2002, one road had been built that ran more than 20 kilometers from the Tjóngalángapási to the Kleine Saramacca River, over which the Chinese had constructed a bridge and then extended the road almost all the way to the village of Abénasitónu (where we'd stayed in 1966, awaiting the *gaamá*'s permission to continue upriver). This incursion was seen as the beginning of the opening up of the whole of Saramaka territory to the destruction accompanying logging as well as permitting Brazilian small-scale gold miners to move heavy equipment into the area. It also destroyed several of the Saramakas' most sacred First-Time sites, where large villages and cemeteries once stood and where great battles had been fought.[31]

From the perspective of the Saramakas, it was a time of considerable confusion and fear. A crisis was looming.

Resistance Redux

Initial Protests

Within weeks of the first Tacoba incursions into their territory in 1996/1997, a group of Saramaka leaders had created a formal association—the Association of Saramaka Authorities (*Vereniging van Saramakaanse Gezagsdragers*, hereafter VSG)[1]—to educate their communities about land rights and to fight against the foreign loggers. The initial impetus came from the three largest villages lying within a few hours' canoe travel from the lake—Pikísééi (home of the Dómbi clan), and Tutúbúka and Guyába (both home to the Awanás). Headcaptain Wazen Eduards, from the village of Pikísééi, and Hugo Jabini from the village of Tutúbúka, a law student at the university in Paramaribo, took the lead. With the help of an NGO, they obtained a map of the concessions that had been handed out by the government and discovered that logging and mining concessions already encompassed most of the fifty-eight Saramaka villages above the lake.[2] In March 1997, at a large meeting in Pikísééi, the VSG asked human rights lawyer Fergus MacKay to help instruct them about protecting their land.[3] He first asked the Saramakas to make sketch maps of their territory and then engaged Peter Poole, a specialist in indigenous mapping who had done extensive work with Canadian Arctic peoples, to help the VSG with a larger-scale mapping project.[4]

Four months later, in July, Jabini was playing soccer with some friends at Tutúbúka when five Chinese men suddenly appeared and asked, in English, to be shown where they could begin logging behind the village. "Have you spoken with the captain?" the youngsters asked. "We don't need to," replied the Chinese. "We have this paper from the government." They explained that they worked for Tacoba and planned to log all the way up to Guyába (upstream from Tutúbúka). When the soccer players refused to help, the Chinese went down to Guunsí (a tiny village just below Tutúbúka), where they found people who were willing to show them around the neighboring forest.[5]

Wazen and Hugo traveling the river.

The government's concession map that the VSG had obtained showed that Tacoba's concession ended far below Tutúbúka, near Pókigoón, a couple of hours by motor canoe downstream. At least ten villages were threatened by this newest Tacoba claim.[6]

The VSG's immediate concern that some third-party concession holder was permitting Tacoba to log on its lands seemed to be confirmed by a remark from the head of the government forestry agency who said that "the Chinese have agreements with other concession holders in that area to cut timber." He further explained that "since many concession holders don't have money or equipment to cut logs, these people make deals with companies that do have money and equipment to work in their concessions."[7] The VSG had heard a rumor that Gaamá Songó had received a logging concession covering this whole area. And in fact, during the wholesale granting of logging concessions of the mid-1990s, Songó did apply for such a concession (apparently on the principle that if all the other political leaders in Suriname were getting rich in this fashion why shouldn't he).[8]

An initial delegation went from the VSG to speak with Gaamá Songó in August 1997 and there were seven further such meetings, but Songó consistently refused to address the issue.[9] It took until March 1998, when some thirty captains from villages within Songó's putative concession came to Asindóópo and forced a large council meeting with the *gaamá*, for the matter to be finally resolved. Songó's chief advisor, Basiá Amèèkán-óli (a.k.a. Aduéngi) of Dángogó, was able to persuade the *gaamá* that the VSG was not trying to wrest power from him (for example, by trying to install an alternative *gaamá* downriver), and Songó finally declared himself. He admitted that he had indeed asked for the concession, but claimed that his motive was altruistic—to protect Saramakas' rights against outsiders—and he reported that in any case the government had refused him the concession. Henceforth, he declared, he would lend the full authority and powers of his office to the VSG in their fight against foreign exploitation of Saramaka territory.[10]

After many meetings between the VSG and village leaders up and down the river, the organization sent a formal petition addressed to His Excellency the President of Suriname, dated 24 October 1999.[11] It read, in part:

— Under section 1b of article 41 of the *Wet Bosbeheer* [the 1992 Forestry Act],

— under the Peace Treaty concluded in 1762 between our ancestors and the Netherlands, of which the Suriname government has been the legal successor since 1975,

— and under international human rights treaties ratified by Suriname, the undersigned, present at the council meeting . . . held on 24 October 1999 at Nieuw Aurora [Tutúbúka], wish to submit the following request to you by means of this appeal. They also make this request on behalf of their paramount chief Songó Abóikóni, who has given assurances that he backs the above-mentioned association.

The undersigned have gathered from maps issued by CELOS [the Center for Agricultural Research in Suriname, part of the University] in September 1999 that concessions were granted to third parties within their territory without the inhabitants being consulted beforehand.

They are of the opinion that this act on the part of the government, or the granting of said concessions,

1. constitutes a threat to their endeavors to have their land rights recognized,

2. is a repudiation of the traditional authorities and the inhabitants,

3. poses a threat to their physical and cultural survival; they wish to
    mention in particular:
    - the plots that provide them with food,
    - the rivers and streams that supply fish and pure drinking water,
    - the hunting grounds where they find their meat,
    - the plants and trees, which they use to build their houses and
      boats and which give them forest fruits, weaving material, and
      medicines,
    - the places where they practice their culture and religion.

The undersigned wish to emphasize that they are not against the
exploitation of timber in their area, but they think that it should be
carried out in consultation with the villages concerned. Besides, they
think that the exploitation should also benefit the entire population of
the interior. Their experiences with the construction of the reservoir
[the Afobaka project] are still fresh in their memory. They also think
that the exploitation of the forest should be carried out in a sustainable manner.

They refer to the promises made in the so-called Lelydorp Peace
Accord in 1992 [which ended the civil war] and the resolutions
adopted at the *Gran Krutu* held at Asindóópo in 1995 and at Galibi in
1996, guaranteeing the right to decide themselves what development
they wish to occur in the area where they have lived for centuries.

Finally, the undersigned refer to the various international human
rights conventions, declarations, and resolutions that recognize the
land rights of indigenous and tribal communities.

They urge you to take measures in order that the above-mentioned
concessions may be revoked without delay. They also insist that they
be consulted by the competent authorities before concessions are
granted in their territory.

In spite of the fact that this appeal is based on, among other things,
article 41 of the Forestry Act, they also request you to have the mining
concessions (stone, gold) in their area cancelled.

It seems a good idea to them to discuss this matter with you. They are
looking forward to hearing from you, in any case, within two weeks.

Within the next twelve months, the VSG submitted two more petitions to
the government in Paramaribo. None received an answer from the president
or anyone else.

A meeting about land rights, with Hugo at the microphone.

*   *   *

Discouraged and frustrated by their inability to get any kind of hearing from the government, the VSG decided to seek the protection of the Inter-American Commission on Human Rights. In October 2000—more than three years after the initial incursions of Chinese loggers—the VSG, along with twelve village captains representing each of the major matrilineal clans, filed a petition with the Commission.[12] This document called attention to Suriname's failure to recognize Saramaka rights to land and resources as defined by the American Convention on Human Rights and its active violation of those rights due to the logging and mining concessions it had granted in Saramaka territory.

I participated in this initial filing by writing a ten-page report that was included as Annex D, as well as by having my testimony about Saramaka society and history, from the Aloeboetoe case, cited in the body of the petition. MacKay had asked me to address the issue of Saramaka territory (its geographical extension and the nature of its legitimacy), Saramaka land ownership (the definition of the matrilineal clans—the *lôs*—that are the land-holding units), and Saramaka land use (the myriad ways that men and women use the forest and river for subsistence, construction, medicinal, and spiritual purposes), all of which I did. I then added a note on sovereignty, stressing the strength of Saramaka notions of territorial control and its historical origins.

Suriname's president, Ronald Venetiaan, reacted to this filing with anger. According to the national newspaper, he equated Maroons who file petitions with armed insurrectionists. He told the National Assembly that "when you open a website you see that there are people who say that they will start a guerrilla war with the help of some really impressive names of guerrilla organizations in Colombia, if their wishes are not being met." According to the head of state, the newspaper continued, "there are indeed elements who are trying to get a permanent armed struggle started in Suriname, such as is the case in countries like Colombia and Sri Lanka. Is that what one wants in Suriname?" he asked. "And let us not think that people don't have such wishes for our country," he warned. He also said that "if people think that this is just bluffing, they should take into account that the little people of Brokopondo [he is referring here to Ndyuka Maroons from Moiwana] and Sipaliwini [Saramaka Maroons represented by the VSG] are capable of going to neighboring countries and of offering petitions to the OAS."[13]

In June 2001 and May 2002, the VSG submitted additional materials to the Commission, each time providing updates on ongoing logging depredations, citing new legal arguments, and reiterating the demand expressed in the initial petition that the Commission issue precautionary measures (in effect, an injunction) to halt further logging activities while the case was being adjudicated. Once again, I participated in these filings from afar.

In early August 2002, the IACHR finally responded to these requests by issuing an order for precautionary measures, requesting that the government of Suriname take appropriate measures to suspend all concessions, including permits and licenses for logging and mine exploration and other natural resource development activity on lands used and occupied by the twelve Saramaka clans, until the Commission had the opportunity to investigate the substantive claims raised in the case.[14]

On 21 August, Hugo Jabini, on behalf of the Saramakas, sent a polite letter to Attorney General Subhaas Punwasi, asking how the government was planning to honor the Commission's request, and suggesting that

In light of the preceding, we encourage you to seek all available means to give effect to the precautionary measures issued by the

Commission, including obtaining "stop-work" orders, other adequate and appropriate administrative measures and, if necessary, judicial orders to suspend all logging and mining operations on lands occupied and used by the twelve Saramaka *lôs*. This includes a total withdrawal of all Surinamese military units guarding logging concessions in this area, or, at a minimum, an order to these military units that they shall cease any interference with the traditional subsistence and other practices of the members of the twelve Saramaka *lôs*.

But following its longstanding pattern of non-response to requests from Saramakas, the government remained silent. Punwasi, like many of his colleagues widely rumored to be involved in the drug trade, was apparently busy with other matters.[15]

Similar letters, including a formal petition to President Venetiaan, were sent during 2002 and 2003 by Jabini on behalf of the VSG (which had formally met and passed resolutions urging the government to act), but none received a response.[16] The Saramakas then submitted further information to the IACHR, arguing that since Suriname had ignored the Commission's requests for precautionary measures and that since considerable further destruction of Saramaka territory had taken place in the intervening twelve months, the Commission should now put some teeth behind its request by asking the Inter-American Court of Human Rights to issue an order for provisional measures.

Specifically, Petitioners' request that the Commission seek a provisional measures order from the Court requiring Suriname to suspend all logging and other natural resource development activities on the lands and territory traditionally owned or otherwise occupied and used by the twelve Saramaka *lôs* (clans) until such time as Case 12.338 has been resolved by the Inter-American human rights protection organs.

As part of this petition, I wrote a report in favor of provisional measures with the subheadings of "Territory," "Saramaka Laws about Territory," "Immediate Threats to the Forest Environment and their Effect on Diet and Material Culture," and "Immediate Threats to Saramaka Religious Life." The final section, "Threats to Cultural Survival—The Specter of Ethnocide," argued that "the destruction of the Saramakas' forest would mean the end of Saramaka culture," and that without protective measures "ethnocide—the destruction of a culture that is widely regarded as being one of the most creative and vibrant in the entire African diaspora—seems the most likely outcome." The report concluded that "the government's unilateral program to abrogate the Maroons' eighteenth-century treaties in the alleged interest of national unity is tantamount to ethnocide."[17]

*   *   *

The doctrine of full disclosure requires me to mention that during this whole period, Sally and I were physically absent from Suriname. In 1986, two heavily armed MPs had pulled us from our bed at midnight in a Paramaribo hotel, where we had recently arrived from Paris and were awaiting a plane to take us to the interior to visit the very ill Gaamá Agbagó, who had asked to see us before he died. This midnight intrusion, and the subsequent several-hour frightening ride through forest and savannas, tailed all the way by another MP vehicle—without any explanation at all from our captors and believing that at any moment they were going to stop and do us in—ended with our being locked in a room until dawn, having our passports stamped all over *ONGELDIG* (invalid), and then being hustled onto a ferry to French Guiana with the warning never to return.

By chance, and completely unbeknownst to us, the civil war between Ronnie Brunswijk's Jungle Commando and the government had begun that weekend and, as stalwart friends of the Maroons, we had apparently been designated personae non gratae. (When we later requested that the U.S. Embassy ask for clarification about our expulsion, the Suriname government responded to them that it had been "an administrative error.") Numerous friends in Paramaribo—people with political street smarts—suggested that such warnings from the military were meaningful and that we would be wise to keep our distance. Gaamá Agbagó clung to life until 1989, when he died quietly at the age of 102. I was badly torn between my wish to attend our friend's funeral and Sally's cautionary stance. In the end, I didn't take the risk and we had to content ourselves with videos and personal reports.

Commander Bouterse's second-hand threat, delivered through Judge Advocate-General de Freitas after my testimony at the 1992 trial in Costa Rica, only increased the pressure. Here we were, scholars whose whole lives had been devoted to Saramakas in Suriname, unable to feel that we would be safe arriving at the international airport, or even walking around the capital. Our solution, begun immediately after the 1986 expulsion, was to shift

Gravediggers, funeral of Gaamá Agbagó, 1989.

the bulk of our attention to Saramakas in French Guiana. In the wake of the civil war, Maroons had poured over the Marowijne, and before long almost one-third of all Saramakas were living in this tiny piece of Europe in South America. In any case, since 1986, we have spent our research time largely in this new site, working with people who—unlike ourselves—could move with ease back and forth across the border with Suriname. In the process, we

Funeral of Gaamá Agbagó.

stayed in close touch with developments in Saramaka territory, but always from a distance, second-hand as it were.[18]

* * *

When Gaamá Songó died in November 2003, Sally and I followed the complex political maneuverings concerning his succession from French Guiana, where we were working at the time.[19] Most Saramakas saw Songó as a weak leader, especially after he suffered a stroke during his final years. His tumultuous funeral, which dragged on until his burial more than three months later, was marked by the coffin's persistent refusal to name a successor (as it should have, through divination) and the *gaamás* in the cemetery refusing (again, through divination), until the final moment, to "accept" Songó for burial as one of their own. Without awaiting the "second funeral" some months later, after which the successor is normally named, Albert Abóikóni (the interim *gaamá* and therefore prohibited from becoming a candidate for the permanent position) quickly went to Paramaribo and announced that his own brother, Otjútju (a.k.a. Belfón Abóikóni), had been chosen as the next *gaamá*, and his picture was duly published in the major Suriname newspaper, *De Ware Tijd*. (Since the eighteenth century, tradition has it that once the Saramakas select and enstool the new *gaamá*, he travels to the city where he is officially installed and given a uniform by the colonial/national government.)

When we arrived in Cayenne on 18 April 2004, Otjútju's formal enstoolment as *gaamá* six days earlier was, for Saramakas, the talk of the town. A Saramaka friend had just returned from a weekend in Paramaribo with photos of the new chief, legs whitened with kaolin according to tradition, head tied in a kerchief, sitting in the ancestor shrine of Asindóópo, and holding the *gaamá*'s staff of office. But only two days later, in the village of Dángogó, another man—Ozéni—was enstooled in the ancestor shrine of that village. The Saramakas suddenly had two rival *gaamás* and no one knew quite what to make of it. Disputes and rivalries for political office have always been part of the Saramaka political scene. But in the past, it had always been rival clans vying for the office. Here, two men who were closely related Matjáu-clan members of the Dángogó community had somehow split it right down the middle.

Otjútju had never hidden his political ambitions. When I knew him in the 1960s and 1970s, he was a close confidant of the wise and respected

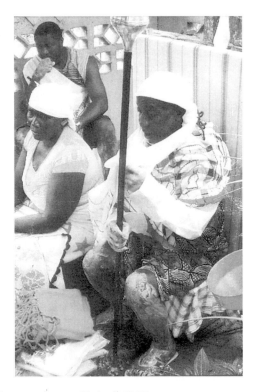

Gaamá Belfón's enstoolment, 12 April 2005.

Gaamá Agbagó Abóikóni and, apparently, his preferred successor.[20] He had long collaborated with outsiders on various projects—he was the first Saramaka to serve as manager of an airstrip in the interior and one of the few to have a small store. In *First-Time*, I described him as "very much caught between the worlds of the coast and Saramaka" and noted that "he gave me some of my most important leads about First-Time, though his information sometimes turned out upon examination to be spurious"—by which I meant "politically motivated." I knew Ozéni only by reputation, as a man from Dángogó, the village where we were based, who had chosen to live and work in Paranam, Alcoa's company town on the coast. Allegedly a mild-mannered man, Ozéni—I suspected—gained his support for the office of *gaamá* less for anything he represented than for not being Otjútju. Many Saramakas, and particularly many from Dángogó, didn't really trust Otjútju, whom they saw as too much of a manipulator. Genealogically, both fit the bill.

The talk among my Saramaka friends in Cayenne was, however, of an entirely different nature. Yes, they all agreed that Otjútju was the consummate political animal, and that this made him well-suited to the office. But more to the point, Otjútju was not to be messed with. First off, he's what is known as "master of the great avenging spirit"—he has in his head one of the most powerful avenging spirits of his lineage. Second his namesake (the ancestor found via divination to have contributed to his birth) is Bôò, the mother of Gaamá Agbagó, and her own namesake was Lukéinsi, the daughter of Adjágbò and Paánza and the medium of the First-Time forest spirit Wámba, giving him a supernatural lineage of great power.[21] Once Otjútju had been ritually enstooled in the ancestor shrine of Asindóópo, who could dare to try and take the office away from him and survive?

A friend who'd just returned from Suriname played us a cassette with the audio of Otjútju's installation. Captain Tooy Alexander, an expert on Saramaka ritual, listened intently to the *apínti* rhythms and commented on exactly what they said: "*Fúndi ofón, fúndi ofón, fúndi ofón, alákatáka fúndi ofón*—The Suriname River is without a headman. The ship has no steersman. The ship turns sideways and drifts dangerously." And then it played, "*Séi kúnya, séi kúnya, séi kúnya, alábatáta séi kúnya*—The river has found a headman. The ship has found a steersman." After that we listened as women sang lively *sekêti* songs composed for the occasion, celebrating Otjútju's enstoolment. "This dispute will have an outcome one way or the other," laughed Tooy. "When a woman's pregnant, if she doesn't have a boy she'll have a girl. Even if she doesn't have a boy or a girl, she'll have some sort of child with teeth in its mouth. Let's just wait and see!"

The next day a Saramaka man arrived with what he said was the inside dope—and it soon seemed he was on to something. The conflict wasn't about personalities or traditional genealogy; it was about the very modern forces of money, corruption, and development. There were credible rumors that a certain "Pésé," a Frenchman who ran French Guiana's largest gold mine, had made a deal with Gaamá Songó shortly before his death to "develop" Saramaka, with plans to build a five-star hotel across the river from Asindóópo, lengthen the nearby airstrip at Djoemoe, build a road linking all the Saramaka villages with the outside world, and open up a massive gold mine inside the sacred Paaba Creek. Songó's death temporarily halted the project, though Pésé sent massive amounts of goods to the funeral, as a show of his respect. (I recall having heard at the time of the funeral that a "Frenchman" had sent a private plane and a number of canoes carrying thousands of dollars of goods, from bolts of cloth to cases of rum and soft drinks as gifts.) Now, according to the latest rumors, Ozéni and his supporters intended to continue with Songó's secret plans while Otjútju wanted nothing to do with Pésé.

My friend Tooy surprised me by saying he knew Pésé. "That man's been in Guyane for years, living in St. Laurent. He once killed seven Amerindian headmen with that *óbia* of his—he keeps it in a sack that he wears over his shoulder. It has an *asamaká* [a dead man's skull] in it.... He would go into the forest all by himself and ask his *óbia* if he should sleep in a certain spot that night, and if it said no, he'd move on. He works with it all the time." Tooy told how Pésé had built himself a house in St. Laurent, but his wife left to go back to her own country. He asked Tooy if he'd pour libations to bring her back. Tooy did and a week later she returned. Since then, Pésé has been a fan. But Tooy warned me about the man. He was once up near St. Elie, where Pésé's company mines gold, and learned that Pésé steals Saramaka children from the coast to sacrifice to the devil who owns the gold in the bowels of the earth—diamonds too, he's heard. Pésé has the children kidnapped and dropped from his helicopters near the goldfields.

One afternoon, Sally and I visited Kalusé, a Dángogó man who's been living in Cayenne for decades. He told us that the week before, both parties to the *gaamá* dispute had agreed to go to the Lángu oracle at Béndiwáta to see what she said—three captains from Dángogó, and three of Otjútju's supporters, all with their cassettes to record the verdict. The oracle tilted in favor of Dángogó, saying that the first person they met when they returned to the landing place should be the next *gaamá*—and it turned out to be Ozéni. Kalusé said he can't see how Otjútju stands a chance, since the only people present at his alleged enstoolment were his brother (the interim *gaamá*), the *apínti* drummer, and a couple of friends.

A few days later, when we were in St. Laurent, the border town just across the river from Suriname, we paid a visit to Saramaka captain Antonísi, who we'd been told was Pésé's middleman with Saramakas. An old friend, he told us that the man's name is really Alain Pichet, that he owns the St. Elie gold mine, and that he employs dozens of Saramakas. He indeed spent some 10,000 Euros for Songó's funeral, entrusting Antonísi to buy and deliver ten cases of Gandia (a sweet, fortified Spanish wine much appreciated by Saramaka women), ten cases of rum, sixteen cases of beer, twenty-five kilos of kidney beans, twenty-five kilos of salted pig's tails, boxes and boxes of shotgun cartridges, three cases of black gunpowder, and a fine shotgun to hang in the house of mourning, which would later be hung by the new *gaamá* in his audience-chamber, and he gave Antonísi another 3,500 Euros to buy whatever he thought should be added. Now, complained Antonísi, some people are claiming behind his back that he took some of the money and others that Pichet is going to reward him with fifty kilos of gold! (I did notice that he's got a massive new flat-screen TV.) Antonísi added that Otjútju was improperly installed because tradition has it that a *gaamá* must be enstooled in Dángogó, not in Asindóópo. So, Ozéni must be the real *gaamá*.[22]

During the following days, rumors continued to fly in Cayenne. A supporter of Ozéni assured us that no one came to Otjútju's enstoolment except his brother and the *apínti* drummer—there were no captains or guests from elsewhere. It wasn't at all like a *gaamá*'s installation, he said. (But the photos we'd seen seem to give the lie to that.) A Dángogó supporter of Otjútju reported that all up and down the river the villages are for Otjútju, that Dángogó is isolated in, for the most part, supporting Ozéni. Otjútju is already sitting in his "office" at Asindóópo, receiving people and acting very much the *gaamá*.

The big news was that Gaama Gazón, the Ndyuka who was the most senior of all living Maroon chiefs, had sent a personal delegation to Saramaka to try to sort out the situation. They found Otjútju in his office and greeted him as *gaamá*, even offering him a "piece" of the Ndyuka god Gaán Tatá, as a gesture of friendship, to help him reign. When they visited Dángogó, Captain Amèèkán-óli (a.k.a. Aduéngi) threw them out. He said this wasn't a Ndyuka matter and they should get back to their own river. But the Ndyukas came ashore and walked right up to Gaán Tatá's house. (Since the early twentieth century, Dángogó has had a branch of Gaán Tatá that serves as the major village oracle. People from Dángogó had brought it over from Ndyuka.) They asked Captain Amèèkán-óli what that "thing" on the plank there was. The *sóói-gádu* of Mamá Ndyuka? "Get outta here!" they said. The Ndyuka captain pointed to his chest and said that the *sóói-gádu* of Mamá Ndyuka was there and that what Dángogó had was worth nothing. The Ndyukas returned to Asindóópo, where they met with Otjútju and his councilors for three days. The Ndyukas said that Otjútju's name had been written in the whitefolks' book in the city for nearly a year already. He's sitting on the *gaamá*'s stool. Who's going to pull him off? No one knows the other man. If Amèèkán-óli enstooled him, he'll be the one to pay his salary and buy him a uniform because the whitefolks never even heard of him.[23]

Tooy concluded that Otjútju will be the winner. "When Agbagó became *gaamá* he sat on the stool with Todjê [his tutelary sea-god]. Songó did it all alone—and he did it badly. But Otjútju—he has the great avenging spirit of the Pikílío in his head! Who's about to take the *gaamá*-ship away from him? The person who tries—if they don't bury him in seven days they'll bury him in fourteen days."

A Dángogó visitor reported that in fact large numbers of people came for Otjútju's enstoolment—several planeloads of whitefolks and even some city policemen.

The Saramakas played Nanábulúku,[24] then Apúku, then Komantí! Otjútju has always worked with whitefolks/city folks. Even if only for that, they'll make him *gaamá*. You know that Pésé and Songó had agreed to open up a gold mine in the Pikílío and the others knew if Otjútju won, he'd stop that, he wouldn't want some Frenchman to get all the profits. But if Ozéni won, the contract made by Songó would continue. Otjútju wants a new contract with the city. Nowadays, if you go more than 100 meters from the riverbank, people start telling you that it's not your river anymore. Otjútju will end all that! The city officials have summoned Otjútju to the city, but because of the national elections it's been postponed. Amèèkán-óli and Ozéni are really screwed! Saramakas had decided they'd make Ozéni a headcaptain in compensation for him yielding to Otjútju as *gaamá* but now that Amèèkán-óli insulted the Ndyukas, he won't get a thing.

Tooy remarked that when you take a knife away from a child, you give it a stick. But Amèèkán-óli had ruined all hope of even that happening!

Meanwhile, the city government was at a standstill because of national elections scheduled for 25 May—everyone knew that they would do nothing to sort out the dispute in Saramaka for weeks or months, until a president and a cabinet were in place.

Tooy's elderly blind brother, Sensiló, chimed in with some history, trying to put some perspective on present-day pretenders to the *gaamá*-ship.

Once, District Commissioner Junker summoned Gaamá Djankusó to a meeting. [Junker was trying hard to get the Saramaka *gaamá* under his thumb during the early years of the twentieth century, but Djankusó consistently outmaneuvered him.] Each one knew the other wouldn't kill him in public. So they arranged to meet on neutral ground, at the mouth of Gaánkiíki. The first thing Djankusó said to the white man was, "Anacondas—I'm their boss. Jaguars—I'm their boss. Human beings—I'm their boss. Poisonous snakes—I'm their boss. Do you think you can fool with me? Let's live and work together." That was a *gaamá*! Do you think we've seen another one lately?

Nine weeks after we left Guyane on the final day of May 2005, we got the news in a phone call from Tooy. Otjútju was the new *gaamá*![25]

Yet, the leadership dispute dragged on for years, with a group of youths from Dángogó (some say funded by Pésé) at one point kidnapping Gaamá Otjútju, after which they were arrested and convicted, and served time in a Paramaribo prison—since then, the *gaamá* has had police bodyguards provided by the government. But, by the end of 2006, Gaamá Otjútju (Belfón) had managed to stabilize his position and was functioning as traditional ruler. It was in this capacity that he began cooperating with the VSG, eventually playing an important symbolic role in the hearing before the Inter-American Court of Human Rights in 2007.

The Depredations Continue

Even as the IACHR was deliberating the case of *The Saramaka People* (or *The 12 Lôs*) *v. Suriname*, other kinds of evidence were piling up from international organizations that Suriname was not taking human rights, and especially the rights of the indigenous and Maroon peoples living within its borders, at all seriously. A sixty-eight-page report submitted in 2002 by three Suriname organizations—the VSG, the Association of Indigenous Village Leaders in Suriname, and Stichting Sanomaro Esa—as well as the Forest Peoples Programme to the U.N. Special Rapporteur on the Situation of Human Rights and Fundamental Freedoms of Indigenous Peoples, set the stage for subsequent reports on the situation in Suriname by CERD, the U.N. Committee on the Elimination of Racial Discrimination.[1] It's worth examining that 2002 report more closely. It began by stressing that

> Suriname is the only state in the Americas that has failed to legally recognize and guarantee some measure of protection for indigenous and tribal rights to lands, territories and resources. Coupled with substantial and highly prejudicial resource exploitation operations, this failure to recognize and respect territorial and resource rights has led to gross violations of indigenous and tribal peoples' human rights, undermined their means of subsistence, and severely compromised their physical, cultural and economic integrity. As territorial and other rights are not recognized and protected by Surinamese law, indigenous and tribal peoples are without adequate and effective remedies to assert and defend their rights in domestic procedures leaving them no choice but to seek international oversight, intervention and protection. International attention is urgently needed as violations of indigenous and tribal rights in Suriname are widespread, systematic and substantial and the nature and impact of the violations is immediate, ongoing and, in some cases, irreversible.

The report went on to document and analyze not only the human rights abuses relating to logging but also a number of others, including discrimination against Maroons and indigenous peoples in terms of health care.

Many communities do not have functioning health care facilities. Those that do exist have few, or in some cases no, supplies and are rarely visited by a qualified doctor. Immunization rates are 50 percent lower than on the coast.... Malaria, also related to mining activities, has reached "epidemic" proportions in many parts of the interior. According to the Pan American Health Organization, Suriname has the highest incidence of malaria infection in the Americas.

The report singled out discrimination in education as well—the State provides "an allowance of Sf 26.50 (or US$0.05) per student per year for maintenance of the buildings and school materials" in the interior.[2] And destruction of the environment through mining activities also received a place.

An estimated 15–30,000 Brazilian small-scale miners are operating in Suriname under license from the government as are many thousands of local small-scale miners. It is estimated that 20–30 tonnes of mercury are released into the environment, most of it inhabited by indigenous and tribal peoples, every year. Other sources estimate that between 1993 and 1998, gold miners dumped over 150,000 kg of mercury into the environment. Some indigenous and tribal communities report that their rivers and other water sources are unfit for human consumption and that they catch fish with tumors and soapy white eyes.

But rights to land remained the focus of the report, with several poignant case histories, including that of Nieuw Koffiekamp, one of the transmigration villages from under Alcoa's lake that was then preparing for a second forced relocation to make way for a giant gold mine run by Canadian multinationals Cambior and Golden Star, another that of the Ndyuka Maroon villagers of Adjoemakondre, near the town of Moengoe, who had once lived surrounded by lush forest but now, because of Alcoa's extension of bauxite mining into their lands, "live in a moonscape, surrounded by blasted rock, covered in dust and debris from blasting and are subjected to high intensity lights that allow mining to take place twenty-four hours a day, seven days a week," and that of several other communities threatened by multinational mining

Ndyuka Maroon small-scale gold miners.

companies. The report also introduced the thorny issue of protected areas—nature reserves and the like—which, like mining and logging concessions in Suriname, have been established without regard to the needs (or opinions) of the indigenous and Maroon peoples who live or work within their boundaries. This subject merits our special attention.

In June 1998, Suriname and Conservation International had conducted a remarkable public relations campaign, culminating with a lead editorial in *The New York Times* that was headlined "Suriname's Example." At a press conference featuring Harrison Ford posed in front of the United Nations Building in New York, the rainforest protection group, which was in partnership in Suriname with Bristol-Myers Squibb, announced the creation of a 4-million-acre nature (and bio-prospecting) park in central Suriname. The idea was that it would be free from logging and mining, and maintained with the assistance of funds from Conservation International.[3] A month later, the reserve was officially created by presidential resolution. "Established to protect and preserve the natural resources in Suriname," it was said to amount to nearly 10 percent of the total landmass of the country and to constitute the largest area of protected tropical forest in the world. The designated area was said not to include either Amerindian or Maroon lands. It was soon declared a UNESCO World Heritage Site.

Although *The New York Times* almost certainly did not know it, Conservation International must have been aware that the project provided a timely smokescreen for Suriname's ongoing forestry depredations just to the west of the park. (The situation was reminiscent of that in the 1960s, when Alcoa's hydroelectric project received a great deal of feel-good publicity as part of the International Society for the Protection of Animals' save-the-wildlife project.) It would be legitimate to view the very public announcement of the nature reserve as a magnificent diversion from the vast devastation and abuse that Suriname was simultaneously perpetrating in precisely those areas of the forest where large numbers of Maroons and Amerindians did, in fact, live.

What was not announced was that the Central Suriname Nature Reserve actually expropriated one-third of the territory over which the Kwinti Maroons had exercised ownership and other rights since the eighteenth century as well as areas traditionally owned by the Trio indigenous peoples in the south of the reserve. The presidential resolution, adopting language similar to that found in other Suriname government documents, stated simply, with regard to the rights of the Kwinti and the Trio, that "the villages and settlements of bushland inhabitants living in tribes, will be respected as long as it is

(a) not contrary to the general interest or the national goal of the established nature reserve and if (b) it is not provided otherwise."

Flush with this 1998 success, Conservation International had larger horizons in mind.

*   *   *

The Lángu clan, whose traditional homeland lies above the formidable natural barriers of Tapáwáta and Gaándan falls and includes all the villages on the Gaánlío (the largest tributary of the Suriname River), is among the most powerful of Saramaka *lôs* (matrilineal clans). Its proud history (which I've had the privilege to learn more about from one of its most knowledgeable elders, Captain Tooy Alexander, during the past decade), includes the early eighteenth-century escapes from slavery of Kaásipúmbu and Wíi—the iconic African-born ancestors who index the clan's two segments, the Kaapátu and Kadósu. Kaási first led his people south to a village near the pool of Ma Pugúsu where Wíi's people joined them, and which they miraculously crossed when government troops attacked in 1712.[4] Soon, they founded a short-lived village at Mindindéti Creek, and then moved into the area of the Kleine Saramacca River where they lived until the fierce battles of 1730–31.[5] Then, after two decades moving southward, through various village sites still remembered today, Kaási and his people settled in the great mountaintop redoubt of Bákakúun, just behind the distant mountains that appear as clouds on the horizon from the Gaánlío territory that his Lángu descendants call home today.[6] On the journey southward, it was also Kaási who "purified the river," a ritual act that permitted all Saramakas to drink and wash in it and live along its banks.[7]

Saramakas remember the battle at Bákakúun, in 1749, as their finest wartime moment—the defenders, having first hidden their women and children in the forest, lured the white soldiers up a great ditch and then, just as they approached the summit, rolled down mighty tree roots until they were crushed.[8] Soon after, the Lángu people moved down from the mountain toward the Gaánlío and established new villages, playing signal roles in the final battles of the 1750s. Then, in 1762, one of their own brought about the proudest moment in Saramaka history—Wíi, after an extremely complex series of events, became the man who finally "brought the Peace" to Saramaka.[9] And then, throughout the whole second half of the eighteenth century, one of Wíi's sisters' sons, Antamá, acknowledged as the greatest of all Saramaka *óbia*-men, held sway along the Gaánlío.[10] Since settling along the Gaánlío in the eighteenth century, Kaási's descendants in the village of Béndiwáta have controlled the most important oracle in all Saramaka, the one that the *gaamá* must consult, even today, for any matter of national importance.

In other words, the Lángu clan has a great deal to be proud of and possesses a large territory replete with historical and sacred meaning. Imagine then, their reaction when, sometime in 2002, Lángu leaders learned of Conservation International's plan to make all of Lángu territory (as well as a good deal of the lands belonging to the powerful Matjáu clan) part of an expanded Central Suriname Nature Reserve. This was to be a "nature-and-tourist reserve" that would expropriate about 40 percent of remaining Saramaka territory without consultation or consent, and—if current law were to be applied—would legally confirm that this part of Saramaka territory is "state land," and that Saramakas would be prohibited from farming, fishing, and hunting within its borders.[11]

As best I can tell, there were two motives for CI's 2001–2002 initiative to expand the reserve into Saramaka territory. First, CI's master plan called for a "conservation corridor" running from Venezuela through Guyana and Suriname to French Guiana and the states of Amapá and Pará in Brazil, and Saramaka territory was a building block along this corridor. Second, the Gordon and Betty Moore Foundation (with its Intel-generated endowment of $6 billion) had made a $261 million commitment to CI in December 2001, and reportedly required that CI secure a certain amount of protected lands acreage per year.

Soon after they learned of CI's expansion plans, the VSG organized a *gaán kuútu* (tribal council meeting) that concluded with a resolution that Conservation International

> suspend all attempts to incorporate our ancestral lands within the Central Suriname Nature Reserve; that the Government of Suriname revoke any permissions or permits issued to Conservation International by which it may be undertaking the abovementioned activities; and that the preceding applies at least until such time as the case pending before the Inter-American human rights system has been resolved and until full and meaningful consultation with the Saramaka people has taken place and we have given our consent to any activity that may affect our rights to our lands, territories and resources.[12]

And a group of Lángu captains and other village officials, as well as the VSG, wrote additional letters and petitions requesting that the project be shelved until their case before the IACHR was resolved.[13] But, according to one report, CI ignored these requests and instead brought a Saramaka head-captain to Paramaribo to publicly denounce the requests for suspension. CI-Suriname staff members apparently also threatened the Saramakas with legal action for interfering with donor relations and for libel in connection with their opposition to the proposed expansion.

After receiving no response to their requests and complaints, the VSG then raised these issues directly with the IACHR, stating that

Despite repeated requests and formal petitions to State authorities, petitioners have not received any official confirmation about the status of the plans of Conservation International, a United States-based environmental organization, to expand the Central Suriname Nature Reserve. No response to requests for information has been received from Conservation International either. Petitioners observe that these two entities are the only bodies that possess and can share formal information about the plans to expand the CSNR and neither is willing to provide that information.[14]

The VSG also informed the IACHR that

in July 2003, Conservation International presented detailed maps of the proposed extension to twelve Saramaka communities in the affected area. Conservation International explained that these maps were produced as part of its efforts to expand the Central Suriname Nature Reserve and that these efforts had the support of the State.[15]

And then came a potentially incendiary accusation.

Additionally, at least one traditional Saramaka leader has alleged that representatives of this organization [Conservation International] have told him that he will receive US$500 per month once the expansion has taken place. This statement was confirmed by a number of witnesses.[16]

Before long, facing the threat of devastatingly bad publicity and after meeting with the lawyer for the Saramakas to discuss the situation, Conservation

International agreed to shelve its plans to expand the nature reserve into Saramaka territory (at least until the case before the inter-American system had been resolved) and informed the VSG by letter. In a mid-October communication to the IACHR, the VSG noted that they had now "received assurances from the conservation organization involved that it will cease its efforts to expand the nature reserve."[17]

This was undoubtedly good news for the Saramakas. In 2008, Andrew Westoll, a Canadian writer, published an account of five months traveling through what the book's cover describes as "the most surreal country in South America" that details the full range of modern horrors. His take on the kind of ecotourism proposed by Conservation International:

> Ecotourism here looks like a new form of imperialism. The new visitor's centre [in CI's nature reserve at Raleigh Falls, Suriname], financed by money from Wal-Mart and Intel, will dwarf the very forest it was built to promote. Soon, it will host an internet café, crowds of Dutch tourists drinking Coca-Cola, hordes of European teenagers performing cannonballs into the water and getting high on the rocks, gaggles of young women on vacation looking to bed a wild, primitive Maroon.[18]

*   *   *

The U.N. Committee on the Elimination of Racial Discrimination (CERD) issued several condemnatory reports on Suriname during this period, in part reacting to the report submitted to them by Indigenous and Maroon groups in 2002.[19]

In its March 2004 report, for example, CERD noted that after eighteen years of non-compliance, Suriname had finally submitted a report on racial discrimination within the nation (normally due every five years) and had sent a delegation to the Committee. But it went on to deplore Suriname's treatment of its indigenous and Maroon populations, making formal recommendations that there be "legal acknowledgement by the State party of the rights of indigenous and tribal peoples to possess, develop, control, and use their communal lands and to participate in the exploitation, management, and conservation of the associated natural resources." It also recommended "urgent action by [Suriname], in cooperation with the indigenous and tribal peoples concerned, to identify the lands which those peoples have traditionally occupied and used." Noting that the rights of indigenous peoples and Maroons had been violated by logging and mining activities in the interior, the Committee stated that "development objectives are no justification for encroachments on human rights." Among various other recommendations, CERD asked that Suriname "respect and promote the indigenous and tribal peoples' cultures, languages, and distinctive ways of life" and that it conduct "a survey, in collaboration with the groups concerned, of the impact of economic development in the indigenous and tribal peoples' lands on their collective and individual cultural rights."[20] As the press release on this report, written by the Forest Peoples Programme, put it,

> The Committee's observations on the situation in Suriname confirm what indigenous peoples and Maroons have been saying since Suriname's independence from the Netherlands in 1975. Despite a number of agreements and promises and many attempts by indigenous peoples and Maroons to resolve these issues with the government, no progress has been made. Not only has no progress been made, but the situation in the interior continues to deteriorate every year as more logging and mining concessions are granted.[21]

In its July 2005 submission to CERD, the Suriname organizations noted that they had already made four submissions, beginning in 2002, but that dire new developments on the ground—as well as Suriname's failure to heed any of the Committee's 2004 recommendations—necessitated the transmission of further information. They ended their report with the plea that "the Committee elevate the level of its dialogue with and oversight of Suriname by considering the situation of indigenous and tribal peoples under its Emergency/Urgent Action procedure so as to assist Suriname in ensuring that the rights guaranteed by the Convention [International Convention on the Elimination of all Forms of Racial Discrimination] are fully recognized and respected in law and practice."[22]

Over the next four years there were continued submissions to the Committee by the Suriname organizations and continued rulings by the Committee castigating the government of Suriname for various kinds of noncompliance. The 2009 CERD report concludes that Suriname's efforts to implement its "concluding observations" of 2004 and to comply with the Committee's "decisions under the early warning and urgent action procedures in 2003, 2005, and 2006" have simply been "insufficient." CERD's 2009 assessment and recommendations were polite but to the point.

Recognizing the fact that the State Party's national economy heavily depends on the natural resource extraction industry—namely mining and logging—including in ancestral lands and traditional settlements of indigenous and tribal peoples, the Committee remains concerned about the protection of the rights to land, territories and communal resources of the indigenous and tribal peoples living in the interior of the country. Similarly, the Committee is concerned at the nonexistence of specific legislative framework to guarantee the realization of the collective rights of indigenous and tribal peoples. . . .

The Committee urges the State Party to ensure legal acknowledgement of the collective rights of indigenous and tribal peoples—known locally as Maroons and Bush Negroes—to own, develop, control, and use their lands, resources, and communal territories according to customary laws and traditional land tenure system and to participate in the exploitation, management, and conservation of the associated natural resources.[23]

*   *   *

Nearly six years after the VSG submitted its initial petition in the case that came to be known as *The Saramaka People v. Suriname*, the IACHR issued its final ruling. It had been a long haul for all concerned. My rough count shows that some five dozen substantial documents passed back and forth between the VSG, the IACHR, and the State during the years of deliberations. There were a number of meetings in Paramaribo between the State and the Saramakas and several hearings with the parties in attendance in Washington as well.

After carefully laying out the history of the case and the relevant legal considerations, the Commission concluded, in a fifty-four-page decision, that

The State violated the right to property established in Article 21 of the American Convention to the detriment of the Saramaka people by not adopting effective measures to recognize its communal property right to the lands it has traditionally occupied and used.

The State violated the right to judicial protection enshrined in Article 25 of the American Convention, to the detriment of the Saramaka people, by not providing it effective access to justice for the protection of its fundamental rights.

The State of Suriname violated Articles 1 and 2 of the Convention by failing to recognize or give effect to the collective rights of the Saramaka people to their lands and territories.

On June 23, 2006, having received no appropriate response from the Republic of Suriname, the Commission officially passed the case along to the Inter-American Court of Human Rights for legally binding adjudication.[24]

Judgment Day

Pre-Hearing Pleadings

In the eleven months between the Commission's submitting its "Application" to the Court, asking it "to determine the international responsibility of the State of Suriname ... for violations committed by the State against the Saramaka people and its members," and the climactic two-day hearing in San Jose, Costa Rica (9–10 May 2007), three documents passed between the Saramakas, the State, and the Court. In November 2006, the legal representatives of the Saramakas submitted a 62-page document entitled "Pleadings, Motions and Evidence." In January 2007, Suriname responded with a 125-page document of its own (mainly arguing that the Court should declare the case inadmissible), to which the Saramakas' representatives submitted their own lengthy "Observations" in March.

The Saramakas' "pleadings"[1] tell a story that should by now be familiar to readers of this book. They begin by laying out "the facts" of the case in a section called "The Saramaka People and Its Territory."[2] This is followed by sections on Suriname's "Disregard for the Rights of the Saramaka People in Practice" (including subsections on the Afobaka dam and reservoir, logging and mining concessions, and environmental damage), on the "Disregard for Saramaka Rights in Suriname's Constitution and Laws," on "Suriname's Land Titling Procedure," and finally on the lack of "Judicial Remedies" for the Saramakas in Suriname. The pleadings then spell out Suriname's violations of Articles 1, 2, 3, 21, and 25 of the American Convention, discuss the continuing validity of the 1762 treaty, and argue that the State should pay the Saramakas material damages, moral damages, and costs, as well as offering other forms of reparation. The document ends with a conclusion and presentation of evidentiary/testimonial annexes.

As I read them, these "pleadings" diverge from the IACHR's "Application" to the Court in four major respects. The Saramaka representatives insist upon four aspects of their complaint that were hardly mentioned by the IACHR: (1) the continuing depredations caused by the building of the Afobaka dam, (2)

the continuing importance to Saramakas of the Treaty of 1762 and its continuing legal validity, (3) the State's violation of Article 3 of the American Convention (The Right to Juridical Personality), and (4) that the Saramakas are
a self-determining people with attendant rights, including ownership of all
resources within Saramaka territory and the right to freely dispose of them,
as well as the right to freely pursue their own economic, social, and cultural
development, even when this diverges from the State's plans for them.[3]

The "pleadings" include several strong pages on the dam and its consequences, reiterating arguments and a good deal of evidence previously submitted to the Commission in various petitions. After outlining the building
of the dam and expropriation of half of Saramaka territory in the 1960s,
without consultation of any kind with Saramakas, the document discusses
the dam's continuing deleterious effects on Saramaka land use, spiritual life,
and material well-being (including mercury poisoning from small-scale gold
mining in the region now harboring refugees from villages that are now
under the lake). And it ends with a discussion of the State's proposed Tapanahoni River Diversion Project, which would force the displacement of a number of Ndyuka villages on the Tapanahoni, as well as raising the level of the
Afobaka reservoir so that a number of additional Saramaka villages just to
its south would be flooded—all this to increase the generating power of the
Afobaka hydroelectric dam so that Alcoa could reopen and expand its aluminum smelting capabilities. (This project is currently pending before IIRSA,
funded in part by the Inter-American Development Bank, and is slated to
cost US$880 million.)

The Saramaka representatives also insist on the continuing importance of
the 1762 treaty. As we have seen, in *Aloeboetoe v. Suriname* the Court found
it "unnecessary" to investigate whether that document constituted an "international treaty" but commented that, if it were, "it would be invalid today
because it would be contrary to the rules of *jus cogens superveniens*" (where
a new peremptory norm of international law voids any conflicting provisions
of an older international treaty). In their pleadings, the Saramaka representatives make a long argument about the legal separability of the offending
clauses of the treaty (concerning the capture, return, and sale of new runaway
slaves) from its core clauses (granting freedom and territory to the Saramakas), stating that:

It would be a grave injustice if the treaty *in toto* were voided due to
a provision that the Saramakas neither wanted nor complied with,

that has had no effect in law and relations between the parties, since slavery was abolished in Suriname over 150 years ago, and was not central to the consent of the parties when they concluded the Treaty. As noted above and as discussed further below, such a result also contradicts established international law.[4]

They further argued that:

This issue is relevant to the current case because the 1762 Treaty, reaffirmed in 1835, is a foundational instrument for the Saramaka people, an instrument that confirmed their freedom from slavery and their rights to political, cultural and territorial autonomy. In law and principle, the Treaty also established a relationship based on consent and mutual respect between the Saramaka and the Dutch and with Suriname as successor to the Dutch. [Report of Prof. Richard Price, Annex D of the petition of 30 September 2000, in Annex 1 to the Application of the Commission, para. 4.1.] It is a sacred instrument consecrated by the blood oath of their most renowned and powerful ancestors whose spirits are revered and invoked to this day. To disregard the Treaty would, from the Saramaka perspective, constitute a gross and spiritually reckless offence against these most powerful ancestral spirits.[5]

Given that Saramakas—in their own terms—base their collective territorial rights, as well as the rights that undergird their ongoing relationship with the city government, on the 1762 Treaty, it seems entirely fitting that they should wish to reiterate its significance to the Court and plead here for the Court to reconsider its summary dismissal of the issue in *Aloeboetoe*. For Saramakas, the treaty represents their fundamental definition of the situation (see the King Nothing-hurts-him folktale in an earlier chapter) and, in this logic, it is only by insisting on this definition—and rejecting outsiders' definitions—that they can ultimately triumph.

Finally, the Saramakas argue in their pleadings that the State violated their rights under Article 3 of the American Convention, which provides that "Every person has the right to recognition as a person before the law." This right is significant because the enjoyment of domestic legal protections depends on legal personality. As the pleadings point out, "Denial of the right to legal personality precludes the vesting, exercise, and enjoyment of fundamental human rights and renders persons and collectivities invisible to domestic law and the protections that it may provide."[6] Under the laws of Suriname, only individuals, corporations, or nonprofit organizations have legal personality. This means that indigenous or tribal peoples (or their communities as collectivities) cannot be recognized as legal persons for the purposes of applying for and holding title to land. As the pleadings argue, "That this is the situation in Suriname was acknowledged by the Court in *Moiwana Village*, by the Commission in *Twelve Saramaka Clans*, and by the U.N. Committee on the Elimination of Racial Discrimination."[7] The Saramakas here insist on their right to self-determination and definition as a people and argue that Suriname's unwillingness to grant these rights constitutes a violation of Article 3 of the Convention.

> As discussed above in connection with the property rights protected by Article 21, Article 3 of the Convention must also be interpreted in light of the Saramaka people's right to self-determination, as guaranteed by common Article 1 of the Covenants and as affirmed in the United Nations Declaration on the Rights of Indigenous Peoples. This necessitates that Suriname recognize the juridical personality of the Saramaka people as a distinct *people* rather than simply as communities or some other sub-entity of the people as a whole.[8]

Compared to these pleadings, the other two documents that precede the hearing before the Court seem lightweight. Suriname's submission[9] is a scattershot defense of the State's behavior that is fraught with accusations, insinuations, and *ad hominem* attacks leveled at the Saramakas' legal representatives and expert witnesses. For example, referring to "the foreign attorney Fergus MacKay," it states that he "has proven that his main purpose is not the acknowledgment by the State of the land rights of the Saramaka people but the accomplishment of his own personal agenda"[10] and that he "is single-handedly destroying the culture and customs of the Saramaka people."[11] It claims that attorney David Padilla, who had formerly served as assistant executive secretary of the IACHR, created a conflict of interest by now joining MacKay as legal advisor to the Saramakas.[12] It refers to Hugo Jabini as "an active member of the National Democratic Party, the party headed by Mr. D. D. Bouterse, the same military ruler who committed the coup d'état in 1980, the same military ruler who was heading the government when the killings in the Maroon village of Moiwana took place"[13] and claims that "individuals [i.e., Jabini] are being used as instruments of the same person or persons who were in charge of or in fact executed several human rights violations in Suriname."[14] It states that the meaning "is not clear . . . [but] vague" when Dr. Peter Poole, an environmental expert, writes about "environmental damage" caused by logging.[15] And it claims that the testimony of "the expert witness Richard Price is totally outdated . . . and legally unfounded."[16]

This submission asks the Court to grant a separate hearing on its various preliminary objections—that the petitioners lacked legal standing to present a petition to the IACHR and lacked standing before the Court (only the *gaamá*, not the VSG, would have such standing, they argue); that the petitioners had not exhausted domestic remedies before submitting their complaint; that the case is a duplication of other proceedings, for example, before the United Nations Committee on the Elimination of Racial Discrimination; and that the Commission abused its rules of procedure "by letting the prescribed deadline" pass to submit the case to the Court. It also includes a slew of more specific objections that it claims contribute to the inadmissability of the case, for example that one of the signatures on the document identifying the Saramaka complainants was written by a grandchild for her grandfather: "The State does not believe that [allowing such a substitution] is a proper conduct for attorneys, certainly not human rights attorneys."[17]

Reviewing the rulings and recommendations of the IACHR in its "Application" to the Court, Suriname's submission repeatedly denies that the State violated any rights of the Saramakas, denies that Saramakas "regulate themselves according to their own norms and customs," denies that Saramakas form a tribal community, and insists that "there are no [logging or mining] concessions granted without the consent of the Saramaka people and authorities."[18] It also includes a number of blatantly inaccurate factual statements (for example, that Saramakas live not only on the Upper Suriname River but also on the Upper Saramacca River—in fact the home of the Matawais—and that Saramaka territory is also inhabited by Amerindians[19]). The submission concludes that "The State denies and contests all statements made in the document 'Pleadings, Motions, and Evidence of the Victim's Representatives'"[20] and insists that "Suriname, with its multi-ethnic and multi-cultural population, is respecting and guaranteeing the fundamental rights and liberties of its population."[21] It therefore recommends to the Court that "Case 12.338, the Twelve Saramaka Clans, . . . be closed."[22]

The "Observations"[23] of the Saramakas' representatives in response to Suriname's preliminary objections is a sober, understated document that replies to these objections point by point. It includes, for example, a detailed statement of the *gaamá*'s support of the VSG in this case and explains that "Captain Paanza is partially blind and for this reason has difficulty writing; preferring to have his name rather than his thumb print affixed to the petition, he personally requested, before numerous witnesses, that his granddaughter write his name for him on the petition."[24] Toward the end of their detailed and lengthy observations, the representatives write:

> While the State would have the Court believe that Case 12.338 is about anything but its own acts and omissions, it is precisely those acts and omissions and the resulting human rights violations that the Court has been requested to adjudicate. While the State would also have the Court believe that it is the victim in these proceedings, the victims have always been and remain the Saramaka people, its twelve clans and the members thereof, and not the State. For these reasons and the reasons stated above, the victims' representatives will not further address the attacks and accusations made by the State herein.[25]

The stage was set for the hearing of 9–10 May 2007, during the seventy-fifth regular session of the Court.

The Hearing

Even if you live on the moon, you are still a Saramaka.
Saramaka Headcaptain Albert Abóikóni, witness

Early May. Men and women are packing their suitcases and readying their papers and laptops in Saramaka villages, Paramaribo, Washington, D.C., Baltimore, New York, and Amsterdam. In Suriname, those coming as part of the Saramaka delegation include Hugo Jabini, the Saramaka law student who has worked closely with the VSG from the outset; Headcaptain Wazen Eduards,[1] who has proved to be the most energetic of the Saramaka captains in organizing meetings and spreading news; Captain César Adjako, an older leader from a transmigration village who has been chosen in part to speak about the effects of the dam; and Gaamá Belfón (Otjútju) Abóikóni, who has decided to lend the full weight of his support to the delegation by accompanying them to Costa Rica.[2]

The official delegation of the State of Suriname is much larger and includes Attorney General Subhaas Punwasi; President Venetiaan's trusted legal advisor Hans Lim a Po; two law professors from Suriname's Anton de Kom University, Eric Rudge and Margo Waterval (both describing themselves as experts in international human rights law); legal advisors Reshma Alladin and Lydia Ravenberg; translator Monique Pool; District Commissioner Rudy Strijk; Acting Director of the Foundation for Forest Management and Production Control René Somopawiro; Saramaka Headcaptain Albert Abóikóni (Gaamá Belfón's brother); and a Saramaka man identified as a cultural anthropologist, Salomon Emanuels.

From Washington, the Commission's delegation is led by Professor Paolo Carozza, a specialist in international human rights law at the University of Notre Dame Law School, and includes human rights lawyers Elizabeth

Abi-Mershed and Juan Pablo Albán, who are employed by the IACHR. Fergus MacKay and David Padilla, the legal representatives for the Saramakas, are flying in from Amsterdam and Washington, respectively.[3] Adiante Franszoon, a Saramaka who has lived for years as a woodcarver in the United States and who will serve as simultaneous interpreter for the *gaamá*, leaves from Baltimore. And Sally and I, having just finished a semester of teaching at the College of William and Mary, pick up a flight to Costa Rica from New York.

By the evening of May 7, the Saramaka delegation, including Adiante and ourselves, are set up in a pleasant, garden-style hotel. The IACHR people are at a more international-style business hotel. And the Suriname delegation is at yet a third hotel, somewhere else in the city.

Our own first day is devoted to preparations for the hearing at the Commission's hotel, with Elizabeth Abi-Mershed laying out what will happen over the two-day hearing, as Adiante translates into Saramaccan for the benefit of the *gaamá* and captains Wazen and César. She describes how there will be seven judges from various countries—Mexico, Costa Rica, Chile, Peru, Argentina, the Dominican Republic, and Jamaica—plus an extra one from Suriname. The proceedings will look very formal, she warns, with the judges in robes on a high bench, but in the end they are interested only in getting at the truth. Elizabeth asks for questions and Wazen expresses his concerns: "We won't know how to phrase things properly since we haven't been educated in this sort of way." And he asks that "the important men and women assembled here put things in the most helpful and correct fashion." Elizabeth stresses the importance of truth and accuracy in each person's testimony. The next day, she tells us, the hearing will begin at three in the afternoon. Headcaptain Wazen will be the first witness and Captain César, who will follow him on the witness stand, will be sequestered outside the courtroom during Wazen's testimony. Each person, she says, should talk about his own, personal, first-hand experiences. Since there is only very limited time for each witness, answers must be brief and to the point. She stresses that the Court has a lot of experience getting at the truth and bypassing politically motivated testimony, so it's important just to stick to the facts.[4]

Fergus says that we're going to practice questions today and then continue tomorrow morning. The role of the expert witnesses—which in the Saramaka case, means only me—is to translate Saramaka sociocultural realities to people who come from very different backgrounds.

Preparing the witnesses: Elizabeth, Fergus, R.P., Wazen.

The second day of the hearing will end with half-hour concluding arguments from the Commission, the Saramaka People, and the State.[5] At each
stage of the hearing, the judges will be able to pose their own questions of
witnesses and attorneys. Once the hearing is over, the judges will deliberate. It
will probably be a good six months before they hand down their judgment.

Gaamá Belfón is given the floor and says he will speak to the background
of this case.

It all began around 1963. At that time, the *gaamá* had been co-opted
by the city government. When I saw the dam being built—at the time
I was working as a manual laborer on the project—it really hurt me.
Years later, when I became *gaamá* and was told that there was a land
problem, I said to myself "This is not a new problem. We have been
living with it since 1963."

That's why I am here in Costa Rica, to see if things can be straight-
ened out properly. I am not here to claim that Maroons should have

absolute sovereignty. I want Suriname to do the right thing for the sake of the whole nation's future.... Headcaptain Wazen is one of the real warriors of the Maroons, as is Captain César. I'm here to join their battle, to support them. That's my proper role as *gaamá*, to help Maroons move forward in the world. When someone tries to hold us back, he becomes my enemy. That's why I am so pleased with the work of our lawyer, Fergus MacKay, who helps us move forward. It is very sweet to me that Richard Price is here to help us, because he knows the inside of my house. I hope and pray that the Saramaka people may move forward. As *gaamá*, I will support their efforts at this trial in every way.

The government claims that it is giving us Maroons all sorts of good things—welfare payments, old-age pensions, and so on—but I believe, to the contrary, that the government is keeping us in poverty. We are Surinamers. We want to cooperate with other Surinamers. I have come here to see who will tell lies about Saramaka history and who will tell the truth. Seeking the truth is always the best way forward for your country. I want to make clear that I'm not coming here as a supporter of one or another political party. I do want Suriname to move forward, but above all I want my own people to move forward, because they've been held back for too long. We're behind in terms of electricity, we're behind in terms of schools, we're behind in terms of housing, we're behind in terms of roads, we're behind in terms of everything in our forest domain.

I have come to Costa Rica to bear witness that blood mustn't stain the ground again because of disputes about territory. Many people have said that the *gaamá* is too important to bother to come to a hearing such as this. But I don't see it that way. My duty is to help my people find the path to justice. At the hearing, I plan to remain silent and simply bear witness. Now that I've said what is on my mind, I will not speak again. Thank you.[6]

Elizabeth then begins the practice questions, which go very poorly at first, as both Wazen and César have difficulty giving answers to some of the kinds of questions she poses: "How does political authority work in Saramaka?" "What is the role of captain?" They do better in answering queries such as "Is life better or worse since Chinese companies began logging?" Fergus, more experienced with Saramakas, asks questions that give them less

The Inter-American Court at night.

trouble: "In addition to your meetings with the *gaamá*, did you hold meetings in the various villages?" (Answer: We held more than 120 meetings all
told.) "Do you know where Saramaka territory ends and Matawai territory
begins? (Yes...) "How can the Chinese cut wood in Saramaka territory if the
Saramakas don't want them there?" (They are protected by soldiers from the
Suriname army...).

After sunset, our delegation takes several taxis to the Court, where
there is a reception designed in part so that the participants can visit the
imposing building and not be intimidated the next day. Adiante, always
the extrovert, tries out his minimal Spanish on the two guards at the gate,
asking them—when they get a chance—if they might be willing to climb up
on the roof of the sentry-box to harvest some of the luscious-looking man-
goes that are dangling just above, since he hasn't eaten a mango in a long
time. We walk through the impressive hearing room with Hugo, Wazen,
and César, staring at the framed photos of previous justices and historic
events, examining the witness stand, the raised row of seats that the justices
will occupy, and the booths where simultaneous interpreters will work.
Elizabeth is especially concerned about locating the shortest path from the
hearing chamber to the men's room, since César's prostate problem seems
to be acting up and she wants to be sure he can make it through his testimony the next day.

The rest of the evening is spent in friendly socializing back at the hotel.
Sally and I meet for a couple of hours with Gaamá Belfón, whom we haven't
seen in thirty years, in his room. We have a lot of catching up to do. In the
colorful poncho (bought in Spain) and dark felt fedora he favors, he seems
very much in charge and his face has come to resemble that of his grandfather, Agbagó, who was *gaamá* during our stays in Saramaka in the 1960s and
1970s.

The next morning is a replay of the previous afternoon, with Wazen and
César trying to get the knack of giving reasonably brief answers to the lawyers' questions. I take notes, on a sheet of hotel stationery, for my own fifteen-
minute presentation scheduled for the second day of testimony.

*   *   *

The sentries greet us with a smile as we emerge from our taxis. After
swinging open the tall metal gate, one of them presents Adiante with a large
plastic bag filled with ripe mangos. Court employees escort us down to the

The Saramaka witnesses and their interpreter the day before the hearing: Wazen, Sally, and César.

Pre-trial pleasantries: Vice President Medina Quiroga, President García Ramírez, and Judge Ventura Robles.

Hugo with a photo of some former judges.

Wazen, the Gaamá, and César.

courtroom, where the several delegations are eventually seated, the Commission in the center in front of the raised platform of the judges, the Saramaka delegation to its left, Suriname's delegation off to the right. The *gaamá* and Adiante, accompanied by Hugo, sit farther back in the room, along with various spectators. All rise as the justices file in.

The president of the Court, Sergio García Ramírez from Mexico, opens the proceedings with some warm words of welcome and comments on the complications of simultaneous interpretation between Spanish (the official language of the Court), English, and Dutch—which will be handled by the Court's professionals—and the translations between Saramaccan and English that Sally will be making for the Saramaka witnesses.

The Court's secretary, in black robes like the judges, adds further details about translations and then opens the courtroom to photographers, who have three minutes to shoot away, after which photos are prohibited.

The secretary states that the purpose of the public hearing is, first, to hear the declarations of the two witnesses and one expert witness provided by the Commission and the Saramakas and then the three witnesses and one expert witness provided by the State. After that, the Court will hear the final oral arguments by the Commission, the representatives of the alleged victims, and the State.

President [in Spanish]: Mr. Secretary, please call the first witness.

Secretary: Wazen Eduards. [Wazen sits down in the witness box with Sally right next to him.] Good afternoon. Will the witness please state his name before the Court.... [etc.] Will the witness now stand?

President: Mr. Witness, do you swear or solemnly declare upon your honor and conscience that you will speak the truth, the whole truth, and nothing but the truth?

Wazen Eduards [leaping to his feet in his bright yellow Saramaka cape and stretching both arms toward heaven, speaking in Saramaccan]: I stand before you and the Great God. I have come here today to talk about the poverty and oppression of my people which has been caused by our brothers from the city. We all came over from Africa together. We are brothers yet our particular rights have been violated. We are deeply aware of the injustice. I stand before you and before the Great God because he is the one who made all the birds, all the animals, all the things in the entire world. He is the one we are standing before today. I speak nothing but the truth. There is nothing aside from the truth that I have to tell you today.[7]

After this dramatic beginning, Wazen proceeds to answer a series of friendly questions from Elizabeth Abi-Mershed regarding his people's history, its territory, and its recent violation by Chinese multinationals. Eventually, she asks "Were the traditional Saramaka authorities consulted before the concessions were granted to the outside companies?" "No, no, no, no," is Wazen's emphatic response.

Elizabeth Abi-Mershed [in English]: After the logging, what is the condition of the land?

Wazen Eduards [in Saramaccan]: It is completely ruined.

E. A.-M.: Can you describe what it looks like?

W. E.: They come in and cut with machines. They clear-cut everything. They cut down absolutely everything. There is nothing at all left in the areas where they work. There isn't a single tree left standing.

E. A.-M.: The people of the Dómbi *lô* [Wazen's clan], do they use the forest for different purposes?

W. E.: The forest is like our marketplace. It is where we get our medicines, our medicinal plants. It is where we hunt to have meat to eat. The forest is truly our entire life. When our ancestors fled into the forest, they did not carry anything with them. They learned how to live—what plants to eat, how to deal with subsistence needs—once they got into the forest. Today it is our whole life. . . .

E. A.-M.: Are there *lôs* within the Saramaka people who have escaped the effects of logging by outside companies?

W. E.: There is absolutely no one in Saramaka territory who has not suffered from the arrival of the companies that are cutting the trees. We all share the same problem.

E. A.-M.: Did the traditional Saramaka authorities take action with the [national] government to try to oppose the logging by outside companies?

W. E.: We did our very best to speak with them about the problem but they would not talk with us. They don't regard us as human beings. They think we are animals. If someone told you that the government treats us with respect, you would know they were lying—which is the reason I have come here today. That is why I have sworn to tell the truth and nothing but the truth because it is very important to me to tell the truth in the face of the lies that have been told. . . .

E. A.-M.: Just one final question. Do the laws of Suriname protect the rights of the Saramakas to the land they live on?

W. E.: No, no. We can count only on our own laws. The laws of the coast do not provide protection for us. We have our laws, they have their laws. Let me give you an example. When I was a child, we lived at a very great distance from the city. Then they came and built a dam that closed off the river. All the trees, all the riches, everything was ruined above the place where they blocked the river. They didn't even take away the trees for lumber before they built the dam and flooded the forest. When they built the dam, it flooded the villages and they moved people into areas where other people were already living, making for tremendous overcrowding. It was not only the people from the villages that were sunk who had a problem. It was also those of us who lived in villages where suddenly all these new people were brought to live. Everybody was impoverished by this. Nobody had much to eat. We all had to share with each other in ways we never had done before. And then logging concessions were granted by the government that have allowed outside people to come in and ruin what is left of our lands. It is a very important thing for me to be able to be here today to present these problems to you. They are very serious problems, very extreme for us. We tried and tried to speak with the government. They refused to deal with us because they don't consider us to be human beings. I have no fear of speaking to the Court today because I am telling the absolute truth. . . . I wish to thank the Great God for allowing me to speak to the Court today. I give the Court a thousand, thousand thanks.

Fergus MacKay then continues the friendly questioning of Headcaptain Wazen, asking him, among many other things, to estimate the number of meetings that were held by the VSG in various villages. Wazen replies that he doesn't know the exact number but that there were several meetings in each of the more than sixty Saramaka villages. Fergus' final question to Wazen concerns the continuing effects of the Afobaka dam. In response, Wazen

Fergus dressed for the hearing.

paints a bleak picture of the economic and social deterioration of Saramaka
life due to the dam and the later granting of logging concessions.

> We continue to have terrible problems. Our schools are simply not
> functioning. We no longer have decent health services. They built the
> dam to produce electricity but our villages remain without electricity.
> Our problems continue to get worse and worse.... Our water is pol-
> luted. We and the city people, we black-skinned people, we all came
> over on the same ships from Africa. We are brothers, we had the same
> mothers and the same fathers. We should be living together as broth-
> ers but that is far from being the case.

In its hostile questioning of Headcaptain Wazen, the State tries to undercut the authority of the VSG by insisting that it is the *gaamá* who is the ultimate Saramaka authority. During this cross-examination, Wazen displays both his pride and pique, often responding to questions with irritation.

Reshma Alladin [in Dutch]: If you say that the *gaamá* is associated with the petition, why is his name not included on it?

Wazen Eduards [in Saramaccan]: The president of Suriname didn't come to this hearing. The underlings of the president came. Does this mean the president doesn't support the position of the State? The *gaamá* is a very distinguished gentleman. He has accompanied us to these hearings. But it is not fitting that he sign or be called to testify.

R. A.: Does this mean that you represent the *gaamá*?

W. E.: As I explained earlier, the VSG met with all the Maroon *gaamás* and they all agreed to support our position here before the Court. So, in that sense I am representing the *gaamá*'s wishes.

R. A.: The fact that you claim to be above the *gaamá* confirms that there was really no internal consultation. . . . Why did you not take steps to obtain a consensus?

W. E. [angrily]: What in the world makes you think that there was no consensus? I have just described the meeting that was held with all the *gaamás* in Dritabiki. I would like to know whether your ears are working properly. . . .

R. A.: You've mentioned that your association has been in existence for ten years. Why, then, did you hold your first meeting with the *gaamá* only last year?

W. E.: I do not have the education that you do, in school, a Western education. But I can tell you that I am a leader of that association and you are lying! We have been meeting time and again with the *gaamá* over a period of many years. If you want to tell me that's not true, then I have nothing more to say to you. . . .

R. A.: Can you tell me the names of the people who have mining concessions in your *lô*'s—the Dómbi *lô*'s—territory?

W. E.: Of course I could. But you're the ones who know it. You're the ones who send them.

R. A.: I'd like you to answer the question.

W. E.: Why should I answer? You're the one who sends these people. If I were the one to send someone to you, I'd be the one who knew who was sent. I am not going to answer these kinds of questions!... [The President makes a plea, saying that the Court would appreciate answers to the questions.] I understand. I have never been to school. I have seen names of concession-holders on pieces of paper but I don't know how to read and I cannot tell you what the names are. But I know that they are very well-known. I apologize that I cannot tell you the names.

R. A.: My last question. According to the Bureau of Statistics, some 21,532 Saramakas no longer live on the Upper Suriname River, approximately 67 percent of the entire Saramaka community.[8] There is a great exodus of Saramakas from their traditional area of residence. How do you explain that so many Saramakas live in the city or in foreign countries? How can you maintain that there is still a common cultural identity?

W. E.: Just because some people have gone to Holland or other places doesn't mean they lose their cultural identity, their way of life. Those Saramakas who are living in the very many villages along the Suriname River are living according to the traditions of our ancestors. Yes, some people have left, but when you are a person of a certain culture, you never lose that culture. You never leave it behind. If you go to Holland, the time will come when you return. But even while you are away, you conduct your life according to Saramaka values and Saramaka beliefs, you hold on to your whole cultural essence, and then when the time comes, you return home. What is ruining Saramaka life is not people leaving Saramaka territory. What is ruining it is the Chinese companies that are coming in and destroying our land. You can't claim that you don't know the names of the Chinese companies!

The State having used up its time, the president asks the judges if they have questions for Wazen. The ad hoc justice from Suriname asks him whether he ever tried to contact appropriate authorities in Suriname with his problems. Wazen replies, "I already told you. We went to them time and again. We kept trying to speak with them, over and over, but they refused to meet with us. They would not treat us as human beings. They treated us as creatures from the forest whom they did not need to deal with."

There is further back and forth between the ad hoc justice and Headcaptain Wazen, some of it contentious, but it yields little useful information. The other judges do not have questions so, after more than an hour and a half of what seems to me strikingly effective testimony, Headcaptain Wazen is permitted to step down and a fifteen-minute recess is called.

The Court reconvenes and Captain César is called to the stand, accompanied by Sally. César appears to be in his seventies and has an expressive face and deliberate manner. He is as far from being comfortable among non-Saramakas, including city people from Suriname, as a Saramaka could be. By his very presence, he exudes "foreignness" or "exoticness"—which is, of course, one of the reasons he was chosen to testify. Most of the questioning for César brings out nothing substantively new. But a few times, the answers are telling.

Elizabeth Abi-Mershed [in English]: Is the way Saramakas cut timber similar to or different than the way the outside companies do?

César Adjako [in Saramaccan]: There is a very big difference and that's what causes problems. When we fell trees, we are thinking of our children and grandchildren, of the future generations. When the outsiders come in they just clear-cut a whole area and then take away what they want.

E. A.-M.: When the workers of the foreign companies are doing the logging on lands that belong to your Matjáu clan, are the Matjáu people free to use the area that is being logged? Can they come into the area?

C. A.: When the Chinese companies come in and start felling trees, they prevent us from entering the area. They don't allow us to go hunting, to do our farming or anything else that we have always done in the area. They don't even allow us in.

E. A.-M.: How do they actually keep you out? How do they physically prevent you from going in there?

C. A.: When they first came into Matjáu territory, I myself tried to go into the area where they were working. And when I went in and said "Here I am," they said, "You can't come in here and if you try to come in here again, we'll call the police and have you arrested." ...

E. A.-M.: What activities were you doing in those areas prior to the logging?

C. A.: Our whole life is centered around the forest. That's where we get medicinal leaves for rituals and for medical purposes. That's where we go hunting. That's where we get our food. That's where our whole life is centered. I could go on about this if you wish. . . .

E. A.-M.: I have just one more short question in the time I have left. When you talk about clear-cutting, is this a kind of damage that lasts a short time or a long time?

C. A.: OK. It's just like in the city. Paramaribo used to be filled with trees. But they were all cut down. There are no more trees in the city. That will last forever. What is going on now is the permanent destruction of the land, of the forest that we have inhabited harmoniously for hundreds of years.

Fergus continues the friendly questioning of César, eliciting further details of the environmental damage caused by Chinese logging, but then turns to the effects of the Afobaka dam, which are especially meaningful to this captain. César was born and brought up in the village of Bèdóti, which was sunk and destroyed by the dam. When still in his twenties, he was forcibly moved to the new transmigration village of Kayapaatí, upstream from the lake, where he now resides and serves as headman. "The problems," he insists, "have certainly lasted into the present. Indeed, they are getting worse. Our whole way of life was destroyed by the flooding."

Fergus MacKay [in English]: Can I ask you one last question? Can you give one example of how you're still experiencing problems today? How is your life worse because of the dam? And explain how you feel about that.

César Adjako [in Saramaccan]: When there is a development project, the idea is to make things better in the end. But exactly the opposite has happened. We have been impoverished by the dam. First, the government made us move to a different place and now they've started to take even that territory away from us, not to allow us to use it as we have in the past. So, first we were moved and then, on top of that, we are now not being allowed access to the new land where they put us. We didn't come all the way to this foreign country [Costa Rica] to make trouble for Suriname. We are simply asking to be able to continue our lifestyle, the way of life that we had for hundreds of years without being impeded by foreigners coming into our midst and taking away access to our land.

The State's questioning of César is an exercise in frustration, with most of the questions relating to arcane aspects of Suriname's land-titling procedures. Sally has to be a little creative in converting this line of questioning into Saramaka concepts, and César's answers don't always address the questions. The State tries to demonstrate that somehow César, as captain, actually invited the Chinese into his clan's forest, something that César tries to show is incomprehensible and unthinkable.

Eric Rudge [in Dutch]: Your honorable president, the questions are not being answered, that's the problem. The State feels that it is not being given the opportunity to put forward what we wish to here....

César Adjako [in Saramaccan]: I'm being told that Suriname considers that I'm not answering their questions directly, but they have to understand what's going on here. The government of Suriname has called outsiders from another country, China, to come into land that belongs to us and to use that land to our detriment and they seem not to understand what that means to us. Let's see, if the lawyers for the State of Suriname would like, I would be happy to bring them into my land in Saramaka, which belongs to us, and show them what the Chinese people, the Chinese loggers, have done to our land. Then they would understand that I am in fact trying to answer their questions....

E. R.: The State will put forward information during the hearing that will show that the Saramaka people themselves give access to others to come into their territory... and my question relates to damage being done by third parties on the concessions where the Saramakas live. My question is, aren't the Saramakas themselves partially liable for the damage that is being done?

C. A.: We the Saramaka people cannot imagine causing damage to the land because we live there. This is our home. This is the place where we live. We have always been very careful about the environment. There is no way that we would stop-up a creek.... This is where our children and grandchildren will live. It is the people from the city who are inviting the Chinese to come, people who don't own the land, who don't live here, who have no concern for the future, for the ecological future of that land, and they are the ones, because it is not their land, who are causing all the damage. Saramakas could never even imagine dealing with land in anything like that fashion.

The judges then begin their questioning of the witness. Judge Ventura Robles, from Costa Rica, is the only one with questions at this time.

Judge Ventura Robles [in Spanish]: Do the Saramaka people have their own customary laws, their own values, and mores according to which they have been living for more than three hundred years? Are you familiar with Western codes, with Western law, or do you have a different system that you use?

César Adjako [in Saramaccan]: We have lived in our territory since slavery times three hundred years ago. We have well-developed laws and customs and values and ways of doing things. When our brothers living in the city, who came over on the same ships from Africa, begin causing problems for us, we do our best to deal with them in line with the kinds of laws, customary laws, ways of life, values, and beliefs that we have held for roughly the last three hundred years in the forest.

Judge Ventura Robles: The Peace Treaty of the 1760s was alluded to, which was signed by the government of the Netherlands and the Saramaka people. I understand that under the peace treaty, part of the territory that is now Suriname was granted to the Saramakas. I would like you to tell me if that is the way your people see it and whether those state obligations are still in force.

C. A.: As far as we, the Saramakas, are concerned, the treaty of 1762 was a sacred act, a sacred treaty that granted us the lands that were designated there, and it's our brothers in the city who are contesting the land ownership that was established by the treaty of 1762.

The president then thanks the witness, who takes the microphone for one last thought. "According to our customs, I would like to thank the Court for this opportunity as well. I beg the Court to find a just solution to our problems. Because our brothers in the city won't give us justice. They claim that we are just night watchmen for *their* forest. But we are human beings, not their servants. And they must be made to give us justice." As César stands to leave the witness box, Sally breathes a sigh of relief that he's made it through his appearance without a trip to the men's room.

The president declares a ten-minute break, after which the State calls its own first witness, veteran District Commissioner Rudy Strijk, who until very recently presided over the district that covers all of Saramaka territory. They begin their friendly questioning, first by Mrs. Alladin, then by Attorney General Punwasi, and then by Mr. Rudge.

Reshma Alladin [in Dutch]: As district commissioner, you have an important role in granting timber and mining concessions.... How would you characterize the relationship between the central government and the *gaamá* and other traditional authorities?

Rudy Strijk [in Dutch]: It is one of mutual respect and cooperation....

R. A.: In your whole period as district commissioner, have any Saramakas ever complained about the effect of the Afobaka dam or reservoir?

R. S.: Not during this period. For as far as I can remember, no.

R. A.: In your frequent consultations with local and traditional authorities was it ever a subject of discussion?

R. S.: No, I cannot remember this....

Subhaas Punwasi [in Dutch]: As district commissioner, how long have you been in touch with the traditional authorities?

R. S.: I think since the end of the 1980s, that would make about twenty-six years.

S. P.: In these twenty-five years, were you ever confronted by tensions between the traditional authorities and the central government? Were you ever presented with conflicts between them?

R. S.: No, as far as I remember, no. If there were misunderstandings, we would hold a meeting... until we reached a consensus. But nothing really important....

Eric Rudge [in Dutch]: During the time you were district commissioner, were there ever concession applications from Saramakas?

R. S.: We do not immediately look at whether a request is from a Saramaka or not but there probably were some.

E. R.: Are you aware that the late Gaamá Songó Abóikóni applied for one or more concessions?

R. S.: Yes, that is my understanding....

E. R.: Did this involve a timber concession or were there other kinds of concessions?

R. S.: It was a very long time ago. I really can't say exactly.

The Commission then takes up the questioning of District Commissioner Strijk.

Paolo Carozza [in English]: During your years as district commissioner, was there any logging occurring on Saramaka territory by outside companies?

Rudy Strijk [in Dutch]: Yes. Certainly.

P. C.: Were those companies logging pursuant to concessions that you, as district commissioner, had approved?....

R. S.: In one case, yes.

P. C.: Is it the case that the logging in this concession did no damage to Saramaka sacred sites, farms, cemeteries, and so forth?

R. S.: As far as I could ascertain at the time, no.

P. C.: You have testified that consultation with Saramakas, getting a consensus, is necessary before you grant a concession. Did you do such consultation and get a consensus in this case, before you granted this concession?

R. S.: There was no need to approach it in this way in this particular case.

P. C.: Just to clarify, then. In the concession that you granted, there was no consultation with the Saramaka people before you granted this concession?

R. S.: In this specific case it was not necessary.

Fergus, on behalf of the Saramaka people, continues the questioning of District Commissioner Strijk.

Fergus MacKay [in English]: The State has argued in its pleadings submitted to the Court, and I quote, "There are no concessions granted without the consent of the Saramaka people and authorities." This is in paragraph 218 of the State's "Official Response." Is that your understanding of the law and practice of Suriname? That no concessions are granted without the consent of the Saramaka people? You're the district commissioner. Your job was to take care of that procedure. Is it your understanding that concessions cannot be granted unless the Saramaka people have consented?

Rudy Strijk [in Dutch]: For as long as... There were no concessions granted without consultation or permission from the Saramaka people....

F. M.: There is expert testimony before the Court in the form of affidavits that says that numerous farms planted by Saramaka people were destroyed in concessions held by the companies called Ji Shen and Tacoba... concessions within Saramaka territory that were granted during your tenure as district commissioner.... How do you explain this expert testimony showing that there are these farms destroyed in these concessions yet the concessions were nonetheless given?

R. S.: These complaints never reached me. If they had been brought before me or to my office I would have known how to deal with them.

F. M.: So, there were no complaints. However, you testified that you would investigate this before giving advice about whether a concession should be granted or not.... You have testified before the Inter-American Commission in the hearing on this case that there has to be a report produced on whether there are farms, whether there are sacred sites, and a number of other things you mentioned in the area, before a concession can be given. Have you ever seen such reports in relation to the concession given to Tacoba or Ji Shen? Have you personally ever seen these reports?....

R. S.: You force me to go back into administrative documents I don't have with me here, so I would have to think long and hard about this.... If these matters had been brought up at my office, I would have known how to deal with them.

By the time Fergus finishes with District Commissioner Strijk, the official seems distinctly uncomfortable. After several of the judges continue the less-than-friendly questioning, Judge Cecilia Medina Quiroga, from Chile, notes (in Spanish) that she remains "a little confused about the questions and the answers."

Based on what I understood, and based on your answers to the Inter-American Commission's questions, concessions had been granted to outsiders before you left office [in March 2007]. And when you were asked whether these concessions had been approved by you, you said that, at least in one case, yes. Then you were asked by the Commission whether this had caused any damage to the Saramaka and you said no. And then you were asked whether you had obtained consent from the Saramaka and you said it wasn't necessary in this case.... What I can't understand is that you also said that there is always consultation and consensus.

District Commissioner Strijk replies, "I really don't understand what you are asking," to which Judge Medina Quiroga repeats her observations in full, this time in English, ending by asking him, "If you granted a logging concession in Saramaka territory, why was there no need for consultation in that case?" Strijk explains that there is a standard procedure "*if* there are sacred sites, cemeteries, and agricultural plots in a proposed concession, then, we have a consultation. But if there are no sacred sites and agricultural plots, then no consultation takes place." He gives no indication of how he, a complete outsider to Saramaka life, would have the faintest idea on his own whether a particular stretch of forest contained sacred sites. It is becoming clear that the State is completely unable to support its contention that it consults with Saramakas before granting concessions.

The State calls the final witness of the day, Saramaka Headcaptain Albert Abóikóni, the brother of Gaamá Otjútju. Their purpose in calling him seems clear. Albert is both a "traditional" Saramaka—he served as interim *gaamá* during the interregnum following Songó's death—and has also served as the representative from the Saramaka region to the National Assembly, the equivalent of a U.S. congressman. He can therefore be touted as a signal example of the extent to which Saramakas participate in government and are, in the State's terms, becoming fully integrated or assimilated. But in the end, through his testimony, Albert becomes almost a witness for the Saramaka plaintiffs. His Saramaka identity is so strong, despite his speaking Dutch and having served in parliament, that in the end his testimony comes across as a strong defense of the need for Saramakas to obtain title to their territory.

The State's questioning is done by Lydia Ravenberg, who first goes over details of Saramaka political authority with him. Eventually, the dialogue becomes more interesting—in ways not anticipated by the State.

Lydia Ravenberg [in Dutch]: Do Saramakas all live in Saramaka territory or are there other countries where Saramakas live?

Albert Abóikóni [in Dutch]: Saramakas live in the United States, for example, in French Guiana, in the Netherlands, perhaps even in England. They also live in . . .

L. R.: Does the *gaamá* have authority over these people in these other countries?

A. A.: Yes, even if you live on the moon, you are still a Saramaka. The *gaamá* is still your *gaamá*.

After Attorney General Punwasi steps in to ask a single question of the witness, regarding the participation of Maroons in the central government, the Commission takes over the questioning.

Paolo Carozza [in English]: During the time you were a parliamentarian [between 2000 and 2005], was there ever any legislation proposed, or was there ever discussion in parliament about the possibility of a law in Suriname that would allow the Saramaka people, or any tribal or indigenous people, to hold title to land collectively?

Albert Abóikóni [in Dutch]: I personally tried to put this forward, this land rights issue, and it was discussed but never acted on. . . .

P. C.: So, your efforts to promote such legislation were unsuccessful. Is that correct?

A. A.: Yes, you could say yes.

Fergus MacKay then takes up the questioning, on behalf of the Saramakas.

Fergus MacKay [in English]: Do you believe that it is still necessary today to have a law protecting land rights, the property of indigenous and tribal peoples in Suriname?

Albert Abóikóni [in Dutch]: Yes, I certainly think that's necessary. Yes, I do think so.

F. M.: For the Saramaka people?

A. A.: Of course!

Soon, after the judges have asked their questions of the witness, the president adjourns the Court and announces that the hearing will resume at 9 A.M. the next morning in order to hear the remaining witnesses and the closing arguments. After dinner at the hotel, we spend the evening chatting with the Saramakas in the hotel and turn in early, exhausted from the day's events.

*   *   *

The next morning, after permitting photographers to snap away for three minutes, the Court gets back in session with the day's first witness, Rene Ali Somopawiro, being called to the stand. Having served for years as deputy director of the Foundation for Forestry Management and Production Control, he is in a key position regarding the granting of logging concessions, and the State has brought him to Costa Rica to demonstrate the care with which concessions are granted and managed. He begins his testimony with confidence, but by the end looks like a beaten man—less corrupt or uncaring than like a bureaucrat caught up in a system quite completely beyond his control. The State begins the questioning, which drags on considerably longer than that of previous witnesses. At one point, the State's representative, Margo Waterval, asks whether the Foundation had granted a concession to a Chinese company called Tacoba. The witness replies that it had not.

Margo Waterval [in Dutch]: If Tacoba never received a concession, how is it possible that they are conducting logging activities in the Saramaka area?

Rene Somopawiro [in Dutch]: I have no idea. But it is possible for a person who has a timber concession to ask a contractor to come in and log it. I think this is the only possibility here. . . .

M. W.: What role does the Foundation have in teaching people to use the forest in a sustainable manner?

R. S.: One of the key roles of the Foundation, since its establishment, is to insure the sustainable harvesting of the forest. That is why we need forest rangers and vehicles, so we can go into the forest and check on ongoing operations. The rangers go into the field and do inspections as frequently as possible. . . .

M. W.: In your inspections, have you found damage done to the forest in the concessions owned by Saramakas?

R. S.: Let me be quite clear. Whenever there are activities in the forest, be they agricultural or logging, there will always be damage, though that damage may be minimal. In our inspections, we have sometimes seen some damage but there is no clear-cutting in Suriname.... The damage that has been done is not in such a manner that the forest cannot restore itself.

M. W.: You talk about selective timber management and you mention clear-cutting. Which is the practice in Suriname?

R. S.: In Suriname in general, there is only selective timber logging. What does this mean? Our forests are not homogeneous, we have heterogeneous forests. There are more than three hundred species of trees. In any hectare, you would only take a certain number of trees. That's what I mean by selective timber logging.

In its back-and-forths with the witness, the State has been touting a special kind of land-use permit for logging called "community forests," designed for Maroons and indigenous groups, in which a village can request such a designation for its surrounding forest, for their own exploitation. When Paolo Carozza, who heads the Commission, takes over questioning of the witness, he homes in on this claim.

Paolo Carozza [in English]: You mentioned that the communal forest system provides that the property is to be used for the benefit of a particular village.

Rene Somopawiro [in English]: Yes.

P. C.: I want to make sure that you mean exactly the word "village" there. For example, our understanding from prior testimony is that a Saramaka clan consists of many villages. Are the communal property rights specifically for a village, then, and not for the *lô* or the clan as a whole?

R. S.: It is for a village or settlement. Nowhere is it stated that it is for a *lô*.

P. C.: Given that property within traditional Saramaka law is held by the *lô* and not by the village, then, do I understand correctly that the communal forest system does not follow the same structure of ownership that traditional Saramaka law follows? Is that correct?

R. S. [in English]: That is correct, yes. . . .

P. C.: Mr. President, my advisor Ms. Abi-Mershed would like to ask a few questions on behalf of the Commission.

Elizabeth Abi-Mershed [in English]: Good morning. When a company is granted a logging concession, what other rights does it get? . . . Can it cut roads, can it put up buildings, can it have people living in the concession area?

R. S. [in English]: Yes, yes, yes. . . .

E. A.-M.: What kind of monitoring of concessions does your office do? Do people from your office go out to look at what is happening every so often?. . . .

R. S.: We try to go to the field at least twice a month, so it's a regular thing. . . .

Fergus MacKay then takes over the questioning on behalf of the Saramakas, asking Somopawiro about a series of letters between the Forestry Foundation and Ji Shen, to whom Somopawiro admits the State had granted a concession. He hands Somopawiro a copy of one of the letters and asks him to read it out loud.

Rene Somopawiro [in English]: "To the concession manager of Ji Shen Forestry and Timber Industries . . . On 5 January 2001, a delegation of the Foundation for Forest Management and Production Control has visited under my command your operation at Pokigron to gain insight into the activities that have been performed by Suriname Ji Shen Forestry and Timber Industries. . . . "

Fergus MacKay [in English]: Sorry, let me interrupt you for a second. Is Pokigron a Saramaka village?

R. S.: Pokigron is a Saramaka village.

F. M.: Can you show it to me on the map there? And how far, approximately, is the Ji Shen concession from Pokigron?

R. S.: I think it's about 15 kilometers. [Continuing to read the letter] "During the discussion we had with Mr. Wong and the camp manager Mr. Yang, it appeared that Ji Shen had already cut seven thousand trees that are still lying in the forest. They had constructed an access road of 55 kilometers and have plans to log the complete plot of land within eighteen months."

F. M.: So, this concession is in Saramaka territory, within about 15 kilometers of a Saramaka village, and did you tell this company to stop its work?

R. S.: We didn't say they had to stop logging. We said that if they wished to continue, they would have to meet certain conditions. . . .

F. M.: In your opinion, do these letters prove that there was a concession issued by the State within, as you describe it, the area claimed by the Saramaka people?

R. S.: Yes. . . .

F. M.: Can you tell me, when you are looking over applications for logging concessions, is there a requirement under Suriname law that an environmental impact or a social impact assessment be conducted?

R. S.: No.

F. M.: The State has argued in its pleading before the Court that while there is no framework environmental law in Suriname, that the State nonetheless uses World Bank standards. Are you aware of these World Bank standards? Do you apply these World Bank standards in your work?

R. S.: No.

F. M.: Why do you think the State is saying that you use World Bank standards then?

R. S.: I'm not sure.

Fergus MacKay then comes back to the issue of community forests, which is part of the State's boast that they provide a legal means for Saramakas, and other Maroons and indigenous peoples in Suriname, to control forest areas of their own.

F. M.: Community forests are issued under Article 41, subparagraph 2, of the Forestry Management Act. It says, and I quote, "Upon consultation with the minister responsible for regional development, the minister will declare certain forestry areas to be community (or communal) forests for the benefit of the tribal inhabitants of the interior." . . . Do so-called "tribal inhabitants" in fact have a right to obtain a communal forest?

R. S.: If they meet the requirements, the government can give them a title of this sort.

F. M.: Is the minister required to do this, if he doesn't want to make such a grant?

R. S.: No, he can refuse.

F. M: In the area you have marked on the map as being claimed by the Saramaka people, can you show the Court how many community forests there are? . . . Are there any?

R. S.: No.

F. M.: There are none.

R. S.: No.

F. M.: So, within the area claimed by the Saramakas, there is not one single community forest.

R. S.: No. . . .

The judges then take their turns questioning the witness, one asking whether the reason that there are no community forests in the Saramaka area is that no Saramakas have ever made application. Somopawiro replies that this indeed is the case, "No Saramakas ever made application. There were no applications from any of the villages in Saramaka territory." Judge Diego García Sayán, from Peru, adds (in Spanish) that it seems to him that "the position of this population is that they do not request these concessions because they consider that the forests are their right, their ancestral right." After some further questions from the judges, the president then dismisses the witness and calls for a fifteen-minute break.

*   *   *

Once everyone has returned, the president makes a speech outlining the procedure for this final portion of the hearing. Each of the two expert witnesses will have fifteen minutes to speak freely and without interruption before being questioned by the lawyers for the three parties and by the judges, who will prepare their questions in writing. Then, after a fifteen-minute recess, each of the three parties will present its closing argument, followed by rebuttal arguments and questions from the judges.

I am called as the first expert witness and, after stating my name and place of residence, am read the standard instructions before being sworn in. I'm struck, as it's read out loud, by one section in the instructions, "Let the witness be advised, in accordance with Article 51 of the Rules of Procedure of the Court, that States may neither institute proceedings against witnesses or expert witnesses nor bring explicit pressure to bear upon them or their families on account of the statements or opinions they have delivered before the Court"—exactly, it seems to me, what happened in 1992, at the end of my *Aloeboetoe* testimony. In general, I am feeling excited and nervous. For more than forty years, my career (and Sally's), as well as much of our lives, has been built on what we have learned from Saramakas. Now, more than ever before, I have an opportunity to do something significant in return, to give them a precious gift. If I can be sufficiently persuasive in the next hour or two, I can build on all the knowledge that Saramakas have shared with me to try to help the judges understand their need for title to their territory and for a significant amount of self-governance. I glance at the sheet of hotel stationery containing my brief notes for the speech.

After thanking the Court for the privilege of testifying before them, I remind them that after my 1992 testimony, the judges asked that I send copies of our Saramaka books for the Court's library but that since that time we have written a number of additional books which we would be pleased to send when we get back from Costa Rica. To emphasize the length of my experience working with Saramakas, I point out that when we first lived with them in 1966, Headcaptain Albert Abóikóni, the State's witness from the previous day, was four years old and Gaamá Otjútju still in his twenties. I also acknowledge the presence of the *gaamá* in the chamber, pointing in his direction (he nods and raises his hand in acknowledgment), and say that he told me before sitting down that there was no way he would miss this hearing, which is so crucial for securing his people's territorial rights.

At that point I begin unrolling a very large map, which I have also had projected as a slide on screens and walls around the hearing chamber.

Richard Price [in English]: I think that the best way to talk about the land and territory of the Saramakas is to direct your attention to a map that was made by the captains in the Association of the twelve *lôs* who are bringing their complaint before the honorable Court.... The first thing one notices when one looks at this map is the fantastic *density* of activities that Saramakas are doing on these lands, on their territory. I want to mention just a few of the symbols that are in the legend of the map. The Saramakas themselves decided what symbols they wanted to put on the map, in the legend.

Gaamá Belfón, posing in the courtroom before the trial.

Of course, there is a symbol for villages, one for former villages, one for cemeteries, one for former cemeteries, and so on. Besides those, there are farms, agricultural plots. Those are the green places you see, the large green places you see scattered all over the map. Each one is a farm that is currently being used by a Saramaka woman. And I should explain, perhaps, that the very great bulk of the food that Saramakas eat comes from those farms, from those gardens. Every Saramaka woman has a farm, a garden, which is cut for her by her husband. Every two years he has to cut a new one, and then the forest is left for another twenty or thirty years until it grows back, and then it is used again—which is why Saramakas, like indigenous peoples in Brazil, in the Amazon forest, need a great deal of land.

They live in a very sustainable relationship with their environment. They protect it in such a way that their children and grandchildren will be able to use it. And it's been this way for the last 300 years in that territory.

I then describe in some detail how Saramaka women spend about half of their time in their gardens, where they have houses, and half in their villages, moving back and forth every couple of weeks, with their menfolk coming to visit them in their gardens, going hunting and fishing while they're there. I move on to the symbols on the map for hunting grounds, discussing how men hunt wild pigs, deer, tapirs, several kinds of monkeys, and many kinds of birds. Then I go through the symbols for fishing areas—including special named ponds spotted through the forest where fish are plentiful. Next, I speak about the symbol for the tree species that men use to make canoes, describing how every man and every woman owns at least one canoe, which is their main means of transportation. The symbols for these trees literally dot the giant map. I discuss the symbol for the reeds Saramakas use to make the baskets women carry on their heads and how these reeds grow only in certain places in the forest. Next, I run through various symbols the Saramakas have put on the map for particular wild fruits they gather—certain kinds of mango, various palm nuts (which women process into cooking oil), and other fruits. Here's an example, taken off the recording of the hearing, of how I say this last bit:

They show you on the map, different species of palm groves, palm trees, that they use for different things. For example, and it's only one example, they have put on the map a symbol for *pína*, which is a kind of palm that they use for roofing their houses. They have another symbol on the map for another species of palm, *tási*, that they also use to roof their houses. And they have another symbol for a third kind of palm, called *maipá*, which is very important because women go into the forest to where these trees grow and bring back the fruits of this tree and they process them into cooking oil. Now, all of you, or I, are used to going into a supermarket to buy cooking oil, you buy it in a bottle. But Saramaka women have to go into the forest, get the nuts off these trees, bring them back to the village, break up the nuts by pounding, it's a very arduous process, and cook it until they get the oil, so they can use it to fry food, just the way we do. So, the Saramakas chose to put that on their map too.

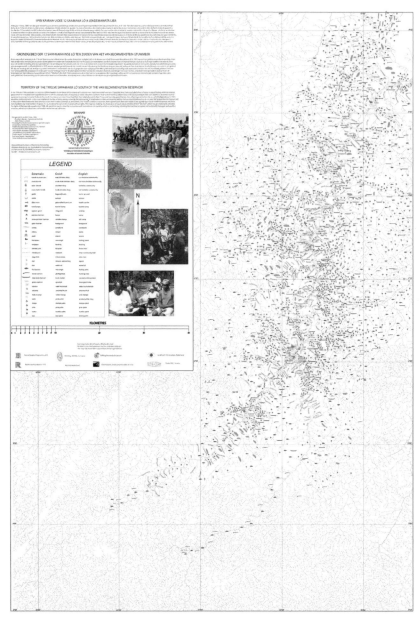

The Saramaka map.

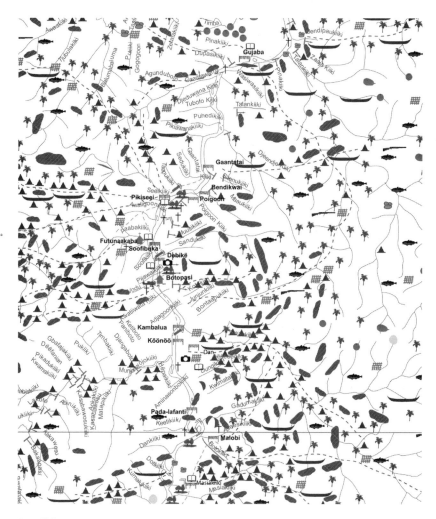

Detail from map.

I discuss *keéti*, the white clay (kaolin) that is so central to Saramaka ritual life and can be mined only at certain places along the river—the Saramakas had chosen to mark those places on their map. In short, I try to bombard the Court with the density of different kinds of symbols on the map, each indicating a specific place where Saramakas directly engage the forest in complex ways. And throughout, I stress Saramakas' fidelity to the notion of environmental sustainability.

Switching gears, I point out that this map, for all its detail and impressive-
ness, only covers about one half of traditional Saramaka territory, explicitly
showing only that part of their territory that lies south of the lake. I then
speak for some time about the treaty of 1762 (drinking the blood oath, and so
forth) and its meaning, in terms of territory and sovereignty, to Saramakas.
And I explain how the building of the Afobaka dam in 1962, without consultation with the Saramakas, violated the treaty and everything it stood for,
from a Saramaka perspective.

I end my fifteen minutes (it's actually eighteen minutes, according to the
recording) by speaking about some of the things that the Saramakas have
deliberately not shown on the map, in particular the places where major
historical events occurred (for example, eighteenth-century battles with the
whites) and places that have special religious significance (sites where particular gods or spirits live). I suggest that although the Saramakas do not wish
to share this information with the public through their map, these places
remain deeply meaningful to them and would constitute a very dense map
of their territory in its own right. In other words, the forest—I argue—is as
filled with places of specific historical and religious meaning to Saramakas as
it is with garden or canoe-building sites, hunting areas, or fruit groves.

The president then invites the Commission to begin its friendly questioning. The first questions, from Elizabeth Abi-Mershed, are of a general
nature—to what extent are Saramakas similar to or different from other
Maroons in Suriname? What is the relationship in practice between Saramaka customary law and the national legal system of Suriname?—and I offer
two- or three-minute, almost lecture-style, answers to each. But in answering,
I manage to discuss government depredations during the civil war including
the events at Moiwana village, which I'm sure Suriname would best like for-
gotten. Elizabeth then homes in on logging and issues more directly related
to the Saramaka complaint.

> Elizabeth Abi-Mershed [in English]: Can you explain what is the cul-
> tural or social significance of cutting timber as a traditional Saramaka
> activity?
>
> Richard Price [in English]: Certainly. Saramakas have always cut trees
> for their own use to make houses, to make canoes. But since before
> the peace treaty, they have also cut timber and made rafts and floated
> them down the river all the way to the coast to sell them to coastal
> plantations. There is evidence for that in the Treaty of 1762, which I

believe has been submitted to the Court as a document, where there is a clause that says Saramakas shall be permitted to continue to float rafts of logs to the coast and sell them to people on the coast. And that has been going on for more than 250 years. So, Saramaka men of my age, for instance, have all participated when they were younger in cutting trees, building rafts, floating them down to the coast and selling them to sawmills there. The time when that ended was when the Afobaka dam was built, since it was no longer possible to float rafts down the river because the lake, the dam, blocked it off. So, that's another serious economic consequence of the dam.

E A.-M.: Could you please share with the Court your expert opinion about the logging by outside companies on Saramaka lands? What is the impact of that outside logging in Saramaka territory?

R. P.: As the two Saramaka captains testified yesterday, the difference between the way that Saramakas have always engaged in logging and the way outside companies do it is like night and day. Saramakas cut several trees to make a raft. They go into the forest and find those trees that are commercially viable that they want to sell and that they know people want to buy and they cut ten or twelve or fourteen trees. What those outside companies, like Tacoba, do in Saramaka territory is come in with heavy machinery, bulldozers, all kinds of heavy tractors. And they first of all build roads right across the creeks that Saramakas drink from. They block the creeks, they ruin the gardens, and they do what is called clear-cutting. They cut everything that is standing. They just bulldoze everything. So, they have absolutely no concern for the environment.... When the Saramakas do anything in the forest, it is done with the utmost concern for their children who are there in the gardens, for their grandchildren, and for future generations. So, there is no relationship between what Saramakas have done for three hundred years in terms of logging and what these outside companies, which are commercial companies who are trying to make a profit, do.

E A.-M.: With commercial logging by outside companies, is there a cultural or spiritual effect on the Saramakas?

R. P.: Absolutely. As I said before, the forest is like the church of the Saramakas. It's as if you went in and just bulldozed the church. All of the sacred places that are there are gone, they're destroyed. The

Saramakas who live in a particular village know that that boulder there is the home of a certain forest spirit who speaks through so-and-so's head, my sister's head, let's say, whenever we have ceremonies for forest spirits. Well, what do you think that forest spirit thinks when the Chinese have come in and bulldozed the rock away? These people are going to suffer with a vengeance from those spirits for time immemorial. And they're very concerned about it.

The Commission continues its questioning, asking about the differential impact of logging on Saramaka men and women, the impact of foreigners coming into Saramaka territory uninvited, the impact of there not being any legal way for Saramakas to gain collective title to their territory, and whether Saramaka customary laws in respect to property are well developed. Each such question gives me a chance to expand on issues of value to the case the Saramakas wish to put forth. After a few minutes of this friendly question and answer, some of which has been led by the Commission's main attorney, Paolo Carozza, the president passes the questioning along to Fergus MacKay, speaking on behalf of "the alleged Saramaka victims."

MacKay begins by asking for details of the definition, by Saramakas, of the notion of a collective territory and the ways this fits with the idea that matrilineal clans (*lôs*) are the ultimate land-holding units. He probes further into Saramaka property law asking whether a Saramaka could sell land (to an outsider or anyone else) or whether a *lô* could do so. After giving detailed answers to these questions, I explain that ultimately, the land belongs to the Saramaka people collectively.

By ultimately, I mean that the land belongs to the Saramaka people. The *lô* stewards that particular piece of land where its villages are. And I might add that we're not talking about just twelve slices of land. We're talking about a number of pieces of land that aren't contiguous, so that the Matjáu clan, for instance, who own the Pikílío, also own lands along other, far-away parts of the river. It owned the land around Bèdóti, where the Captain of Kayapaatí [César Adjako] was brought up before his village was sunk under the lake. So, any clan has different, separated pieces of territory and this has been so since the eighteenth century. And every knowledgeable Saramaka knows that exactly from this rock past that sand bank to the mouth of such-and-such creek, that is the territory of such-and-such clan, such-and-such *lô*.

MacKay then states that the Saramaka witnesses testified yesterday that under their laws, the *lôs* are the owners of all the resources, including sub-soil resources, and asks me whether this is my understanding of Saramaka law. I reply, "Absolutely. What they said is true—from the tops of the tallest trees, way down into the ground. They see all of the territory you could mark on a map as including all of that—it's three-dimensional." MacKay then asks whether there has been spiritual damage to the forest as a result of outside incursions.

As I said, the forest is the Saramakas' church. Their gods and spirits live in it. Their named spirits, the gods, the powers that they deal with on a daily basis, live in particular places in the forest. Their ancestors—whom they speak with at ancestor shrines and who protect their villages and their lives—are vested in particular places. When the dam was built and the lake came and flooded not only all these villages, it flooded their forest, it also flooded their cemeteries. And I hear all the time, every day from Saramakas whom I meet, Saramakas of my age, like Captain César Adjako, how much pain they feel because of the fact that their ancestors, people whom they speak with at the ancestor shrine, are underwater. They've been covered by meters and meters of a lake that the government imposed on them. So, they suffer very terribly from this and in very specific ways. These spirits, which are avenging spirits, come and get everyone in the matrilineage for time immemo-rial. So they have to do rituals all the time to try to appease these spirits who are angry because of what was done to the forest.

MacKay follows up by asking what percentage of Saramaka territory was lost when the dam was built and I reply "about 50 percent." He then points out that the witness for the State estimated, this morning, that 10 percent of the territory claimed by Saramakas has been given out in logging con-cessions, meaning that only 40 percent of traditional Saramaka territory is left for them to use. Fergus then questions me for several minutes about the impact of the dam on Saramaka life, eliciting numerous kinds of suffering that continue today, including the serious land scarcity for agriculture above the lake and the extreme poverty and ghettoization of the people who were moved below the lake. He then asks about the impact for Saramakas of hav-ing soldiers from the Suriname national army in their territory to guard the Ji Shen concession and prevent them from entering it.

As I testified in *Aloeboetoe* in 1992, when that was an issue, . . . the very presence of soldiers in Saramaka territory is something that never, never happened before the civil war, before the government simply imposed this on Saramakas. For Saramakas, soldiers are the enemy. Those are the people their ancestors fought against, black and white. As I have said, in the 1960s, no one could come into Saramaka territory without very special permission. There were no tourists. It was their territory. There has been a gradual erosion of this, and since the civil war the government acts as if this is their territory and not Saramaka territory. And, legally, from the government's point of view, that is true. But it is not true from the Saramakas' point of view. As the Saramakas say over and over again, "We did not abrogate the 1762 treaty that our ancestors fought for, the government is abrogating the treaty of 1762." The government says, "This isn't yours, it belongs to the State." But the Saramakas say "This has always belonged to us, since the treaty, it is ours and you can't come here." And the idea of having soldiers of all people coming in is a very frightening thing for Saramakas.

The president then invites the State to begin its cross-examination. Attorney General Subhaas Punwasi explains that he will begin the questioning and then pass the baton to two of his colleagues. He starts by asking how the requests of Gaamá Belfón for police protection, after his kidnapping by people supporting the rival *gaamá*, square with my "story" that Saramakas wish to run their own legal affairs. I deny any special knowledge about these requests. He reminds me, pointedly, that as attorney general, he is in charge of all police in Suriname, that the police force and its activities fall under his jurisdiction. He then asks how it could be that many important Saramakas are supporters of the political party headed by former dictator Desi Bouterse, and says that "some of them" (presumably Hugo Jabini and Albert Abóikóni) "are in this room." I answer that it is not for me to say why someone chooses to be in a certain political party, that I cannot speak for someone else—and in any case the State asked one of these people that very same question directly yesterday. I also take the opportunity to speak about the brief time period, from the mid-1960s to the mid-1980s, when schools actually functioned in the interior and when people like Albert Abóikóni were able to get an education. I further describe how the school system and health system have fallen apart since that time. The attorney general stops me and insists he is not talking about the ability of Saramakas to participate in government but rather their "active participation in a political party that is dominated by the former military commander of Suriname" (now the leader of the major opposition party, a serious electoral threat to the party of the attorney general). I decline to answer, pleading that I am not qualified, and Punwasi passes the questioning on to attorney Eric Rudge, who asks (in Dutch) what happens after the death of a Saramaka official, how political succession is decided.

R. P. [in English]: Whenever a Saramaka dies, divination is held to find out the cause of the person's death. This is done once the body of the deceased is put into the coffin. The coffin is then carried on the heads of two men, one in front and one in back.

E. R. [now, excited, in English]: Excuse me, excuse me. This is all very interesting but . . .

R. P.: It's the answer to your question.

E. R. [continuing in English]: No, it's not the answer to my question! How is this particular problem solved within the tribe? That's my question.

R. P.: That's what I'm . . .

E. R.: No, you're taking too long to explain it, Sir. Please.

R. P. [speaking more rapidly]: There are judicial procedures which begin with what anthropologists call divination, to determine the cause of death. When it is found that the death is caused by a third party, by supernatural means, by sorcery, when there's a problem between the family of the person who died and another group. . . .

E. R.: Presidente, may I rephrase the question, please? When there is a problem like that, is it solved within the Saramaka tribe?

R. P.: These kinds of cases are solved by very strict laws within Saramaka about which I could explain further . . .

E. R.: So, it's a Yes?

R. P.: Yes.

E. R.: OK. Then how do you explain that such problems are now brought to the central government if there are really two separate systems of law?

R. P.: I am not aware of these cases so I cannot tell you anything about them.

The State continues to hammer away, trying to get me to explain, or acknowledge, that in the case of Gaamá Songó's succession, the State was called in to adjudicate, because of the dispute between two Matjáu-clan factions in Dángogó. I deny any firsthand knowledge of these intricacies, saying I wasn't there. This leads to a very sharp exchange in which I say that during the civil war the central government was fighting against the Jungle Commando, which included Saramakas and Ndyukas, and Rudge angrily says, "That's not true!" Both of our voices are raised.

Rudge then passes the questioning duties on to his colleague, Reshma Alladin, whose job seems to be to attack my credibility as a witness. I have been expecting this but still become somewhat testy as I answer.

Reshma Alladin [in Dutch]: Mr. Price, we would like to know when was the last time you visited Suriname?

R. P. [in English]: 1986. At that time, we were going to visit the *gaamá*, who was dying in the hospital and we were picked up by military police of the government and expelled, in the middle of the night, with guns . . .

R. A. [in English, interrupting]: No, nay. I just want to know . . . [Switching back to Dutch] That means that for approximately twenty-one years you haven't visited Suriname. Is that correct?

R. P.: Yes.

R. A. [in Dutch]: After that, did you ever do any more research in Suriname?

R. P.: I don't understand what you mean, "in Suriname." I said I have not been to Suriname since 1986. But I have been studying Saramakas all this time and have written ten books, including a very large book which is coming out later this year about Saramakas and their land, because I have been working with Saramakas who live in French Guiana . . .

R. A.: Thank you. *Dank u wel.*

There then follow some exchanges in which my expertise about the numbers of Maroons is questioned (as my published figures on Maroon population are more than double those of the Suriname census), and I try to explain why, but the State's representative seems to take my explanation—which focuses on the inadequacies of the Suriname Bureau of

Statistics—as an insult. She says (in Dutch), "Dr. Price, I am very shocked by your statement just now and would like to ask for a clarification." She then asks whether, since Saramakas benefit from various government benefits, such as health and education, they should not be required to participate fully in the government legal system, rather than—as she seems to think I have argued—have some sort of legal autonomy. I reply that I have never said that Saramakas want a separate state—they make clear that they are Surinamers and wish to remain so. But, I say, "What Saramakas ask for is to be treated like other Surinamers, to be treated with *respect*, to have the same kinds of hospitals and the same kinds of schools that you have for your families on the coast." She then asks a question about whether the tourist initiatives that some Saramakas have begun don't undermine Saramaka cultural integrity. I claim that, as far as I know, when Saramakas run such initiatives, they do so in a way that is compatible with cultural norms. And that it's one of the ways that indigenous peoples around the world do it. There is a back and forth in which she says that tourism is culturally destructive and I say that as long as Saramakas run it, it's OK and one of the few ways they have to earn money. I argue that if Chinese tourist agencies were to bring Japanese tourists into Saramaka, that would be quite a different matter. She again raises the fact that I haven't been in Suriname in more than twenty years and that, therefore, my knowledge of Saramaka realities is woefully out of date. I reply, a bit angrily:

I would say that during the last twenty-one years, my knowledge of Saramaka has deepened much more than during the first twenty years. I have been working for many months every year for the last twenty-one years with Saramakas. There are now about 15,000 Saramakas in French Guiana. Since the civil war, one in three Saramakas live across the border in French Guiana. Those people go back and forth to their villages in Suriname many times a year. You can now go by road in four hours to Paramaribo [from French Guiana]. You can then very easily go back to Saramaka. So I am living with people in French Guiana who came, yesterday, from the southernmost villages of the Suriname River. And talking to them about what's happening and what they're seeing. So, it's true that it's hearsay evidence legally, but it's true evidence because these are people whom I've known for forty years, and I speak with them and learn from them. And if you read my new book which is coming out in four months [*Travels with*

Tooy] you'll see that I know much more about Saramaka life now than I did the last time I was in Suriname.

The State's representative asks whether in my testimony about Saramaka sovereignty I am not suggesting that the government shouldn't maintain schools or medical facilities in Saramaka territory. I say:

I think in a way that when Sally Price and I lived in Dángogó and Gaamákóndê [Asindóópo] in the 1960s and 70s, that region of Saramaka was experiencing a golden age in terms of schools and medical facilities. The hospital at Djoemoe had a well-trained Dutch doctor and a very good Dutch head nurse as well as about a dozen nurses from Suriname working at the place. The school had a Dutch schoolteacher with assistants from Paramaribo. It was excellent. What has happened since the civil war is that the hospital at Djoemoe has been largely shut down, it hardly functions. There are no medicines. The schools are in much worse shape than they were in the 1960s and 70s. So, if Suriname, if your government, were to fully accept its responsibility, it would put a great deal of resources into the interior, into where so many of your citizens live. And the reason that they say that they feel that they are treated like dogs, like animals, and not like human beings, has to do with exactly these matters.

Reshma Alladin [in English]: Thank you, but you did not answer my question.

R. P.: Ask it again.

President [in Spanish]: *Perdone, perdone.* This is not the time for debate. Each party will get their chance during the closing arguments . . . There is a request from Judge Ventura.

Judge Ventura Robles then describes how he went to the Court's library after the session yesterday and asked for the books I'd sent in 1992. He learned that, in the interim, they have all disappeared from the collection. Could I, he asks, send new copies to the Court, especially those more recent works that deal with Saramaka culture and their relationship to land ownership? The president says that "We'll all be waiting for those books" and thanks me for my testimony, which has now lasted more than an hour and a half.

I feel wound up and ready for more but my part is over and done. (Two years later, at a meeting in Amsterdam, Fergus tells me that one of his biggest regrets about the hearing was that he didn't intervene during the State's questioning to ask the president of the Court to require the State to explain its hostility toward me and to instruct the State to allow me to answer the questions posed, including *why* we hadn't been to Suriname since 1986. I also learned that during my testimony about the map and the meaning of territory to Saramakas, Albert Abóikóni, the *gaamá*'s brother and witness for the State, was quietly weeping, which touched me deeply.)

The president asks the secretary to call the State's expert witness, Salomon Emanuels. In a somewhat confused ten-minute presentation, Emanuels, an educated Saramaka speaking Dutch, tries valiantly to lay out the political structure of Saramaka society, particularly the authority of the *lôs* in terms of land rights and the importance of the meetings of the leaders of all the clans, in the presence of the *gaamá*, at which tribal consensus is established. As best I can tell, nothing that he says seems to support the State's claims in this case in any way—it's as if they told him what subject to address but didn't tell him what points they were trying to make.

Attorney General Punwasi begins the friendly questioning by asking whether Saramaka society has experienced changes during the past fifteen or twenty years. (I understand full well where this line of questioning is leading. . . .) Emanuels replies, "Of course."[9] Punwasi then observes that "One expert witness here based his explanations on the situation as it was twenty-one years ago. Can you conclude that, perhaps, his statement should therefore not be considered here?" Emanuels replies that since he didn't hear the statement (he was sequestered), he can't answer yes or no, leaving the State without the confirmation they are seeking. Punwasi continues to question Emanuels for several minutes, trying to get him to confirm that the VSG really does not have any authority, but Emanuels consistently fails to give him satisfaction, either denying knowledge about the intricacies of the present case or saying things like, "I assume that the Saramakas who are here for this matter know the rules of the Saramaka people and have acted in accordance with them"—not at all what the State wants to hear. After the Commission asks but one question, about which the witness says he had no information, MacKay asks a single question, to which the witness replies "I don't know." The president then adjourns the session until 4 P.M., when final arguments will begin.

*　*　*

After the delayed close of the morning session, each delegation heads its separate way for a late lunch. Crossing the traffic-filled avenues with the

Saramakas in tow, we find an open-air restaurant where Sally and I figure out who wants fish, who wants meat, and what color soft drinks we need. César is especially happy to have a men's room nearby. It's nice to have a change of scenery. The hearing has become rather tense.

Once we're settled back in our places at the Court, the president outlines the ground rules for the closing arguments and rebuttals, and turns the floor over to the Commission.

Paolo Carozza takes the floor for an eloquent 25-minute presentation that effectively summarizes the legal conclusions that the IACHR had drawn in their 2006 "Application" to the Court. He begins by refuting certain claims made by the State—that Saramakas do not constitute a community which is entitled to the rights that the Court has previously recognized for tribal peoples, that the State has respected the land rights of the Saramakas in accord with the American Convention, and that the State provides sufficient judicial protection for the Saramaka clans. He goes on to review testimony given at the hearing about Saramaka "difference" in the Suriname context, their unique spiritual relations with the land, their separate system of laws and justice, and their multifarious uses of their territory. "All together," he says, "the land constitutes for the Saramaka their history. It is the source of their story as a people, it is a record of their historical existence. The testimony portrayed an intimacy of knowledge of the forest, almost as if every tree in the whole territory were known to them." He speaks about the coming of the Chinese loggers, their clear-cutting practices, and the ensuing "forever destruction" of the environment. And he concludes this portion of his argument, referring to other cases recently adjudicated by the Court, by asking the Court to find violations of Articles 21 and 25 ("right to property" and "right to judicial protection"), in connection with Articles 1 and 2 ("obligation to respect rights" and "domestic legal effect") of the Convention.

Carozza then makes arguments about reparations, stressing that they, like the property rights, need to be communal, collective, and "they need to take into account the full scope of the spiritual and religious suffering of the Saramaka as we've heard in testimony today and not merely their material deprivations." He concludes the Commission's arguments by insisting that:

> The case today is about nothing less than the cultural survival of the Saramaka people. Without a right to their land that is backed by effective judicial protection, the right that grants them effective

control, today their forests will be taken, tomorrow their land will be mined, and eventually, nothing will be left of their ongoing relationship which until now has endured for centuries. In the *Sawhoyamaxa* case, just one year ago, this Court found there to be a violation of the right to life and it noted, with great wisdom, that the right to life had been violated in that case because the State of Paraguay had failed in a timely manner to recognize and protect the right to land. It was a link that the Court made explicitly. The right to life is not yet an issue in this case before the Court today, but from what the Court learned in the *Sawhoyamaxa* case, it will be tomorrow, unless the right to land and property is protected today.

The president thanks the professor and turns the floor over to Fergus MacKay, speaking on behalf of the Saramakas. MacKay begins his twenty-minute summation in measured tones but becomes increasingly passionate as his arguments build toward a conclusion. He first summarizes the Saramakas' complaints—that their possession and ownership of traditional lands is not recognized or protected by the laws of Suriname, that they have lost 50 percent of their territory to a hydroelectric dam that was imposed on them, and that they are suffering further depredations to their territory because the State is issuing logging permits to foreign companies to exploit their forest. And then he goes on, using testimony that has already been given during the hearings or submitted to the Court as affidavits, to demonstrate Suriname's violation of Saramaka property rights and rights to judicial protection, under the American Convention. For example, he quotes the affidavit of Robert Goodland, who served as head of the World Bank's environmental department for over twenty years, regarding the logging practices on the Ji Shen and Tacoba concessions, which he characterized as "among the worst planned, most damaging and wasteful logging possible."

MacKay devotes some time to discussing the continuing effects of the Afobaka dam, "including the continuing deprivation of access to those traditional lands and resources that have been submerged as well as irreparable harm to numerous sacred sites and ongoing disruption of the Saramaka people's traditional land tenure and resource management systems which has placed a severe stress on the capacity of Saramaka lands and forests to meet basic subsistence needs." He goes on to say that "The Court has observed, for concrete and justifiable reasons, that if a State is unable to return indigenous peoples' traditional lands and resources, compensation or the provision of alternative lands is required." After further argument about Suriname's acts and omissions, MacKay states that Suriname is responsible for violations of the Saramakas' rights guaranteed by Articles 3 ("right to juridical personality"), 21, 25, 1, and 2 of the Convention. The final part of his summation makes the case for reparations, where MacKay stresses that both the material and non-material harm in this case has a collective dimension and that damages, therefore, need to be collective as well.

The president gives the floor to the State for its closing arguments. Eric Rudge begins by arguing, in Dutch, that testimony has shown that the respective roles of the traditional authorities and institutions—captains, *lôs*, and *gaamá*—is very unclear. "Who can act for the tribe? . . . Who in fact acted for the tribe in this case?" "It has been clearly shown," he argues, "that the Saramakas have been sufficiently incorporated into the political, social, and economic life of Suriname that they have a very different status from the tribes that have so far presented other cases to the Court." He also dismisses any claims made by the Saramakas on the basis of their 1762 treaty, since the Court already threw out consideration of the treaty in *Aloeboetoe*.

Rudge then passes the questioning on to Attorney General Punwasi, who, speaking in Dutch, summarizes the preliminary objections of the State— objections that were already submitted to the Court in a 125-page document in January 2007 and which were answered by the Commission and then point-by-point in the "Observations" of the representative of the Saramakas in March of that year. The same claims are reiterated—"the State denies all accusations that have been put forward by the Commission and the original petitioners," the case should be declared inadmissible because "procedural mistakes have been made" (the case was not submitted to the Court on time, "the term of one month was not respected by the Commission as February has only 28 days." . . .), the Afobaka dam was constructed before Suriname became a republic, and there has been a duplication of procedures since the core of the case has already been presented to the U.N. Committee on the Elimination of Racial Discrimination. He concludes by stating that "The Commission has incorrectly declared the case to be admissible," and then invites his colleague, Attorney Hans Lim a Po, to address the merits of the case.[10]

Lim a Po, reading out loud from a prepared text in English, announces that he will first treat the facts of the case, then the relevant law, and finally the issue of reparations. He brings up the 1762 treaty, only to dismiss its relevance. He then argues against "the distinctiveness" of the Saramaka people from other Surinamers, saying that during the past twenty years, their cultural distinctiveness has been "severely affected" by "voluntary political, cultural, and social inclusion of the people of the tribe into Western society." "Mr. President," he interjects. "I do not want to miss this opportunity to make a brief reference to the testimony of Dr. Price. I must say, as a Surinamer, I have taken offence at his observation that Suriname is treating any one of its citizens as dogs, as animals. . . . It is a pity that this qualified expert was so much carried away in his presentation that I think that the facts and the judgment have very much been overstated and tainted in an improper way."

He goes on to present Suriname as a poor, young democracy, trying its best to do the right thing under difficult circumstances.

The country and its people face an issue that is very hard to resolve. They are between a rock and a hard place. It's the dilemma of modernization vs. tradition. It's the dilemma of economic progress vs. cultural preservation. It's the dilemma of exclusion vs. inclusion. . . . The president of the country told me explicitly to state here how much he regrets the fact that citizens of this country have to stand here before you to quarrel over something that we think is the kind of issue that we should be able to resolve amongst us. Because only that would be a sustainable resolution.

He speaks for some time about the "confusions" in the petitioners' ideas about the structure of Saramaka political authority, a "lack of clarity" that makes it impossible for the government to act. The Saramaka and Suriname legal system are intertwined, he argues, and not in conflict "as Professor Price has so forcefully tried to make the Court believe."

The State does not agree with the petitioners' premise that traditional territorial boundaries are well understood, scrupulously observed, and encoded in history and tradition. This is highly overstated. . . . Mr. President, from my own personal experience, what has been dramatized here goes far beyond reality. . . .

All nations, Mr. President, and all peoples have suffered in their history one way or another, from acts of others that are now considered substandard and even immoral. Think about slavery—but that in itself is no basis for liability. . . . It takes Suriname and many other developing countries longer than the Western countries to implement modern environmental legislation. The matter is complex. . . . The position adopted by the human rights advocates in the present case shows signs of postulating a role for international law that is unrealistic in the practice of national sovereignty and smells of arrogance. Mr. President, the rights of the Saramaka people lie in our own legal system.

Lim a Po then speaks for some time in defense of the Suriname legal system, trying to show all the ways that it permits Saramakas and other citizens to enjoy property rights and legal protections. He goes on to defend the Suriname legal system regarding logging and mining, as well as judicial protections of various sorts. When the State's summation passes the one-hour mark, Attorney General Punwasi asks, on behalf of his colleague, for ten minutes of additional time, which the president grants on condition that the other parties receive the same additional time for their rebuttals. Lim a Po then continues, speaking about case law in Suriname and other technical matters that, to me, seem to have little specific bearing on the present case. He goes on to claim that the petitioners' pleas are contradictory, that their requests lack clarity, and that they should therefore be rejected. As Lim a Po continues to read from his text, the president interrupts to say that time is up, to which Attorney General Punwasi asks whether they could borrow their ten-minute rebuttal time and use it now. The president suggests that they simply finish up now in five more minutes but the attorney general says they really need at least ten. The president says he's granting only five minutes, and Lim a Po begins speed-reading his text out loud. The president objects and asks Lim a Po, instead, to please summarize his text, which he tries to do for a minute or two but then begins speed-reading again, until the time is up. The State's summation has lasted for an hour and twenty minutes.

The president offers the Commission the opportunity for rebuttal. Paolo Carozza takes the opportunity to make several points, first clarifying that the Commission, in its pleadings, did not in any way depend on the 1762 treaty, and pointing out that in *Moiwana v Suriname*, where the treaty was not at issue, the Court nevertheless acknowledged the community's historical right to land. He then questioned the State's claims of "ambiguity or lack of clarity in the structures of authority and in the customary laws of the Saramaka people," stating that the witnesses—including the witnesses called by the State—had, on the contrary, depicted "a great deal of coherence." The State cannot "rely on its own failure to understand the traditional structure as an excuse not to move forward with the recognition of traditional land rights," he suggests. Carozza then discusses rights to natural resources, claims by states and tribal peoples, and the nature of sovereignty in international law, citing other cases. And he ends by saying that the Commission is very sensitive to the very difficult decisions that states must make regarding development and the common good. "We do not presume to tell governments how they should balance the demands of modernization and preservation.... We simply demand that whatever balance domestic authorities reach with regard to these sensitive questions be done with full respect for the human rights of the individuals affected."

MacKay is given the floor and says he'll be very brief. "As the member of the Commission has touched on many of the points I was going to raise, I would concur with him at the outset and say that I agree with him—with one exception that I'll raise in a minute." His first comments point to a contradiction in the State's arguments. Throughout the many years of petitions and litigation, Suriname has claimed that the Saramakas do not have rights as a people, but now Mr. Lim a Po seems to be defending the ways that Suriname's laws do protect these rights. MacKay wishes aloud that he could ask the state for a clarification. Then turning to the issue of modernization versus tradition, MacKay argues that "the dichotomy of modernization vs. tradition is a false one. And I don't think it's one that's appropriate to discuss in the context of indigenous peoples, [who] live in today's world as much as anyone else." He continues,

The final declaration of the Vienna Conference on Human Rights says that underdevelopment cannot be used as an excuse for violating fundamental human rights. The rights of indigenous and tribal peoples to their lands, to their cultures, are fundamental human rights. Now, I see no contradiction between the State developing itself in one way or another for the benefit of its entire population, including indigenous and tribal peoples, and full respect for the rights of indigenous and tribal peoples. It sounds to me as if the State sees a contradiction here and I'd like to understand what it thinks that contradiction may be.... I'd also point out that the vast majority, if not all, of American states are grappling with this issue. If you look at the constitutions and legislation of the states in Latin America, in North America, all of them to varying degrees recognize that indigenous and tribal peoples have rights to their lands. Now, I'm not saying that these instruments are perfect, some of them aren't. Yet these states are managing to grapple with these issues of modernity vs. tradition, to use the State's formulation, which I think is a false dichotomy. But why is Suriname a special exception to this? . . .

The president turns the floor over to the State, which has already sacrificed half of its ten minutes in order to extend its summation. Lim a Po shouts across the courtroom, "Obviously, my question to the esteemed representative of the petitioners is whether he is going to give me extra time [from his own remaining time] to respond to his questions. Because if he isn't, I'm not going to respond to them and will instead deal with my own issues." He then begins to deal with his own issues, arguing at some length that the alleged ambiguities and lack of clarity about Saramaka political structure make it impossible for the State to know who it should deal with or who would be the appropriate unit to have certain rights. "Is it the *lô* or the tribe? It's that simple." He insists that this is not the government's responsibility. "They [the Saramakas] should know their own business. That's why they're not objects anymore, they are subjects. But here we are saying that the State must do this and that. The State can't do it! The government can't do it! They [the Saramakas] have to share the responsibility of resolving the problems." And he then lays out in more detail what he has in mind, which is that Saramakas should use current Suriname laws and procedures to assure whatever rights they seek, rather than seeking assistance from international tribunals.

> Why I am pursuing this is not because I am trying to get any responsibility away from the State in this matter. I am doing this because I believe that it is the most effective procedure to follow in a country like ours, in which twenty or twenty-two different populations live together. I want to avoid getting judgments or rulings that our country is simply not capable of following because there is no machinery for it. Our democracy does not give that scope. If we had a dictatorship it would be easy to comply. . . . And my esteemed colleague can say this is all about human rights but what I'm saying is how are we supposed to make legislation of such a complex nature? How do you do it in a country like ours? So, I'm suggesting that rather than seek a pyrrhic victory it makes sense to find something that will work for all of us.

At the end of his diatribe, Lim a Po makes a telling admission that almost makes me feel some sympathy for him.

The last point I will make is that we, the government of Suriname, believe that traditional rights should be recognized. Traditional possession and traditional use. That's the genesis of the rights.... But the government of Suriname is very concerned about any development that would reinforce the concept of creating states-within-a-state in Suriname. The political and democratic stability we have built up over so many years still remains fragile... In such a situation, any talk about heterogeneity is almost taboo in our country, because we want to preserve it as a whole. We must make sure that the rule of law and democracy prevail and bind us together. Which is why we have such concern about this talk of human rights for tribal and indigenous peoples—we have twenty-two of them!—becoming little states-within-a-state. It would be good for the Court to acknowledge that human rights don't work in a vacuum. They operate in a context.

The president asks the judges for their final questions. Judge Margarette May Macauley of Jamaica asks the State what the juridical balance is between the rights of the Saramaka people, under Article 21 (right to property) of the Convention, and the prerogative of the State to subordinate those rights in the general interest of the country. She also asks why those Saramaka people who live near the dam are still without electricity if it was built for the general good.

Lim a Po describes the technical difficulties of delivering "very high voltage power from huge turbines over a distance of two hundred kilometers before it is transformed into electricity that people can use," adding that there is no national power grid and ending by saying that "One shouldn't have the idea that when you put in a dam, you can put in your plug and take power for a computer. It's not that way. It's just impractical. The complaint is, philosophically, a good one but practically, this doesn't make much sense."[11] The other, more complex question is answered with a barrage of words and ideas that make little sense to me, either in their written version on the transcript or on the audio recording (which, admittedly, has several gaps in it).

Judge Macauley then asks the Commission two questions. Does it agree with the representative of the Saramakas that the State has violated the right to juridical personality, Article 3 of the Convention, in this case? And does it consider the facts presented by the representative regarding the ongoing effects of the dam "new facts" (in which case they might not be admissible) or do they represent explanations and clarification of facts included in the "Application" to the Court (in which case they would become part of the deliberations)?

Paolo Carozza answers that the Article 3 violation was never brought to the Commission by the representative and that the Commission cannot therefore take a position on it one way or the other. And concerning the dam, he says that he is uncertain whether it was ever discussed in a more than passing way before the Commission and that the Commission's "Application" to the Court contained only a single sentence referring to the dam and its effects.

Judge Macauley then questions Fergus MacKay.

Could you tell me please whether there are any circumstances where the Saramaka people would *not* object to logging or mining concessions being given in their territory? A second question: Under what article of the Convention are you asking the Court to deal with the ongoing effects of the dam, the flooding and the alleged displacement suffered by the people of Saramaka? And could you also elaborate on exactly what the public interest exception in Article 21 protects? And the Saramaka rights to cultural survival? . . . I am interested in the Saramakas' right to cultural survival and the balance with the State's duty to ensure economic development. And finally, if you can answer it, should the one supersede the other, and if so, on what terms? And please answer any of the questions I have asked the State or the Commission.

MacKay, with his plate full—and a good opportunity to have the last word—begins by asking, rhetorically (but perhaps he himself was wondering) "Where to start?"

He first offers some key corrections to what Carozza has just said, describing how the petitioners indeed invoked a violation of Article 3 before the Commission both in writing and at the hearing in Washington in 2004. He adds that the right of self-determination—which does not, he says, mean a state-within-a-state—has been invoked by the petitioners from the very beginning. He then speaks for several minutes about the balance between the State's responsibilities for economic development and for protecting the rights of its citizens, referring to the jurisprudence developed by the U.N. Human Rights Committee, particularly Article 27 of the International Covenant on

Civil and Political Rights, which says, in effect, that minorities should not be denied the right to enjoy their culture.

The Human Rights Committee applies a test to see whether the right to culture has been denied. It's a threshold test. Does the development activity rise to such a level so as to deny the right to culture? . . . If it passes that threshold, it's a violation of Article 27. It's not a case of weighing the state's economic development initiatives against the right to culture. If the right to culture is violated, it's violated. The Committee has been quite explicit in saying that they recognize that a state has the right to develop economically, but that does not mean that the rights of minorities, in this case indigenous and tribal peoples, can be violated, the right to culture in particular. . . .

I'll refer you to the case called *Apirana Mahuika v New Zealand* [adjudicated by the Human Rights Committee in 2000] . . . which deals with the intersection between Articles 1 and 27. The Committee has some very interesting *obiter dicta* in that case, where it addresses the resource rights of indigenous peoples. It states that the test really is, "Do indigenous peoples actually enjoy effective possession of and effective control over those resources?" Presumably, if they do not, rights with regard to Article 1, subparagraph 2, are implicated—in fact, the Committee stated that.

You have a former member of the Committee on the Court [Judge Medina Quiroga] and I feel I have to be a bit humble in expressing my opinions about all this. She was also on the Committee at the time that case was heard, so you have your own resident expert on that. . . .

I think that the question of how you balance economic development against human rights has been addressed by political declarations coming out of conferences—I mentioned the Vienna Conference on Human Rights, where the political declaration explicitly says that underdevelopment cannot be used as an excuse for violating human rights. . . . The Inter-American Commission has said the same thing. The U.N. Committee on the Elimination of Racial Discrimination has said the same thing. The Committee of experts of the International Labor Organization has said the same thing. So, there is quite a bit of jurisprudence out there. . . . The question to my mind is, what is the public interest [that justifies development]?—particularly, if you happen to be a minority indigenous people who is going to lose that argument every time. Why? Because "public interest" is essentially a majority rules test. The majority is going to determine what the public interest is, and if you have a state that does not consider protecting peoples' human rights to also be in the public interest, there is going to be a problem. . . .

I do not pretend to know all the answers but I think we have to look at it from different perspectives. We have to look at how it works from the perspective of indigenous peoples. If the state is the sole determiner of what is in the public interest, and you take for example the Saramaka people, who may amount to five or six per cent of the population, you're essentially saying that a majority will decide what happens to the Saramaka people's property, to their cultural integrity, and they can't do anything about it. It has been claimed [by the State] that you can challenge these decisions in a court. But I have yet to see a court . . . that overturned a political decision that said that something was in the public interest. Judges stay out of these decisions.

The Court has to deal with the text of the Convention. Are there any limitations that may be interpreted with regard to Article 21(1) and Article 21(2) ["right to property"]? I think this is a very important point, and is actually the reason that the right to self-determination has been invoked in this case. The right to self-determination contains a limitation on the extent to which a state may extinguish the property rights of indigenous and tribal peoples. . . . The Human Rights Council in June 2006 approved the U.N. Declaration on the Rights of Indigenous Peoples. Article 3 states that indigenous peoples have the right to self-determination. By virtue of that right, they freely determine their political status and freely pursue their economic, cultural, and social development. . . . This is not about creating states-within-a-state. It is about recognizing that indigenous peoples are peoples, and peoples have certain rights as collectivities, and those rights include resource rights and limits on the power of states to expropriate those resources and those property rights.

MacKay then takes a breath and addresses Judge Macauley's initial question. "Are there any circumstances where Saramakas would not object to logging or mining? I can't speak for them." But he explains how indigenous peoples in other countries have negotiated with, and ultimately agreed to, mining or other extractive industries on their traditional lands, and discusses the type of conditions and safeguards that they have insisted on as part of their agreement. "I can refer you to the Northern Territories in Australia, where the aboriginal peoples have the right to say yes or no to mining. Three billion Australian dollars comes from mining aboriginal lands in the Northern Territories. They say yes almost as much, in fact more, than they say no. Would the Saramaka people do it? I don't know, I can't speak for them."

He then moves on to the question of the dam, trying to explain once again that the issue is not what happened in the 1960s but, rather, the continuing suffering of the Saramaka people because of its construction. For the Saramaka people, the issue concerns property rights and they are therefore invoking a violation of Article 21. Because of the stress brought about by overcrowding on the land and other kinds of suffering they continue to experience, he says, they are seeking moral damages, as well.

Once several other judges pose largely informational questions of the State, at the end of this very long day, the president graciously thanks all the participants, including the translators and interpreters, and adjourns the hearing.

* * *

I walk over to where the Suriname delegation is gathered and stick my hand out to Attorney General Punwasi. (In retrospect, I'm not sure why I made this gesture but suppose it was an attempt to break what I'd felt was a tense situation, and to do it from what I suddenly felt was a position of strength.) He declines the handshake and begins berating me, "You called us dogs, you said that Surinamers are dogs! After all Suriname has done for you . . . " I interrupt, trying to explain that I was merely repeating the words of the two Saramaka witnesses the day before who said that they often felt as if the government of Suriname treated *them* like dogs. "I never called Surinamers dogs." "Yes you did!" he says very deliberately. "And if I have anything to do with it, you will never set foot in my country again." At this point Lim a Po, through clenched teeth, turns to me, "Tomorrow night, as soon as we get back to Suriname, I will be meeting with President Venetiaan and the first thing I intend to tell him is that you called Surinamers dogs. . . . I can assure you he will see that you never come to Suriname again." Meanwhile, Fergus, having seen me walk over to the Surinamers, tells Sally to get over there fast and pull me away. In the event, since things are getting heated, both Fergus

and Sally rush over and get between me and the other men and pull me over
to the other side of the room.

*   *   *

After a late dinner at the hotel, we pull up wicker chairs with Fergus
and the Saramakas in an outdoor patio to try to wind down. Fergus brings
out the bottle of duty-free tequila he bought on the way down, and we all
relax. Adiante shows up with a good-looking woman, whom he introduces
as his date. (When he had the time to meet her is anyone's guess.) We're all
exhausted but feeling positive about the case. Fergus tells us that we can
expect the judgment in about six months.

The Judgment

The Court's Judgment of November 2007 begins with a disappointment for the Saramakas—their complaints about the ongoing effects of the Afobaka dam were ruled inadmissible.[1] It turns out that according to its own rules (as well as an apparently new rule adopted in the judgment), the Court depends on the Commission to determine the issues to be adjudicated, and in this case it found that the Commission, in its "Application" to the Court, had hardly mentioned the dam and then (the new part) only in its "factual" presentation, rather than in its legal arguments. The Court reasoned that since the legal arguments about the effects of the dam came from the representatives of the Saramakas, and were never mentioned by the Commission, they could not be considered by the Court. "The Tribunal considers that the factual basis for the representatives' arguments in this regard falls outside the scope of the controversy as framed by the Commission in its application." Therefore, all the Saramakas' complaints about the effects of the dam and reservoir on their lives, and all the affidavits, expert testimony, and witnesses' statements about it were ruled inadmissible.[2] (Further litigation about the effects of the dam will need to await other potential cases, such as complaints involving the land rights of those Saramakas who live in transmigration villages below the dam.) However, the rest of the judgment may be considered a signal victory for the Saramakas.

Having ruled out issues related to the Afobaka dam and reservoir, the judges went on to dismiss Suriname's seven preliminary objections one by one, concluding that the Court did indeed have jurisdiction for this case and could properly proceed with the consideration of evidence.

The Court then outlined the kinds of evidence it had received in various affidavits from people who did not testify in person at the hearing. On behalf of the Saramakas or the Commission, the Court had heard from Silvi Adjako (the Saramaka woman who originally heard the Chinese loggers from her peanut garden), Hugo Jabini (Saramaka law student and Paramaribo representative of the VSG), Saramaka Headcaptain Eddie Fonkie (who testified about the dire situation of the transmigration villages below the dam, which

he represents), George Leidsman (a Saramaka who testified about the sink-
ing of his village, Ganzee, by the dam), Peter Poole (international authority
on geomatics), Mariska Muskiet (property law lecturer at the University of
Suriname), Robert Goodland (former Chief Environmental Adviser for the
World Bank Group who drafted and implemented the Bank's official policy
on Tribal and Indigenous Peoples adopted in 1982), and Martin Scheinin
(Professor of Constitutional and International Law at the Åbo Akademi
University, Finland, and a former member of the United Nations Human
Rights Committee). On behalf of the State, it had heard from Jennifer Vic-
torine van Dijk-Silos (chairperson of Suriname's Presidential Land Rights
Commission) and Magda Hoever-Venoaks (an authority on legal remedies in
Surinamese administrative and constitutional law).

The Court next cited the people who provided testimony and expert
opinions at the public hearing, all of whom should by now be familiar to
readers. For the Saramakas or the Commission: Headcaptain Wazen Eduards,
Captain César Adjako, and Richard Price. And for the State: former District
Commissioner Rudy Strijk, Saramaka Headcaptain Albert Abóikóni, Acting
Director of the Forestry Foundation Rene Ali Somopawiro, and Saramaka
anthropologist Salomon Emanuels.

The Court then commented on certain of the witnesses and their
testimony, deciding to "incorporate into the present body of evidence
the transcript of the expert opinion rendered by Dr. Richard Price during the public hearing held on July 7, 1992 in the case of *Aloeboetoe* et
al. *v. Suriname*," to admit into evidence, over the State's objection, "the
statement made by Ms. Mariska Muskiet before the Commission," and to
admit into evidence "the statements made by Dr. Richard Price before the
Commission," despite the State's objection that his declaration "is totally
outdated."

At this point in the Judgment, "having examined the evidentiary elements
that have been incorporated into the present case," the Court proceeded with
its analysis of the alleged violations of the American Convention of Human
Rights.[3]

*   *   *

Citing "the interrelatedness of the arguments submitted to the Court
in the present case," it decided to address "in a single chapter" Suriname's
alleged noncompliance with Article 2 (Domestic Legal Effects), and violations of Articles 3 (Right to Juridical Personality), 21 (Right to Property),

and 25 (Right to Judicial Protection), in relation to Article 1(1) (Obligation to Respect Rights) of the American Convention.

The Court broke down its analysis into eight specific issues:

1. whether the members of the Saramaka people make up a tribal community subject to special measures that ensure the full exercise of their rights;
2. whether Article 21 of the American Convention protects the right of the members of tribal peoples to the use and enjoyment of communal property;
3. whether the State has recognized the right to property of the members of the Saramaka people derived from their system of communal property;
4. whether and to what extent the members of the Saramaka people have a right to use and enjoy the natural resources that lie on and within their alleged traditionally owned territory;
5. whether and to what extent the State may grant concessions for the exploration and extraction of natural resources found on and within alleged Saramaka territory;
6. whether the concessions already issued by the State comply with the safeguards established under international law;
7. whether the lack of recognition of the Saramaka people as a juridical personality makes them ineligible under domestic law to receive communal title to property as a tribal community and to have equal access to judicial protection of their property rights; and
8. whether there are adequate and effective legal remedies available in Suriname to protect the members of the Saramaka people against acts that violate their alleged right to the use and enjoyment of communal property.

The Court first addressed the question of whether the members of the Saramaka people make up a tribal community subject to special measures that ensure the full exercise of their rights. In answering, the Court cited detailed evidence, much of it anthropological (I omit the Court's footnotes referring to testimony given at the hearing):

Their social structure is different from other sectors of society inasmuch as the Saramaka people are organized in matrilineal clans (lôs), and they regulate themselves, at least partially, by their own customs and traditions. . . . Their culture is also similar to that of tribal peoples insofar as the members of the Saramaka people maintain a strong spiritual relationship with the ancestral territory they have traditionally used and occupied. Land is more than merely a source of subsistence for them; it is also a necessary source for the continuation of the life and cultural identity of the Saramaka people. The lands and resources of the Saramaka people are part of their social, ancestral, and spiritual essence. In this territory, the Saramaka people hunt, fish, and farm, and they gather water, plants for medicinal purposes, oils, minerals, and wood. Their sacred sites are scattered throughout the territory, while at the same time the territory itself has a sacred value to them. In particular, the identity of the members of the Saramaka people with the land is inextricably linked to their historical fight for freedom from slavery, called the sacred "First Time." . . . Furthermore, their economy can also be characterized as tribal. According to the expert testimony of Dr. Richard Price, for example, "the very great bulk of food that Saramakas eat comes from farms and gardens" traditionally cultivated by Saramaka women. The men, according to Dr. Price, fish and "hunt wild pig, deer, tapir, all sorts of monkeys, different kinds of birds, everything that Saramakas eat." Furthermore, the women gather various fruits, plants and minerals, which they use in a variety of ways, including making baskets, cooking oil, and roofs for their dwellings.

And the Court concluded that

The members of the Saramaka people make up a tribal community whose social, cultural and economic characteristics are different from other sections of the national community, particularly because of their special relationship with their ancestral territories, and because they regulate themselves, at least partially, by their own norms, customs, and/or traditions.

The Court then turned to its second question, whether Article 21 of the American Convention (the right to property) protects the right of the members of tribal peoples to the use and enjoyment of *communal* property. After citing its ruling in the *Moiwana* case, the Court stated that it saw "no reason to depart from this jurisprudence in the present case" and ruled that

The members of the Saramaka people are to be considered a tribal community, and that the Court's jurisprudence regarding indigenous peoples' right to property is also applicable to tribal peoples because both share distinct social, cultural, and economic characteristics, including a special relationship with their ancestral territories, that require special measures under international human rights law in order to guarantee their physical and cultural survival.

Then, after a lengthy and often technical discussion of relevant jurisprudence (involving, among others, the cases of the *Sawhoyamaxa, Awas Tingni,* and *Yakye Axa* that the Court had ruled on previously, as well as precedents carved out by the Human Rights Committee and rights guaranteed in the International Covenant on Civil and Political Rights and the International Covenant on Economic, Social, and Cultural Rights), the Court ruled that "the State has an obligation to adopt special measures to recognize, respect, protect and guarantee the communal property right of the members of the Saramaka community to said territory."

Taking up its third question, whether the State of Suriname has recognized the right to property of the members of the Saramaka people, derived from their system of communal property and guaranteed by the American Convention, the Court concluded, after a long consideration of possible domestic legal remedies claimed by the State, that no, "the State has not complied with its duty" in this respect.

The Court next moved to its fourth and more politically dicey question, "whether and to what extent the members of the Saramaka people have a right to use and enjoy the natural resources that lie on and within their alleged traditionally owned territory." The State had asserted that "all land ownership, including all natural resources, vests in the State, and that, as such, the State may grant logging and mining concessions within alleged Saramaka territory, while respecting as much as possible Saramaka customs and traditions." (The State had long held the position that "Indigenous peoples and Maroons are permissive occupiers of privately held State lands and that whatever rights they may have will always be superseded by the larger interests of the State. Further, these rights are simply temporary protections conceded by the State during a transitional period in which Indigenous peoples and Maroons are to be assimilated into the larger, and inherently superior, Surinamese society and economy."[4]) In contrast, the representatives of the Saramakas had argued that land concessions for forestry and mining awarded by the State to third parties on territory possessed by the Saramaka people, without their free, prior, and informed consent, violates their right to control their territory and the natural resources that lie thereon and thereunder, and that all these resources belong to the Saramakas pursuant to the right to self-determination. They requested that the Court interpret and apply the right to property in the American Convention in accordance with this self-determination-based argument.

Here, after an analysis of prior jurisprudence, the Court decided that the only natural resources "found on and within indigenous and tribal people's territories" that are protected under Article 21 are "those natural resources traditionally used and necessary for the very survival, development, and continuation of such people's way of life."[5] Thus, proof of *traditional use* of a resource by the Saramakas becomes a prerequisite for establishing their ownership rights in that resource. The Court therefore set out to "determine which natural resources found on and within the Saramaka people's territory are essential for the survival of their way of life, and are thus protected under Article 21 of the Convention." In this regard, the State had argued that the Saramakas (whom it claimed were in the process of modernization and assimilation) no longer use the resources of the forest and therefore no longer have any claim to them. But the Court patiently sorted the evidence from the hearing and affidavits. I quote from their deliberations on logging, as an example:

> Thus, with regard to timber logging, a question arises as to whether this natural resource is one that has been traditionally used by the members of the Saramaka people in a manner inextricably related to their survival. In this regard, Dr. Richard Price, an anthropologist who gave his expert opinion during the public hearing in the present case, submitted a map in which the Saramaka people made hundreds of marks illustrating the location and variety of trees they use for different purposes. For example, the Saramakas use a special type of tree from which they build boats and canoes to move and transport people and goods from one village to another. The members of the Saramaka community also use many different species of palm trees to make different things, including roofing for their houses, and from which they obtain fruits that they process into cooking oil.

The Court concluded that the natural resources of the forest and the river, as outlined in the map made by Saramakas, are indeed essential to their continued physical and cultural survival as a people, that these resources therefore fall under the protection of the American Convention, and that these resources form part of the Saramakas' corporate ownership rights.

Continuing with politically dicey issues, the fifth and sixth questions addressed by the Court regard the right of the State to intrude on (or grant third parties concessions to intrude on) Saramaka territory under certain circumstances for resource extraction (so-called "development projects") as well as whether the logging and mining concessions already issued by the State comply with the safeguards established under international law. The Court concluded that:

In order to guarantee that restrictions to the property rights of the members of the Saramaka people by the issuance of concessions within their territory does not amount to a denial of their survival as a tribal people, the State must abide by the following three safeguards [in addition to the general requirements applicable to all persons, such as necessity and proportionality].[6] First, the State must ensure the effective participation of the members of the Saramaka people, in conformity with their customs and traditions, regarding any development, investment, exploration or extraction plan within Saramaka territory. Second, the State must guarantee that the Saramakas will receive a reasonable benefit from any such plan within their territory. Thirdly, the State must ensure that no concession will be issued within Saramaka territory unless and until independent and technically capable entities, with the State's supervision, perform a prior environmental and social impact assessment. These safeguards are intended to preserve, protect and guarantee the special relationship that the members of the Saramaka community have with their territory, which in turn ensures their survival as a tribal people.

And finally, "the Court considers that, regarding large-scale development or investment projects that would have a major impact within Saramaka territory, the State has a duty, not only to consult with the Saramakas, but also *to obtain their free, prior, and informed consent*, according to their customs and traditions" (my italics). In its 2008 Interpretive Judgment (Para. 17), the Court further specified (and expanded) the conditions under which free, prior, and informed consent would need to be obtained: "Depending on the level of impact of the proposed activity, the state may additionally be required to obtain consent from the Saramaka people. The tribunal has emphasized that when large-scale development or investment projects could affect the integrity of the Saramaka people's lands and natural resources, the state has a duty not only to consult with the Saramakas, but also to obtain their free, prior and informed consent in accordance with their customs and traditions."[7]

So the test would seem to become the extent to which a large project affects the integrity of indigenous and tribal territories. Nonetheless, in its Interpretive Judgment, the Court stressed that the State's right to restrict the Saramakas' right to property can occur only "under very specific, exceptional circumstances," suggesting that such restrictions must be truly extraordinary.[8]

Regarding the prior logging concessions granted by the State to Chinese and other multinationals without Saramaka consent, the Court noted, on the basis of the testimony it had heard, that "The Saramaka people have been left with a legacy of environmental destruction, despoiled subsistence resources, and spiritual and social problems, but they received no benefit from the logging in their territory. Government statistics submitted into evidence before the Court prove that a considerable quantity of valuable timber was extracted from the territory of the Saramaka people without any compensation."

And the Court ended its considerations of the State's rights to grant concessions in Saramaka territory by concluding:

First, that the members of the Saramaka people have a right to use and enjoy the natural resources that lie on and within their traditionally owned territory that are necessary for their survival; second, that the State may restrict said right by granting concessions for the exploration and extraction of natural resources found on and within Saramaka territory only if the State ensures the effective participation and benefit of the Saramaka people, performs or supervises prior environmental and social impact assessments, and implements adequate safeguards and mechanisms in order to ensure that these activities do not significantly affect the traditional Saramaka lands and natural resources; and finally, that the concessions already issued by the State did not comply with these safeguards. Thus, the Court considers that the State has violated Article 21 of the Convention, in conjunction with Article 1 of such instrument, to the detriment of the members of the Saramaka people.

After deliberations about the value of the timber extracted and the environmental damages caused by outside logging in Saramaka territory, the Court ruled that the State must pay US$75,000 for material damages into the development fund to be established for the Saramaka people.[9]

And finally, the Court considered its seventh and eighth questions: does the lack of recognition of the Saramaka people as a juridical personality make them ineligible under domestic law to receive title and judicial protection of their property rights, and are there adequate legal remedies in Suriname to protect the Saramakas against acts that violate their right to communal property? In answering, the Court underlined what it saw as a key element of its Judgment: "The Court considers that the right to have their juridical personality recognized by the State is one of the special measures owed to indigenous and tribal groups in order to ensure that they are able to use and enjoy their territory in accordance with their own traditions. This is a natural consequence of the recognition of the right of members of indigenous and tribal groups to enjoy certain rights in a communal manner."

The Court continued,

In conclusion, the members of the Saramaka people form a distinct tribal community in a situation of vulnerability, both as regards the State as well as private third parties, insofar as they lack the juridical capacity to collectively enjoy the right to property and to challenge before domestic courts alleged violations of such right. The Court considers that the State must recognize the juridical capacity of the members of the Saramaka people to fully exercise these rights in a collective manner. This may be achieved by implementing legislative or other measures that recognize and take into account the particular way in which the Saramaka people view themselves as a collectivity capable of exercising and enjoying the right to property. Thus, the State must establish, in consultation with the Saramaka people and fully respecting their traditions and customs, the judicial and administrative conditions necessary to ensure the recognition of their juridical personality, with the aim of guaranteeing them the use and enjoyment of their territory in accordance with their communal property system, as well as the rights to access to justice and equality before the law.[10]

In other words, Suriname must rewrite its laws, including the Constitution if necessary, both to recognize indigenous and Maroon groups as legal personalities and to permit such groups to own and effectively control property communally.

*   *   *

The Court's ruling ends with a series of ten actions that the government of Suriname must take, the most important of which are that:

The State shall delimit, demarcate, and grant collective title over the territory of the members of the Saramaka people, in accordance with their customary laws, and through previous, effective and fully informed consultations with the Saramaka people.... This must start by 19 March 2008 and conclude no later than 19 December 2010.

The State shall grant the members of the Saramaka people legal recognition of the collective juridical capacity, pertaining to the community to which they belong, with the purpose of ensuring the full exercise and enjoyment of their right to communal property, as well as collective access to justice, in accordance with their communal system, customary laws, and traditions.

The State shall remove or amend the legal provisions that impede protection of the right to property of the members of the Saramaka people and adopt, in its domestic legislation, and through prior, effective and fully informed consultations with the Saramaka people, legislative, administrative, and other measures as may be required to recognize, protect, guarantee and give legal effect to the right of the members of the Saramaka people to hold collective title of the territory they have traditionally used and occupied as well as their right to manage, distribute, and effectively control such territory, in accordance with their customary laws and traditional collective land tenure system. (This must be done within the three-year period established to comply with the order pertaining to delimitation, demarcation and titling, because the State will be unable to issue title without first adopting the legislative means for doing so.)

The State shall adopt legislative, administrative and other measures necessary to recognize and ensure the right of the Saramaka people to be effectively consulted, in accordance with their traditions and customs, or when necessary, the right to give or withhold their free, informed and prior consent, with regards to development or investment projects that may affect their territory, and to reasonably share the benefits of such projects with the members of the Saramaka people, should these be ultimately carried out.

The State shall allocate the amounts set in this Judgment as compensation for material and non-material damages in a community development fund created and established for the benefit of the members of the Saramaka people [a total of US$675,000]. The State must allocate at least US$225,000 to the development fund no later than 19 December 2008, and the total amount no later than 19 December 2010.

*   *   *

In January 2008, the government of Suriname publicly declared that it would implement the judgment of the Court and do so within the schedule set by the tribunal. At that point, according to a government minister, the government was "doing everything to prevent other tribal peoples from following the path of the Saramakas and filing a case against Suriname with the Court."[11]

But only two months after making this statement, the government submitted a request to the Court asking for an interpretation of key aspects of the judgment, resulting in the Court's Interpretive Judgment of August 2008.[12] In this document, the State's interpretations of the original judgment—many of which simply reiterated their arguments before the Court and most of which would have severely undermined the Saramaka people's rights—were soundly rejected by the Court, which also took the opportunity to further develop its reasoning on the consent standard and reiterate key aspects of the original judgment.

As the Court moved into what it calls its "monitoring" mode—assuring that the various measures in the Judgment are carried out by Suriname in a timely manner—the Saramakas, represented by the VSG, moved into their own monitoring mode, actively keeping track of developing events on the ground.

American Dreams

Developments on the Ground

As I write this in the spring of 2010, Suriname has done little to abide by the Court's judgment, other than to assert its good intentions. It has complied with the easiest of the rulings, paying the costs of the petitioners in preparing their case ($15,000 to the Forest Peoples Programme, $75,000 to the VSG). But, on the more serious measures—delimiting Saramaka territory and granting the Saramaka people collective title to it, changing domestic legislation to recognize the Saramaka people as a juridical personality, and placing $675,000 in a community development fund for the benefit of the Saramaka people—all of which, according to the Court's judgment, must be completed by December 2010—the State has barely made a start.[1]

In its various pronouncements and communications, the State has taken the position that it can resolve the Saramaka situation only as part of a broader reconsideration of the place of all indigenous peoples and Maroons within Suriname, effectively postponing specific action in response to the Court's judgment. The State points out, for example, that "Suriname has many tribal groups that reside and live next to each other. This circumstance results in added complexity to handle the Saramaka case as an issue that stands on its own. The government is for this reason pursuing an integral approach."[2] Toward this end, the State has proposed a project, "Support for the Sustainable Development of the Interior" (SSDI), sponsored a public meeting in a theater in Paramaribo devoted to "The Judgment of the Saramaka Los: Next Steps?" (December 2008) and a conference ("National Land Rights Conference," in June 2009), and established an interministerial executive committee to coordinate implementation of the judgment. As far as I can determine, there has been no further concrete action to implement the Court's orders.

Since the judgment of 2007, the Saramakas have remained vigilant and proactive. In September 2009, their representatives submitted comments to the Court, responding to Suriname's claims about the progress it had made on implementation of the judgment.[3] They assert that Suriname has taken no steps at all to "delimit, demarcate, and grant collective title" to Saramaka territory, nor has it consulted with the Saramakas on these issues—despite the Saramakas having requested meetings in several formal yet friendly letters that reminded the government of its obligations under the judgment.[4] They refer to Operative Paragraph 5 of the judgment, which orders the State to "evaluate whether a modification of the rights of existing concessionaires operating within Saramaka territory is necessary in order to preserve the survival of the Saramaka people," and say that they "have no reason to believe that the State has considered complying with this component of the order," despite the fact that "there are large-scale mining concessions and one operating gold mine within traditional Saramaka territory [the contentious Rosebel mine near the village of Nieuw Koffiekamp] as well as a number of logging concessions that require review and potential modification." The Saramakas add that the required review and potential modification of these concessions includes potential benefit-sharing measures required by the Court.

In their "Comments," the Saramakas next discuss the proposed asphalting of the road around the lake, which would make Saramaka villages readily accessible from the coast, and which was supposed to begin before the end of 2009. The State has contracted this project to a Chinese company called Dalian Xinke, with funding from the Inter-American Development Bank for impact assessments. In contravention of the Court's judgment, there has been no formal consultation with the Saramakas.

The Saramakas next roundly criticize the State's SSDI project, which has "as one of its objectives the drafting of legislation on the rights of indigenous and tribal peoples." It is being implemented by an NGO called the Amazon Conservation Team Suriname, which the Saramakas claim has little if any experience in drafting legislation "and whose chair is one of the delegates (legal advisors) who represented (and continues to represent) the State before the Court in *Saramaka People*, thus raising concerns about its impartiality and independence." For these and other reasons (notably the failure to consult with indigenous and tribal peoples about project design and implementation), the Saramakas point out, the SSDI has been rejected by the national indigenous peoples' organization (the Association of Indigenous Village Leaders) as well as by the Saramaka people.

Against the claims of President Venetiaan, Minister Felisi, and Suriname legal advisor Hans Lim a Po, who made speeches at the June 2009 land rights conference, the Saramakas insist simply that the judgment be respected—and implemented according to the schedule mandated by the Court.

In his comments at the conference, President Venetiaan stressed that "in the development of tribal groups, choices have to be made. Are we on the road to modernisation of the total community? Or are we on the road of retreating within the respective tribal groups?" And, alluding to the problems of Suriname's largest gold mine (which the Saramakas say is in their territory) and implicitly criticizing the Saramakas for having taken their case to the Court, he concluded that,

I think we should explicitly emphasize the area of economic rights, the area of economic interests. . . .That is where the big challenge lies for the people of Suriname. It is not about whether one has the right to dance as one dances, to eat as one eats, to sing as one sings, but rather about which economic rights [he mentions as possibilities, "everything that is found under your house, under your village, in the territory you inhabit, above, on, and under the soil"] are linked to the recognition of the rights of tribal groups in this country.

Minister Felisi was equally blunt:

The movement around the recognition of indigenous and tribal rights focuses mainly on the themes of self-government, territories they inhabit, and political participation. It certainly does not concern the demarcation and relinquishing (allocating) a piece of land to one part of the community over which the government then no longer has any say. . . .

In our country the discussions regarding this issue have been hesitant and circumspect. You could almost say that there is a taboo in the relationship between the government. . . and tribal groups. This is how outsiders have been given room to penetrate these tribal communities in our country and succeeded in introducing their own interpretations into these groups—interpretations that often do not correspond to the scope of the treaties and conventions.

And Lim a Po summarized Suriname's position regarding the order to change its legislation, "The problem is that the Court can say this easily, but implementation is not easy. It is a complex issue of much significance, with possibly important political, social, and cultural implications. It is easier said than done."[5]

Suriname has made one positive move toward solving the problem identified by Lim a Po. The State has made a request, which was accepted, that Professor James Anaya, the U.N. Special Rapporteur on the rights and fundamental freedoms of indigenous people, help draft the legislation that will be needed to implement the Court's judgment. In March 2009, this move was welcomed and endorsed by the U.N. Committee on the Elimination of Racial Discrimination.[6]

There is reason to expect further delays in Suriname's making concrete progress on the implementation of the Court's judgment. National elections are scheduled for May 25, 2010. Traditionally, government activity grinds to a halt in the months before an election and, once the election is held, the formation of a new government often drags on for months. Meanwhile, the Court, prodded by the representatives of the Saramakas, will continue its monitoring process. As best I can tell, the main sanctions available to the Court and petitioners in case of Suriname's noncompliance with the judgment (or even substantial malingering in implementing it) would be to follow the money trail. Since Suriname receives substantial development funds from the Inter-American Development Bank (which, like the Court, is an organ of the OAS), the threat of withholding such funds might well tip the balance toward the State's compliance.

In November 2009, when two government ministers flew in to Laduáni to inaugurate a new primary school in nearby Guyába, they were met by Saramaka protesters who were angry about government delays in implementing the Court's ruling. As reported by *De Ware Tijd*, the protesters held aloft handwritten placards saying (in Dutch), "Implementation of the Saramaka judgment now," "Land rights are human rights," and "Legal recognition of the traditional authority of captains and assistant headmen."

Since December 2007, when the Court's judgment was made public, the Suriname government has done almost nothing to recognize the rights of the Saramaka people as ordered by the Court. This week's rally in Laduani was directed at Michel Felisi, minister for regional development, whom the Saramaka captains urged to hasten the implementation process, in order to comply with the Court's deadline of December 2010.... As he climbed down from the plane, the protesters raised placards and shouted. Military men and other security personnel closely guarded the rally, which remained peaceful.... Minister Felisi has expressed disappointment over the protest action. He referred to his own Maroon (Ndyuka) heritage and said he had not expected such a protest from "his own people."[7]

As this book goes to press, I have learned that on 20 April 2010, the president of the Court issued an order ("Monitoring Compliance with the Judgment in the case of *The Saramaka People v. Suriname*") to convene "the Inter-American Commission, the representatives of the victims, and the State to a private hearing that will take place at San José, Costa Rica, on May 26, 2010, in order to receive complete and updated information from the State on the actions taken in compliance with the Judgment issued in this case, as well as the observations from the representatives and the Commission." Clearly, the Court is concerned about the State's lack of progress in meeting its legal obligations.

*   *   *

I offer here my personal summary of current hotspots in Suriname relating to the rights of Saramakas and other tribal and indigenous peoples— ongoing issues to monitor, in addition to the implementation of the Court's judgment. I propose to post periodic updates on the Internet for readers interested in following these developments.[8]

For the Saramakas:

— The asphalting of the Afobaka road (the Tjóngalángapási). It is unclear whether the government has conducted the legally required environmental impact reports. But it is clear that there has not yet been formal consultation with the Saramakas, in whose territory the road lies and whose lives would be significantly affected by the project. On 23 November 2009, President Venetiaan, the vice president, and various government ministers, in the presence of the ambassador of China (with whom the government has contracted to asphalt the road), publicly celebrated the start of the project, stating that it would lead to "the building, renovation, and expansion of various polyclinics, schools, and council houses by the State" and to "the coming of city people who will live, work, and invest" in the region. "The growing number of tourists will bring in foreign currency." And President Venetiaan stressed the benefits that would come once there is a full "North-South highway to

Brazil"—a long-term dream of many a Suriname administration. (If the asphalting of the road is meant to be a step in that direction, the consequences for Saramakas would be that much more enormous.) This ceremony was held, as far as the newspaper reported, without the presence of Saramakas.[9]

— The situation of Nieuw Koffiekamp, the primarily Ndyuka transmigration village of refugees from under the lake that is part of the most lucrative gold mining concession in Suriname, currently owned by Iamgold, a Canadian multinational and the tenth largest gold mining corporation in the world. Iamgold's Gros Rosebel mine, as well as its newer potential mining sites nearby, lie in traditional Saramaka territory. (Iamgold announced record gold production from its "flagship operation, the Rosebel Gold Mine" in 2009: over 400,000 ounces = nearly half a billion U.S. dollars at current prices.[10]) The situation is complicated by the fact that many of the inhabitants of Nieuw Koffiekamp engage in small-scale gold mining on the fringes of Iamgold's commercial mine. I was told by a participant at the Gaán Kuútu (tribal council meeting) of May 2008, that when Gaamá Belfón repeated that the mines were in Saramaka territory—reiterating the traditional Saramaka phrase (enshrined, in their understandings, in the treaty of 1762), "From Mawási on up, the land is ours"—President Venetiaan visibly blanched. The issue of demarcating and titling Saramaka territory, ordered by the Court, will be at its most contentious concerning this area.

— The Tapanahoni Diversion Project, which would force the displacement of a number of Ndyuka villages on the Tapanahoni, as well as raising the level of the Afobaka reservoir so that a number of additional Saramaka villages just to its south would be flooded—all this to increase the generating power of the Afobaka hydroelectric dam so that Alcoa could reopen and expand its aluminum smelting capabilities. This project is currently pending before IIRSA, funded in part by the Inter-American Development Bank, and is slated to cost US$880 million. Because of the complexity of this project, which would require roads to be built into the interior and canals to extend over great distances, it currently seems unlikely that it will be made a reality. The significant and obvious costs, in terms of ecological damage and human rights abuses, seem to me to be so great as to discourage the realization of this project. But who knows?

— Bioprospecting by the Suriname Biodiversity Prospecting Initiative (SBPI), which involves obtaining knowledge about traditional medicine, in particular medicinal plants, from indigenous and Maroon traditional healers and shamans. (The SBPI is a joint effort of Conservation International, the BGVS [a state-owned pharmaceutical company], the National Herbarium of Suriname, the Virginia Polytechnic Institute, and Bristol-Meyers Squibb.) Suriname has no laws that protect indigenous and tribal peoples' traditional knowledge. Indeed, the State maintains that it owns all biological and genetic resources and any exploitation of traditional knowledge pertaining to those resources is the property of the State—a claim exactly like that to the Saramakas' land, prior to the ruling of the Court. Clearly, until the Saramakas gain title to their territory, in line with the order of the Court, it will be much harder for them to negotiate such matters. But once they do gain title, they should be in a better position to begin to protect their rights in these respects, both deciding what they wish to share with outsiders and what benefits they should derive therefrom.[11]

— A "Protected Area" in Saramaka territory. In contrast to earlier projects proposed by outsiders, such as Conservation International's initiative to expand the Central Suriname Nature Reserve into Saramaka territory (discussed above, "The Depredations Continue"), a proposal has been floated by Gaamá Belfón to turn a part of the southernmost portion of Saramaka territory into a protected area managed by the Saramaka people. (Until now, the designation of a nature reserve or other protected area automatically gave title of that area to the State. Given the Court's rulings, the establishment of such an area by Saramakas would not have that effect.) The area under consideration includes a number of eighteenth-century village sites and is of great cultural and religious importance. It also contains an important watershed and the headwaters of the Suriname River, one of the country's main waterways, and a substantial area of primary tropical forest. As part of this proposal, the Saramakas may seek to develop plans for watershed management, eco-tourism, and other community development initiatives. This plan must await the demarcation and titling mandated by the Court.

For other Maroons and indigenous peoples:

— The Nassau Mountains mining project. Suriname has granted exploratory mining concessions to Suralco (Alcoa) for bauxite extraction on lands that traditionally belong to the Paramaka Maroons. As these explorations were progressing, gold was discovered and Alcoa is now partnering in the area with the world's largest gold producer, Newmont Mining. In addition, in 2009, the government signed a memorandum of understanding with the Swiss multinational Glencore International AG for underwriting additional bauxite mining activities in the Nassau and Bakhuys areas. No adequate consultations have occurred with the Paramakas and it is unclear whether sufficient environmental or social impact studies have been conducted or completed. In addition, Alcoa has recently announced plans to build a 125-kilometer road connecting the Nassau Mountain mines to Paranam, to be serviced by bauxitecarrying "road trains," which would require the displacement of five villages belonging to Indigenous peoples.[12]

— The Sarakreek mining project. Owned by Iamgold, and located "100 kilometers south of the Rosebel mine," drilling began in 2009. "The project area covers 743 square kilometers of Golden Star's concession rights in the Brokolonko Range of eastern Suriname. Initial exploratory research indicated possible reserves of up to 3 million troy ounces."[13] Another company, called Sara Creek Gold (listed on the OTC), announced in October 2009 that it is planning extensive exploration and investment in the area.[14]

— The Bakhuys Mountains bauxite project, also known as the Kabalebo Project, is scheduled to begin operations in 2012 (or soon thereafter).[15] Alcoa, which has few bauxite reserves remaining in its current mines and whose smelter at Paranam has been closed since the turbines at Afobaka silted up ten years ago, is about to expand into West Suriname, affecting at least ten villages belonging to the Lokono and Trio peoples. The 2,800-square-kilometer concession and exploration permits were issued without any consultation with the affected communities. The proposed hydroelectric dams on the Kabalebo River would power a new smelter, as part of creating an integrated aluminum industry in Suriname, and would create three reservoirs that would be significantly larger than the one at Afobaka. Dr. Robert Goodland, who helped to create the World Commission on Dams, and was the chief technical advisor to the World Bank's Extractive Industry Review, observes that, "The Bakhuys bauxite mine project is a classic case of asymmetric power. Unsustainable mining confronts sustainable traditional societies. Rich and powerful multinationals will impose potentially severe impacts on inexperienced, weak, largely illiterate and poor Indigenous Peoples."[16]

— The Patamacca palm oil project in the Marowjine District. Suriname has granted permission to a Chinese company, China Sang Heng Tai, to create and operate a 40,000 hectare palm oil plantation at Patamacca, in an area traditionally occupied and used by indigenous Kalina and Lokono villages as well as Ndyuka Maroon communities. There was no prior consultation with the affected communities. The plan is to clear-cut the existing forest and then plant oil-bearing palms, destroying the ecology of the area and its capacity to provide subsistence resources. It will "cause irreparable harm to indigenous peoples and Maroons who count the area as part of their ancestral homeland."[17]

— Gold mining in the Benzdorp region. This area in southeast Suriname was traditionally part of the Aluku and Wayana homelands. Since the 1990s, Brazilian gold miners have flooded into the region creating multiple problems,[18] and the sorting out of land and resource titles has yet to be effected. Kenneth Bilby, veteran ethnographer of the Aluku, wrote me after a visit in late 2009: "I briefly passed Benzdorp on this trip, and the amount of activity (constant air traffic) and the explosion of ramshackle 'development' there is truly incredible—but it's all over the Suriname side of the Lawa and farther upriver." Gaanman Adochini "complained fervently" to Bilby about the wholesale granting of logging and mining concessions in this region by the Paramaribo government, with complete lack of regard for preexisting Aluku claims. He also complained about the large frontier settlement that has mushroomed directly across the river from Maripasoula, on the Suriname side (replete with restaurants, nightclubs, and brothels), populated mostly by Brazilians, Ndyukas, and people from Paramaribo—outsiders living as they wish on Aluku territory, with no respect for Aluku law. Bilby asks, rhetorically, "But what can the Aluku do against this influx, which continues to grow and threatens to outnumber the Aluku and Wayana populations combined?"

Meanwhile, the Alukus (the majority of whom are based on the French side of the border river and are therefore French citizens) feel that the bulk of their territory, which lies on the French side, is under assault from decisions taken in Paris and Cayenne. Having no legal existence as a people—since French law does not recognize minorities of any sort—they are being subjected to having their traditional territory parceled out in individual lots on cadastral maps against their will, to frequent raids by gendarmes to prevent them from gold mining within their territory (an artisanal activity they have conducted for generations), and to a plan to include much of their traditional territory in a national park (which would prevent them from gold mining as well as other traditional activities in their territory). Gaanman Adochini recently asked Bilby whether he had ideas about outside support to protect Aluku rights against these incursions. Might the European Court of Human Rights (in Strasbourg) be an appropriate venue for Alukus (and the neighboring Wayanas) to seek legal protection from what they perceive as imminent threats to their territorial sovereignty?

— The case submitted by the Kalina and Lokono peoples of the Lower Marowijne River concerning their property rights. They are complaining about the establishment of three protected areas in their territory, bauxite mining operations conducted by Suralco and BHP/Billiton in their territory, and wealthy individuals from Paramaribo building vacation homes on the beachfront in four of their villages, which were forcibly allotted by the State in 1975–76 over the communities' vociferous objections. This case was declared admissible by the IACHR in October 2007 and could be sent to the Court as early as mid 2010.[19]

— Micro-hydroelectric projects. In 2009, Suriname announced a surprising number of planned micro-hydropower projects, a number in Saramaka territory. Saramakas—two years after the Court's decision!—have not been consulted. One project is said to be already underway in Ndyuka territory near the village of the *gaamá*, the other near the indigenous village of Palumeu. But there are plans for such projects on some of the greatest rapids in

Saramaka territory, Gaándan (on the Gaánlío), Tápawáta (at the confluence of the Gaánlío and Pikílío), "Felusi Afobasu" (do they mean Félulási?), and "Felusi Mindrihati" (do they mean Bíaháti?), plus three others outside of Saramaka territory.[20]

— Gold mining at "Saramacca." In a press release of 9 November 2009, multinational Golden Star reports that it is "continuing exploration activities at Saramacca, our joint venture with Newmont in Suriname." In a press release of 24 February 2010, Golden Star mentioned an agreement with Newmont to buy its share in this project for "approximately $8.0 million." This project appears to be in Matawai territory. I know nothing more about these developments.

— The Forest Carbon Partnership Facility (FCPF), which purports to assist developing countries in their efforts to reduce emissions from deforestation and forest degradation (REDD), by providing value to standing forests. Suriname is becoming heavily involved in these efforts (see "Broader Implications," below), both to raise cash and to reassert its ownership over forests. This might well lead to restrictions on traditional farming (such as that practiced by Saramakas) which Suriname—like many other nations—claims is bad for a low-carbon economy.

Broader Implications

The landmark nature of the Court's judgment in *The Saramaka People v. Suriname* has been recognized by numerous observers and organizations. The U.N. Permanent Forum on Indigenous Issues acknowledged the global significance of the case in praising the Court's decision and particularly welcoming its reference to the 2007 U.N. *Declaration on the Rights of Indigenous Peoples*.[1] But several authorities on international law who have discussed the judgment have, in my view, not quite grasped its import.

One legal scholar has claimed that this "is the first binding international decision to recognize tribal peoples' rights to the natural resources located in their lands, indicating that tribal peoples are more akin to indigenous communities than they are to other ethnic, linguistic or religious minorities."[2] Another has claimed that "the Court expanded the scope of protection for groups seeking to protect ancestral lands and resources, moving for the first time beyond indigenous peoples to extend protection to other tribal groups."[3]

But the recognition of Suriname Maroons as "tribal peoples" and of tribal peoples as equivalent before the law to indigenous groups was recognized by the Court as early as 1993 in the judgment of *Aloeboetoe v. Suriname* and is based on the Court's use of the definition set forth in Article 1(1)(a) of ILO Convention No. 169, a treaty ratified widely in the Americas and which applies to both indigenous and tribal peoples.[4] And while the Court ultimately did not address territorial rights in *Aloeboetoe v. Suriname* (although it heard a great deal of testimony on the subject), in the case of *Moiwana Village v. Suriname*, it specifically addressed and upheld Ndyuka Maroon land and resource rights, though in a more limited context than in *The Saramaka People v. Suriname*.

From my perspective, the broader significance of the Court's 2007 decision and the related 2008 Interpretive Judgment is, rather, that for the first time the Court addressed a people's *corporate* (collective) rights, instead of viewing them merely as an aggregation of individuals or as a community/

village. In this case, the Court established the Saramaka peoples' right to recognition as a corporate legal identity, despite the lack of such a possibility
under current Suriname law. In addition, the Court awarded monetary damages for the first time to an indigenous or tribal people for a State having
caused environmental harm to its lands and resources.

In his own comments on the significance of the judgment, Fergus
MacKay has stressed its ruling on the right to self-determination. Noting
that "the analysis underlying the Court's orders breaks new ground in many
respects," he singles out its ruling that the Saramaka people hold the right to
self-determination . . .

> and that this right cannot be restricted when interpreting the
> property rights guaranteed under Article 21 of the American
> Convention. . . . The application of the right to self-determination
> thus supports an interpretation of Article 21 that recognizes indig-
> enous and tribal peoples' right "to freely determine and enjoy their
> own social, cultural and economic development, which includes the
> right to enjoy their particular spiritual relationship with the territory
> they have traditionally used and occupied." Consistent with this, the
> Court ordered that recognition of the Saramaka people's territorial
> rights must include recognition of "*their right to manage, distribute,
> and effectively control such territory,* in accordance with their custom-
> ary laws and traditional collective land tenure system."[5]

These newly recognized legal rights have broad potential impact. For
example, in the domain of international agreements regarding climate change,
indigenous and tribal peoples—whose lands include a substantial proportion
of the world's remaining forests—could become significant players. One could
imagine, for example, that the Saramakas (or any other such people whose
territory includes large stretches of rainforest) could be involved directly in
the sorts of carbon reduction and exchange programs that are beginning to
be negotiated around the globe. The government of Guyana, for example,
has signed a memorandum of understanding with Norway that provides up
to $250 million during the next few years for it to implement a low carbon
development strategy and save its remaining tropical forest.[6] (Unfortunately,
Guyana has not adequately consulted with the numerous indigenous peoples
whose traditional territories are covered by this agreement, rendering its
future uncertain.) Meanwhile, Suriname has stated that, rather than seeking

this sort of bilateral (nation-to-nation) agreement, it will seek multilateral compensation, under the REDD program, for "the way it has preserved its forests for so many years."[7] Once the Court's orders are carried out, couldn't the Saramakas—in partnership with a single nation, such as Norway, or some international organization—decide to preserve, for example, the southern-most part of their territory and be compensated for doing so?

The United Nations REDD program (Reducing Emissions from Defor-estation and Forest Degradation in Developing Countries), within which the Norway-Guyana agreement is conceptualized, is designed to assign a financial value for the carbon stored in forests and to encourage developing countries to reduce deforestation and invest in sustainable and low-carbon development. Part of the idea is to reduce carbon dioxide emissions caused by deforestation, which are estimated to be around 20 percent of annual global CO_2 emissions. REDD's home page claims that "it is predicted that financial flows for greenhouse gas emission reductions from REDD could reach up to US$30 billion a year. This significant North-South flow of funds could reward a meaningful reduction of carbon emissions and could also support new, pro-poor development, help conserve biodiversity, and secure vital ecosystem services."

But in reality, it seems likely that much of the potential reduction will dis-appear as part of carbon trading schemes that allow wealthy, mostly north-ern, corporations to continue to pollute.[8] Not to mention that these plans for carbon trading would generate billions of dollars for hedge funds as carbon trading markets are set up on the model of commodities and stock markets, something that hasn't escaped the attention of northern governments and their corporate friends. There is no small irony in the fact that Suriname, which during the 1990s so aggressively sought to sell off its forest resources to rapacious multinational logging corporations (paying no attention to the rights of its tribal peoples), now seeks to promote itself as the most conser-vationist country on the planet, ready to preserve its 90 percent forest cover (again paying no attention to the rights of its tribal peoples). Money talks.[9]

The potential role of indigenous and tribal peoples in these developments seems enormous—but only if states can be held to the sorts of human rights principles that the Court underlined in *The Saramaka People v. Suriname* and that are more broadly expressed in the 2007 U.N. Declaration on the Rights of Indigenous Peoples. The problem is that such rights are only now begin-ning to be seriously considered as part of such agreements.[10] Internationally, to date, indigenous and tribal peoples have generally been excluded from discussions and agreements about mitigating climate change, sometimes with disastrous consequences for their well-being.[11] The discussions, to date, have remained at the level of nation-states, largely excluding the very populations that inhabit, and rightfully own, many of the world's most precious forest resources.[12]

*   *   *

There is no question of the significance of the Court's judgment for the 55,000 Saramakas, for the other 55,000 Suriname Maroons, and for Suriname's 18,000 indigenous people. And its potential significance for indigenous peoples elsewhere in the hemisphere seems equally clear. But its significance for other (non-tribal) poor, rural, and black people in the Americas remains to be worked out in future cases.

A "tribal peoples" argument has been used, based on ILO 169 (and its Article 1 calling for self-identification [consciousness of an indigenous or tribal identity]), for some "rural black communities" in Brazil, Colombia, and Ecuador.[13] But in my view, it remains something of a stretch to argue that most rural black communities are "tribal peoples" (since they do not generally possess "social, cultural, and economic characteristics... different from other sections of the national community," nor do they necessarily "regulate themselves, at least partially, by their own norms, customs, and/or traditions" (the criteria used by the Court in the 2007 Saramaka case). In this sense, the "cultural" argument that formed part of the Court's basis for deciding the Saramaka case—and which was wholly appropriate to the needs of these Maroons, and of other Suriname Maroons (who clearly form culturally distinct groups within the State)—would seem to have more limited application to most nonindigenous rural black communities in the Americas, such as many *remanecentes de quilombos*, who are seeking rights to their traditional territories.[14] In these cases, it may well be that arguments weighted more on grounds of racial discrimination and inequality will be necessary to steer the Court in directions that will more clearly cover rural black communities outside of Suriname. In the Saramaka judgment, the Court did several times invoke the International Convention for the Elimination of All Forms of Racial Discrimination in interpreting the content of the American Convention, and it referred to decisions and reports of the United Nations Committee on the Elimination of Racial Discrimination more than a dozen times. But the Court has not yet directly addressed issues of structural racism of the sort that is so pervasive in Latin America, and rulings affecting the property rights of large numbers of communities in the hemisphere may well depend on arguments that are more heavily weighted in this direction.

In a paper presented at the LASA meeting in Rio de Janeiro in June 2009 ("When Afro-Descendants became 'Tribal Peoples': The Inter-American System and Rural Black Communities"), legal scholar Ariel E. Dulitzky criticized the Court in the Saramaka case for stressing what he considers "cultural" rather than racial criteria in their arguments. But the idea of a one-size-fits-all argument for Afro-Descendants in the Americas (who range all the way from President Barack Obama to Saramakas) belies the variety of historical and ethnographic realities these diverse peoples represent. I would suggest that arguments making the strongest possible case for each particular historical/ethnographic situation continue to be called for, as was done in the Saramaka case, and I would express the hope that, as more cases are adjudicated by the Court, cracks will begin to appear in the widespread systems of structural racism that Dulitzky wishes to target.

In fact, in the Saramaka judgment, the Court deliberated on a set of arguments that went beyond an essentialized notion of culture, including these people's distinct and ongoing (developing) relation to their territory, which they continue to regulate wholly or partially by customary norms. On the other hand, there did emerge a disturbingly essentialist leaning in some of the Court's reasoning: if the use of a resource is not "traditional," it is not covered by property laws, so that, for example, the State could argue that the granting of eco-tourism permits in Saramaka territory need not be approved by Saramakas since eco-tourism is not a "traditional" activity. In the Saramaka hearing, the Court seemed to dismiss the Saramaka witnesses' claims that they considered that the forest belonged to them "from the tops of the trees to below their deepest roots," insisting instead that the Saramakas need to demonstrate that they traditionally used particular resources (trees, clay from the riverbanks, and so forth) in order for them to be fully protected by the judgment. The Court's reliance in this case on common-sense Western ideas about "tradition" recalls, for me, their inability in the Aloeboetoe case to accept the logic of matriliny as being compatible with "human nature," as discussed in the chapter on that case.

It seems worth pointing to the fundamental tension that exists between ideas that undergird relevant aspects of international human rights law and current ideas in anthropology.[15] The category of "tribal" or "indigenous" people (much like the once-prominent category of "primitive" people), which forms the basis of relevant human rights law, carries heavy cultural baggage for many educated Westerners, including many judges, lawyers, and politicians. That baggage begins with the very idea that these peoples (these Others) share certain characteristics that make them different from "us": for example, it is often said that they are bound by "tradition"; their lives are fraught with myth and symbolism; their societies are resistant to change and governed by "custom;" they live outside of history, ruled by the changing seasons and in perfect harmony with nature—you add the rest.[16]

For decades, anthropologists and historians have been criticizing such commonsense Western ideas that essentialize "culture" (and "cultures") and that put a prime on "tradition" as the central diacritic of cultural authenticity. As Eric Hobsbawm recognized in 1983, "'Traditions' which appear or claim to be ancient are often quite recent in origin and sometimes invented."[17] That is, *all* societies change and develop through time. And as anthropologist Eric Wolf reminded us in 1982,

By turning names [such as "culture"] into things we create false models of reality. By endowing nations, societies, or cultures with the qualities of internally homogeneous and externally distinctive and bounded objects, we create a model of the world as a global pool hall in which the entities spin off each other like so many hard and round billiard balls. Thus it becomes easy to sort the world into differently colored balls.... The habit of treating named entities such as Iroquois, Greece, Persia, or the United States as fixed entities opposed to one another by stable internal architecture and external boundaries interferes with our ability to understand their mutual encounter and confrontation.[18]

Wolf showed how, during the course of the nineteenth and early twentieth centuries, the terms "modern" and "modernization" came to stand for a democratic, rational, and secular West (in particular, the United States), whereas "traditional" came to refer to "all those others that would have to adopt that ideal to qualify for assistance." And he suggested that "by equating tradition with stasis and lack of development, [such a view] denied societies marked off as traditional any significant history of their own."[19]

Anthropologists, who in the late nineteenth and early twentieth centuries, focused on custom and tradition in small-scale societies, have for decades routinely emphasized these same societies' openness and historical interactions as well as the importance of change and development in them—as in all societies. No longer do anthropologists work within an "us"/"them" binary, within the ideological framework that created the West and its Others, or in what Michel-Rolph Trouillot has called the "savage slot."[20] As Trouillot puts it, "There is no Other, but multitudes of others who are all others for different reasons."[21]

This tension puts special burdens on a human rights lawyer arguing on behalf of the Saramakas before the Inter-American Court. It becomes necessary, for purposes of argument, to accept the multiple fictions that created the category of "tribal peoples."[22] And it becomes equally necessary to engage in a teaching effort—aimed toward the judges and the State, who are likely to share certain stereotypes about "tribal" peoples—stressing that such peoples live (and have always lived) fully in history, exercise their own agency, adopt (and have always adopted) changes, and possess a degree of historical consciousness that permits them to make sophisticated choices about directions for their society's future. In short, it becomes necessary to insist that "they" are, in every way, as modern as "we." As should be clear from reading the testimony before the Court, the practical need to support the idea that there is such a thing as "tribal peoples" and simultaneously to criticize the cultural baggage that undergirds it created tensions that were not always easily resolved either for the lawyer or for the anthropologist serving as expert witness.

Before such an audience, it is necessary to make clear that a Dutch-speaking Saramaka who wears a Western suit to his job as school principal in Amsterdam can still remain a Saramaka, just as a village on the upper Suriname River that now has piped-in water, gasoline-generated electricity, a Saramaka-run tourist lodge, and an Evangelical church remains a Saramaka village. As Headcaptain Albert Abóikóni said at the hearing, "Even if you live on the moon"—presumably under very different material circumstances—"you are still a Saramaka." (He could have added, to be more precise, "if you still wish to identify yourself as such.")

For the present, the Saramakas and their Maroon and indigenous neighbors will need to be vigilant and proactive in seeing that Suriname implements the Judgment of 2007 (and the Interpretive Judgment of 2008). The coming several years will be pivotal, on the ground in Suriname, in determining whether the rulings of the Court in San José have the desired local—and international—effects. The Saramaka leaders, negotiating with the government of Suriname, will need to draw on all their considerable political and warrior skills to assure that their abstract legal victory brings the desired concrete benefits to their long-suffering, but immensely proud and vibrant people.

Postface

As I finish this book in May 2010, the Saramakas confront two contrastive visions of their future. The first, promulgated by the government in Paramaribo, sees "development" and "integration" leading to their rapid assimilation into some sort of mythically harmonious, multicultural national population. (President Venetiaan continues to contrast such "modernization" with what he views as a "retreat" into tribalism.[1]) The second, made possible by the Court ruling and the militancy of the VSG, sees a self-determining Saramaka people controlling and making the ultimate decisions about what takes place in their territory.

Recently, Vinije Haabo, an educated Saramaka living in the Netherlands, gave this pessimistic prophesy to an interviewer:

In twenty years' time there will hardly be any original inhabitants left in the Surinamese interior. Multiple mixed social groups will live there ... Chinese, Brazilians, and other foreigners who are only there to extract the raw materials and leave as soon as possible.... I expect there'll be an exodus [of Saramakas and other traditional forest dwellers] and we'll see ghettos in the big cities just like in Africa and [elsewhere in] South America.[2]

His prediction fits the government's latest proposals for the interior. These now include a road that continues from the village of Pókigoón (currently the southern end of the road that connects Saramaka territory to Paramaribo) upstream along the Suriname River nearly to the confluence with the Gaánlío, then cuts eastward to the Tapanahoni and upstream along that river through Ndyuka territory, continuing southward until it connects with the Brazilian national highway system.[3] Such a road would make the villages (and forest) in Saramaka and Ndyuka territory easily accessible to tourists, land speculators, miners, loggers, and other outsiders. It is almost as if the government's intention is to steamroller the rights of Maroons and indigenous people before the Court or anyone else really takes notice, and to empty the forest of its current inhabitants in order to permit economic development that benefits the State. Most ongoing government plans for the interior ignore the Court's judgment and proceed as if the judgment had never been issued.

In the other view, the Saramakas—drawing considerable strength from their culture, spirituality, and history of resistance, as well as leaning on their victory before the Court—would insist on their own vision of the future. They would decide, after weighing the pros and cons, what sorts of development would be undertaken within their territory and what sorts of development would be kept out. In this view, Saramakas would remain largely masters of their fate, continuing the struggle their ancestors began three centuries ago. Their relationship to the government would in fact become (as the Saramaka people already consider it) like that of many indigenous peoples in the world who consider themselves "nations" even while recognizing (as they always have) that they live within larger nation-states and must maintain cordial and collaborative relationships with those states.

Will the Saramakas have the collective will and the organizational skills to play the strong hand that the Court has dealt them? Or will they join the long list of peoples who have become proverbial "victims of development"? The next few years will be decisive.

Notes

Preface

1. Frank Bajak, "Indian Political Awakening Stirs Latin America," Associated Press, 1 November 2009.

2. Saramakas are one of the six Maroon peoples of Suriname and French Guiana, who today number some 120,000 people. With Sally Price, I have been studying their lives and history since the mid-1960s. References to relevant bibliography can be found on our website: http://www.richandsally.net.

3. http://goldmanprize.org/2009/southcentralamerica. This website includes a five-minute video about the Saramaka legal victory, narrated by Robert Redford.

4. Conservation International, press release, "Suriname Launches a Bold Plan for a Green Future," 3 November 2009. In 2000, the World Bank ranked Suriname as the 17th richest country in the world in terms of natural resources, the bulk of which are in the interior of the country, where Maroons and indigenous peoples live.

Africans Discover America

Land, Spirits, Power

1. Readers familiar with Saramaka history from my earlier books may wish to skim lightly through this chapter, which draws particularly on *First-Time* (Baltimore: Johns Hopkins University Press, 1983 [2nd edition, Chicago: University of Chicago Press, 2002]), *Alabi's World* (Baltimore: Johns Hopkins University Press, 1990), and *Travels with Tooy* (Chicago: University of Chicago Press, 2008).

2. Price, *First-Time*, 85.

3. David de Ishak Cohen Nassy, *Essai historique sur la colonie de Surinam* (Paramaribo, 1788), 1:56.

4. Nassy, *Essai historique*, 2:40.

5. For documentation, see in particular, John Gabriel Stedman, *Narrative of a Five Years Expedition Against the Revolted Negroes of Surinam*, newly transcribed from the original 1790 manuscript, with an introduction and notes by Richard Price and Sally Price (Baltimore: Johns Hopkins University Press, 1988).

6. The Ndyukas, the other major Maroon group, had signed with the colonists in 1760.

7. Price, *First-Time*, 173.

8. Ibid., 174.

9. For the text of the treaty, see Richard Price, *To Slay the Hydra: Dutch Colonial Perspectives on the Saramaka Wars* (Ann Arbor, Mich.: Karoma, 1983), 159–165.

10. The treaty also obliged the Saramakas to return to the whites any slaves who had joined them since 1760 and who might do so in future, and to pursue any such slaves the government told them about—provisions which the Saramakas managed to successfully subvert throughout the second half of the eighteenth century.

11. For details, see Price, *Travels with Tooy*, 291–293.

12. Stedman, *Narrative*, 409–410.

13. "First-Time" (*fési-tên*) refers to the years of war, the formative years of Saramaka society, the period ending with the Treaty of 1762.

14. Some of this paragraph and the next echoes Sidney W. Mintz and Richard Price, *The Birth of African-American Culture* (Boston: Beacon Press, 1992).

15. See, for example, S. and R. Price, *Maroon Arts* (Boston: Beacon Press, 1999).

16. For details, see Price, *Travels with Tooy*. For the ways that Ndyuka Maroon religion similarly develops through time, see H. U. E. Thoden van Velzen and W. van Wetering, *In the Shadow of the Oracle: Religion as Politics in a Suriname Maroon Society* (Long Grove, Ill.: Waveland, 2004).

Earth, Water, Sky

The Dam at Afobaka

1. A recording of this song, made in 1968, is available on CD: Richard Price and Sally Price, *Music from Saramaka* (Smithsonian Folkways: 4225, Washington, D.C., 1977).

2. In the mid-eighteenth century, the trip from Paramaribo to the heart of Saramaka territory took two to four weeks by canoe, depending on season. The first outboard motors, in the mid-1950s, cut that time in half. With the building of a road to the Afobaka dam in the 1960s, the trip took only four or five days. And with the extension of the road around the artificial lake in the late 1980s, one could travel from Paramaribo to the *gaamá*'s village in two days. (For those who can afford air travel and deal with intermittent scheduling or chartering private aircraft, it has been possible since the 1960s to fly from Paramaribo to Djoemoe, near the *gaamá*'s village, in an hour and a half.)

3. The dam is 2 kilometers long and 54 meters high. There are sixteen related dams filling in low places around the lake, together measuring more than an additional 6 kilometers in length.

4. Some sources, which count only the larger villages, list twenty-five or twenty-eight belonging to Saramakas, plus six belonging to Sara Creek Ndyukas. (John Walsh, who like us was there near the time, also counts forty-three—John Walsh with Robert Gannon. *Time Is Short and the Water Rises* [New York: E. P. Dutton, 1967], 26.) All agree that the number of people whose homes and lands were sunk under the lake was about 6,000, about one-third of the Saramaka population, including the great majority of its

Christian population (who had converted in the nineteenth century). The expanse of the lake is approximately 1,400 square kilometers.

5. Mamádan apparently reappeared during the next dry season and finally disappeared for the last time in 1967.

6. Carlo Hoop. *Verdronken land, Verdwenen dorpen: De transmigratie van Saramaccaners in Suriname 1958–1964* (Alkmaar: Uitgeverij Bewustzijn, 1991). One report, possibly apocryphal, claims that in 1952, Blommestein himself stopped at the main landing place of the village of Ganzee, where he informed the head captain that the region would be flooded within the next fifteen years—which the villagers took as a tall tale (Erney R. A. O. Landveld, *Ganzë: Het dorp dat het meer verdronk* [Utrecht: Drukkerij Nout B.V., 1989]), 89.

7. Hoop, *Verdronken land,* 11–25. See also Ellen-Rose Kambel, *Resource Conflicts, Gender and Indigenous Rights in Suriname: Local, National and Global Perspectives* (Proefschrift Universiteit Leiden, 2002), 39.

8. Michels' mimeoed report entitled "Transmigratie van de Saramakkaners en Aukaners Boven Suriname, 1958," which I examined in 1968, is a thoughtful attempt to deal with the issue, advising—following his own census enumeration of each village to be flooded—that all move south of the lake, retaining a more traditional lifestyle. Hoop claims that Gaamá Agbagó agreed with Michels that the new villages should be above the lake, but that certain villages simply refused to comply (*Verdronken land,* 68).

9. Hoop, *Verdronken land,* 63–64. Michels made his remark to me in July 1968. In 1958, the Paramaribo government had published a pamphlet that claimed that all sorts of development benefits would accrue to the Saramakas as a result of the dam, and that it was really for the development of the interior, not just the coast (Ben Scholtens, *Bosnegers en overheid in Suriname: De ontwikkeling van de politieke verhouding 1651–1992,* Paramaribo: Afdeling Cultuurstudies/Minov, 1994, 129).

10. Scholtens, *Bosnegers en overheid,* 129.

11. Hoop, *Verdronken land,* 64.

12. Translated from a recording made at Asindóópo, 8 July 1978. In that same discussion, the *gaamá* told me how he got the name Abóikóni—which has since been taken as a surname by the following two *gaamá*s and many members of his matrilineal family. He said that as a boy he was embarrassingly scrawny and his father once warned him that he'd have to take responsibility to "bói kóni"—"cook up some way"—to pull himself together and become a man. That name came only when he was a young adolescent but it stuck—for him and, later, for others in his lineage.

13. Hoop, *Verdronken land,* 65.

14. See Walsh and Gannon's *Time Is Short* (also known as "Operation Gwamba: The Story of the Rescue of 10,000 Animals from Certain Death in a South American Rain Forest"), 19–20.

15. RP fieldnotes, especially discussion with B. O. Jackson, 988. There were initially thirteen new villages above the lake.

16. RP fieldnotes, 1,020.

17. Walsh and Gannon, *Time Is Short*, 46. See also Carlo Lamur, *The American Take-over: Industrial Emergence and Alcoa's Expansion in Guyana and Suriname 1914–1921* (Dordrecht: Foris, 1985), 9, 135. The strategic importance of Suriname bauxite for the United States had a long history. Marcus Colchester reports that during World War II, Suriname provided two-thirds of the bauxite used for aluminum production, and it was equally crucial for supplies during the Korean War. By 1994, he writes, alumina and aluminum accounted for 87 percent of Suriname's exports. (*Forest Politics in Suriname*, Utrecht: International Books, 1995), 43–44.

18. The fullest account of the political in-fighting surrounding the transmigration can be found in Scholtens, *Bosnegers en overheid*, 128–134.

19. I. Vrede, "Facing Violence Against Women in Indigenous Communities. The Case of Maroon Communities in Brokopondo District, Suriname." *Symposium 2001.* "Gender violence, health and rights in the Americas." Cancun, Mexico, 4–7 June 2001, 1. Available at http://www.paho.org/english/hdp/hdw/Suriname.pdf.

20. Inter-American Court of Human Rights, Case of *Twelve Saramaka Clans v. Suriname*, Affidavit of Dr. Robert Goodland, Expert Witness, Submitted by the Victims' Representatives, 2 May 2007.

21. Hoop, *Verdronken land*, 97.

22. Ellen-Rose Kambel and Fergus MacKay, *The Rights of Indigenous Peoples and Maroons in Suriname*, Copenhagen, IWGIA, 1999, 105; Kambel, *Resource Conflicts*, 39–40.

23. The handwritten Dutch original, from which I have loosely translated, appears in Hoop, *Verdronken land*, 77.

24. Hoop, *Verdronken land*, 129.

25. Scholtens, *Bosnegers en overheid*, 133.

26. Ibid., 131.

27. Walsh and Gannon, *Time Is Short*, 51.

28. Kambel, *Resource Conflicts*, 40.

Rockets at Kourou

1. Sally Price, *Co-Wives and Calabashes* (Ann Arbor: University of Michigan Press, 1984), 177–178.

2. From De Gaulle's speech in Cayenne, 21 March 1964, http://www.inra.fr/dpenv/vissal6.htm.

3. Marie-José Jolivet, *La question créole: essai de sociologie sur la Guyane française*, Paris: ORSTOM, 1982, 446–447. Missing from this description is the overwhelming militarization of Kourou, and French Guiana more generally. France justifies the presence of a giant Foreign Legion camp in Kourou and large numbers of gendarmes and soldiers throughout the territory as necessary security guarantors, given the massive numbers of poor, illegal immigrants (from Brazil, Haiti, Suriname, Guyana, and elsewhere) who contribute to the social instability of French Guiana. As of 1995, the rocket base generated about half of all economic activity in French Guiana, about one-third of all employment, and more than half of all imports (Peter Redfield, *Space in the*

Tropics: From Convicts to Rockets in French Guiana [Berkeley: University of California Press], 285).

4. See, for example, Evan Fox-Decent, "Indigenous Peoples and Human Dignity," in Frédéric Mégret and Florian Hoffmann (eds.), *Protecting Dignity: An Agenda for Human Rights. Research Project on Human Dignity. "Dignity: A Special Focus on Vulnerable Groups,"* McGill Centre for Human Rights and Legal Pluralism, June 2009, 34–46.

5. Price, *First-Time*, 12.

6. Saramaka folktales are told as part of funeral rites. The tale included here in summary form was told in 1968 by Kasólu, a man then in his late twenties who had been working in Kourou, to an enthusiastically participating group of the deceased woman's relatives, friends, and neighbors back in Saramaka. For a full transcription/translation of the tale, see Richard and Sally Price, *Two Evenings in Saramaka* (Chicago: University of Chicago Press, 1991), 126–138.

7. African American folktales frequently allude, implicitly or explicitly, to equivalences between kings, slave masters, white men, and devils—each of whom controls labor, and money. (In this context, it is worth noting that in Saramaka folktales, the speech of devils is consistently rendered in Sranan, the creole language of coastal Suriname.)

8. At this point in the tale-telling, a woman exclaimed, "What hasn't changed is that they still lop off your ass at Kourou!" (Price and Price, *Two Evenings*, 138).

Sovereignty and Territory

The Aloeboetoe Incursion

1. Price, *First-Time*, 12.

2. Price, Ibid., 153–59.

3. Price, Ibid., 153.

4. Gary Brana-Shute, *On the Corner: Male Social Life in a Paramaribo Creole Neighborhood* (Assen: Van Gorcum, 1979), 119.

5. Ellen-Rose Kambel, "Land, Development, and Indigenous Rights in Suriname: The Role of International Human Rights Law," in Jean Besson and Janet Henshall Momsen (eds.), *Caribbean Land and Development Revisited* (Gordonsville, Va., Palgrave Macmillan, 2007), 69–80, 75.

6. Gerard van Westerloo and Willem Diepraam, *Frimangron* (Amsterdam: De Arbeiderspers, 1975), 157.

7. *Suriname: An International Alert Report* (London, International Alert, 1988), 24.

8. Simultaneously with these murders, "the offices of two radio-stations, a newspaper, and the *Moederbond* [the largest trade union federation] were burnt to the ground. Five newspaper dailies and weeklies were suppressed and two press agencies closed" (Peter Meel, "Money Talks, Morals Vex: The Netherlands and the Decolonization of Suriname, 1975–1990," *European Review of Latin American and Caribbean Studies* 48(1990), 75–98, 85). The International Commission of Jurists, after a site visit, concluded that "an impartial investigation into the killings of December 1982 was an

essential pre-condition for the restoration of the rule of law," and the Inter-American Commission on Human Rights, after its own visit, urged in addition that Suriname pay compensation to the families of the victims (*Suriname: An International Alert Report,* 26–27). The military leadership maintained that "the fifteen were shot while trying to escape" (ibid.). More generally, "Until now [1989], the military authorities have successfully prevented the civil police and judicial authorities from investigating crimes committed by military personnel, by means of claiming the sole responsibility for these investigations" (Manfred Nowak, *Suriname: An International Alert Report* [London, International Alert, 1989], 15). (See, for more details, *Report on the Situation of Human Rights in Suriname,* Washington, D.C., Organization of American States [OAS/Ser.L/II.61/Doc.6 rev. 1, October 5, 1983], *Second Report on the Human Rights Situation in Suriname,* Washington, D.C., Organization of American States [OAS/Ser.L/II.66/Doc.21 rev. 1, October 2, 1985], and S. Amos Wako, "Visit by the Special Rapporteur to Suriname," Geneva[?]: Commission on Human Rights, Economic and Social Council of the United Nations [E/CN.4/1985/17, Annex V]. As I complete this book in early 2010, some of the perpetrators of the "December Murders" of 1982 are, for the first time, standing trial in Paramaribo.

9. David Binder, "Diplomacy and Public Relations: Image Maker Aids New Democracy," *New York Times,* 25 January 1988.

10. Ibid.

11. H. U. E. Thoden van Velzen, "The Maroon Insurgency: Anthropological Reflections on the Civil War in Suriname," in Gary Brana-Shute (ed.), *Resistance and Rebellion in Suriname: Old and New* (Williamsburg, Va.: College of William and Mary, 1990), 159–88, 160.

12. Gert Oostindie, "The Dutch Caribbean in the 1990s: Decolonization or Recolonization?" *Caribbean Affairs,* 1992, 5:103–119, 106.

13. Oostindie, "The Dutch Caribbean," 108.

14. Gary Brana-Shute, "An Inside-Out Insurgency: The Tukuyana Amazones of Suriname," in Paul Sutton and Anthony Payne (eds.), *Size and Survival: The Politics of Security in the Caribbean and the Pacific* (London: Frank Cass, 1993), 54–69, 61.

15. During the 1990s, Rensch was arrested four times and tortured in detention, and there was an attempt on his life by unknown gunmen.

16. *Mensenrechten 1991 Suriname,* Paramaribo, Moiwana'86, 1992, 8.

17. *Mensenrechten,* 20–21; see also *Annual Report of the Inter-American Commission on Human Rights 1989–1990,* Washington, D.C., Organization of American States. [OEA/Ser.L/V/II.77 rev.1/Doc.7, 17 May, 1990], 180–81.

18. Other observers saw the 1992 agreement as driven by clandestine land deals. The Dutch press reported that several months before the signing of the *Akkoord,* Paramaribo businessman Kenneth Tjon A Lio, on behalf of his lumber company, N.V. Inply, signed a private agreement with Brunswijk (in his capacity as de-facto "ruler" of the Eastern half of Suriname's interior) and Tukujana Amazones leader Thomas Sabajo (in his similar capacity for the west). According to these reports, the "peace treaty" was,

in reality, an economic deal, after which Inply would gain nearly unlimited rights to exploit the riches of the interior (see, for example, *NRC Handelsblad*, 1 October 1992, 1–2, *Vrij Nederland,* 21 November 1992, 27).

19. Sally Price and Richard Price, *Afro-American Arts of the Suriname Rain Forest* (Berkeley: University of California Press, 1980).

20. The government had recently built a dirt road around the lake, linking Paramaribo to Pókigoón.

21. Because the report (petition) was written by Stanley Rensch, a Saramaccan-speaker and director of Moiwana'86, in what is his fourth-best language (English), I have taken minor liberties with its phrasing to enhance its clarity. The original petition from which I quote is included in *Report No. 03/90, Case 10.150, Suriname*, Inter-American Commission on Human Rights, OEA/Ser.L/V/II.77/Doc. 23, 15 May 1990, 1–3, which contains a good deal of supporting testimony from other witnesses.

22. The Inter-American Commission on Human Rights has been functioning since 1960.

23. The interview was conducted on 28 January 1988. Padilla's notes are contained in a sworn affidavit, signed in Washington, D.C., and dated 26 March 1991, which constitutes "Annex 1" of the "Memorial of the Inter-American Commission on Human Rights, Case No. 10.150, *Aloeboetoe et al. v. the Government of Suriname*."

24. Excerpts from a videotaped interview made by delegates of the IACHR with Aside's brother, on 15 December 1988 in Paramaribo, add a few final details—see Richard Price, "Executing Ethnicity: The Killings in Suriname," *Cultural Anthropology* 1995, 10:437–471, 463.

25. This retroactive amnesty act was passed by Suriname's parliament in 1992, cancelling all judicial proceedings related to human rights violations committed between 1985 and 1991—except for crimes against humanity (as defined by the 1948 Convention on the Prevention and Punishment of the Crime of Genocide and the 1950 Nuremberg Principles). For a discussion of the Inter-American Court's attitudes toward the 1992 amnesty act, see Thomas M. Antkowiak, "*Moiwana Village v. Suriname*: A Portal into Recent Jurisprudential Developments of the Inter-American Court of Human Rights," *Berkeley Journal of International Law* (2), 2007, 25: 101–115.

26. The Inter-American Court of Human Rights officially came into existence in 1978, when the eleventh member state deposited its instrument of ratification of the American Convention on Human Rights with the General Secretariat of the OAS. The Court held its first session in 1980. As of the end of 2009, the Court's jurisdiction had been accepted by every country in South America except Guyana and every country in Central America except Belize.

27. In what follows, I draw primarily on the following documents: The IACHR's "Report No. 03/90, Case 10.150, Suriname" (OEA/Ser.L/V/II.77/Doc. 23, 15 May 1990); "Memorial of the IACHR, Case No. 10.150, *Aloeboetoe et al. v. The Government of Suriname*" (1991); "Counter-Memorial of Suriname" (1991); "Suriname's Comments on

the Presentation of Evidence" (1991); "Inter-American Court of Human Rights, Judgment of 4 December 1991, *Aloeboetoe et al.* Case."

28. David Padilla has explained that "the Commission sought to establish new Inter-American jurisprudence in the area of cultural rights. Rather than basing its argument on the legal validity of the Treaty, the Commission sought, through the testimony of Professor Price, to show that the character, pride, and very identity of the Saramakas stemmed from their having obtained their freedom from slavery, as enshrined in the Treaty.... The Commission also attempted to demonstrate that the self-esteem of an entire people had been profoundly violated during the... civil war through repeated and pitiless incursions of the army. The Commission then tried to establish that failure to compensate the Saramakas to restore their lost dignity would constitute an irreparable injury to their cultural integrity" (David J. Padilla, "Reparations in *Aloeboetoe v. Suriname*," *Human Rights Quarterly* 17, 1995, 541–555, 547–548).

29. This account is based on the uncorrected official Court transcript (more than 200 typed pages written in "tape-recordese") and my on-the-spot notes. The transcript/translation is partly in Spanish and partly in English. Much of the key testimony and interrogation actually took place in Dutch, as Claudio Grossman (who conducted the examination of witnesses on behalf of the Commission) asked his direct questions in Dutch, and the witnesses from Suriname also spoke in Dutch (except for Stanley Rensch, who spoke in English). Present was a young Curaçaoan staff member of the Court who served as ad hoc (non-professional) interpreter between Dutch and Spanish, and it is her words that appear in the transcripts. Because these parts of the transcript radically foreshorten the actual testimony, as seen by comparing them with my on-the-spot notes from the trial, the account I give here is constructed from a combination of these sources. Fortunately, like Grossman, I was able to understand testimony in the three relevant languages: Dutch, Spanish, and English. Suriname's lead lawyer, who was Costa Rican, posed his questions to me in Spanish and I replied in English.

30. In fact, telephones—mobile phones—did not reach Saramaka territory until fifteen years later.

31. See Richard Price and Sally Price, *On the Mall: Presenting Maroon Tradition-Bearers at the 1992 FAF*, Bloomington, The Folklore Institute, Indiana University, 1995. That I, and not Gaamá Songó or his representative, served as expert witness stemmed from the Commission's belief that academic testimony would be more persuasive to the Court, especially as a complement to the participation of the Commission's other witness, Stanley Rensch, who had been in close touch with Gaamá Songó throughout the preparation of the case.

32. Rensch's briefer testimony in answer to the Commission's lawyer was straightforward, largely dealing with the details of his trips to the interior to get the affidavits identifying the dependents. Suriname's rather contentious cross-examination focused on an attempt to poke holes in my testimony. Throughout, Rensch gave dignified responses that, unbeknownst to him (as he had not been permitted to be present when

I spoke), strongly supported my testimony. In answer to questions from the judges, he stressed the need for some kind of government guarantees of various Saramaka rights. Judge Cançado Trindade: "What form should such a guarantee, that this does not happen again, take?" SR: "I think the Suriname society should give these people [Saramakas] the feeling that they care, that whosoever touches them in the future will be punished, that if their rights are violated, they will be punished, the perpetrators will be punished.... in whatever way the law provides in Suriname."

33. Judgment of 10 September, 17 (section 58).

34. In point of fact, "In the 1987 Constitution, Article 177 states that the National Army is the military vanguard of the people of Suriname, defending sovereignty and the supreme rights of the people, and contributing to national reconstruction and liberation. An even greater opportunity for [military] interference is provided by Article 178" (Marcel Zwamborn, "Suriname," in *Human Rights in Developing Countries*, Utrecht, Studie- en Informatiecentrum Mensenrechten, Rijksuniversiteit te Utrecht, 1992, 1–30, 12).

35. See, for example, A.J.A. Quintus Bosz, *Drie eeuwen grondpolitiek in Suriname*, Assen, Van Gorcum, 1954, and "De rechten van de bosnegers op de ontruimde gronden in het stuwmeergebied," *Surinaams Juristenblad*, 1965, 14–21.

36. Edward Dew, *The Difficult Flowering of Surinam: Ethnicity and Politics in a Plural Society*, The Hague: Martinus Nijhoff, 1978, 194.

37. Harold F. Munneke, "Customary Law and National Legal System in the Dutch-speaking Caribbean, With Special Reference to Suriname," *European Review of Latin American and Caribbean Studies* 1991, 51:91–99, 97–98.

38. Kambel and MacKay, *The Rights*, 73, 79.

39. Ibid., 50.

40. Ibid., 50–51.

41. Ibid., 61, 64.

42. Kenneth M. Bilby, "Swearing by the Past, Swearing to the Future: Sacred Oaths, Alliances, and Treaties among the Guianese and Jamaican Maroons," *Ethnohistory* 1997, 44:655–689, 677.

43. Kambel and MacKay, *The Rights*, 66.

44. It is worth noting that in 1986, with the advent of the civil war, those few schools that existed in the interior were all closed by the military.

45. Of course, it is not *all* ethnicity that the ruling elite wishes to erase, only tribal (primitive) ethnicity. Suriname's urban life and political parties have long been based on ethnic power sharing among blacks or Creoles (non-Maroon Afro-Surinamers), Hindustanis (East Indians), and Javanese (Indonesians), with smaller niches reserved for Chinese and Lebanese. In contrast to Maroons and Amerindians, these other groups (even when they speak their own languages at home) participate fully in the modern state.

46. *Vrij Nederland*, 24 October 1992, 25.

47. CIDH 1993, 18.

48. CIDH 1993, 24.

49. CIDH 1993, 24.

50. CIDH 1993, 19.

51. CIDH 1993, 17.

52. CIDH 1993, 17–18.

53. CIDH 1993, 18. As Kambel and MacKay point out, the application of *jus cogens* means that "with respect to provisions concerning slavery, the 1762 treaty is void—[but] this does not necessarily mean... that the entire treaty would be invalid" (*Rights*, 63). The Saramakas themselves remember nothing about slavery being mentioned in the treaty—other than their receiving their freedom!

54. CIDH 1993, 18.

55. CIDH 1993, 18.

56. CIDH 1993, 26–28. The Court's judgment consistently uses the word "racial" for what I call "ethnic." It is unclear whether it understood that the Commission was not arguing on the basis of phenotype—in fact, the killers and the killed were largely indistinguishable physically—but on the basis of culture and politics and history. (In international law, the definition of racial discrimination incorporates discrimination based on ethnicity—as well as other grounds for discrimination, such as descent or national origin—so there is a tendency to use "race" as short-hand for "ethnicity.")

57. Padilla, "Reparations," 548.

The Moiwana Massacre

1. Joseph Cerquone, *Flight from Suriname: Refugees in French Guiana*, Washington, D.C., U.S. Committee for Refugees, 1987, 5.

2. H. U. E. Thoden van Velzen, "Ten geleide" and "Militaire patstelling beheerst Suriname," in T.S. Polimé and H. U. E. Thoden van Velzen, *Vluchtelingen, opstandelingen en andere Bosnegers van Oost-Suriname, 1986–1988*, Utrecht, Instituut voor Culturele Antropologie, 1988, 7–9, 14–25, 7–8, 19.

3. Kenneth M. Bilby, "The Remaking of the Aluku: Culture, Politics, and Maroon Ethnicity in French South America," unpublished Ph.D. dissertation, Baltimore: Johns Hopkins University, 1990, 505–06.

4. See, for example, *Suriname: Violations of Human Rights*, London, Amnesty International, 1987; Cerquone, *Flight*; Adiante Franszoon, "Crisis in the Backlands," *Hemisphere*, 1987, 1, 2:36–38; *Memre Moiwana*, Paramaribo, Moiwana'86, n.d. [ca. 1990]; and T. S. Polimé and H. U. E. Thoden van Velzen, *Vluchtelingen, opstandelingen en andere Bosnegers van Oost-Suriname, 1986–1988*, Utrecht, Instituut voor Culturele Antropologie, 1988. Amerindians, particularly Caribs (Galibi), had been used as troops against Maroons by colonial armies since the earliest years of the colony (see Price, *Alabi's World*, 403–04). Throughout Suriname's recent civil war, Bouterse—who claims part Amerindian ancestry—manipulated Amerindian-Maroon relations to his advantage, most notably in the creation of the Tucujana Amazones who controlled the whole western part of the country at war's end, and who—along with the Jungle Commando and the national government—were the main parties to the Peace Treaty of August 1992.

5. *Memre Moiwana*, 13.

6. Fergus MacKay (ed.), *Moiwana zoekt gerechtigheid: De strijd van een Marrondorp tegen de staat Suriname*, Amsterdam, KIT Publishers, 2006, 10–11. The Inter-American Court of Human Rights, case of *Moiwana Village v. Suriname*, Judgment of 15 June 2005, lists the names of thirty-nine people killed, as well as 130 survivors, in paragraphs 86 (16 and 17). There were additional people killed, including five children, but they could not be identified with sufficient certainty for legal purposes.

7. Henk E. Chin and Hans Buddingh', *Surinam: Politics, Economics and Society* (London: Frances Pinter, 1987), 116.

8. S. Amos Wako, "Summary or Arbitrary Executions: Report by the Special Rapporteur," Geneva[?]: Commission on Human Rights, Economic and Social Council of the United Nations. [E/CN.4/1988/22, 19 January 1988], 43.

9. French psychiatric nurse Angèle Gilormini, who kindly gave me this drawing, which she had fished out of the wastebasket in the camp, told me that other children drew "helicopters and bombs and masked bandanna-faced heavily armed soldiers— eerie, graphic images of what happened in Moiwana."

10. Suriname News Agency, in *De West*, 15 December 1986, cited in *Memre Moiwana*, 26–27.

11. *Memre Moiwana*, 5; *In Memoriam Herman Eddy Gooding: Viribus Audax, manmoedig door innerlijke kracht*, Paramaribo, Moiwana'86, n.d. [1992], 8.

12. The staff of Moiwana'86 called Inspector Gooding's cold-blooded murder by the military police "the absolute low point, in terms of human rights, during the period 1980–90" (*In Memoriam*, 5). Gooding's civilian police colleagues agreed: soon after his funeral, thirteen of them, "convinced that the future was without any hope," fled with their families to the Netherlands (*In Memoriam*, 16). An investigation of Gooding's death was begun by a special Commission of Inquiry appointed after widespread protests within Suriname and abroad. But within a month, the investigators came up against what the minister of justice and the acting attorney general publicly called "a blind wall" (Zwamborn, "Suriname," 17). "The atmosphere of fear and intimidation made potential witnesses ask for guarantees of their safety; police officers and other law enforcement officers received death threats" (ibid.).

13. See for details, MacKay, *Moiwana*, 13.

14. *Libération*, 9 May 1989, 25.

15. Sophie Bourgarel, "Migration sur le Maroni: le cas des réfugiés surinamiens en Guyane." Mémoire de Maîtrise, Montpellier: Université Paul Valéry, 1988, 71–72.

16. Richard Price and Sally Price, *Equatoria*, New York, Routledge, 1992, 123–127.

17. By the late 1990s, both Bouterse and Brunswijk had transformed themselves into civilian politicians. *The Washington Post* reported that "U.S., European, and Caribbean experts say that Suriname offers the most extreme example of a small nation whose institutions have been corrupted by the drug trade" and quoted a specialist on organized crime in the Caribbean who said that "Suriname is a criminal enterprise. It is barely a country." The article also noted that U.S. "intelligence reports... indicated Suriname is the site of several large cocaine processing plants, operated by Colombian

drug traffickers from the Northern Cauca Valley and under the protection of Bouterse" (Douglas Farah, "Drug Corruption Over the Top: High-Level Suriname Officials Linked to Trafficking," 17 February 1998, A 10).

18. MacKay, *Moiwana*, 14–15.

19. Ibid., 15–16.

20. This history is spelled out in Inter-American Court of Human Rights, case of *Moiwana Village v. Suriname*, Judgment of 15 June 2005, paragraph 7.

21. The Court, which has jurisdiction from the time that a state ratifies the *American Convention* and separately deposits an instrument accepting the Court's jurisdiction to hear contentious cases, only examines violations of the *Convention*.

22. *Moiwana Village v. Suriname*, Judgment, paragraph 36.

23. On the implications of the judgment, in addition to MacKay, *Moiwana*, see Antkowiak, "*Moiwana Village v. Suriname.*"

24. *Moiwana Village v. Suriname*, Judgment, paragraph 93.

25. Ibid., paragraphs 101–102.

26. Ibid., paragraph 129.

27. Cf. Case of the Mayagna (Sumo) Awas Tingni Community. Judgment of 31 August 2001. Series C No. 79, paragraph 151.

28. Ibid., paragraph 149.

29. Ibid., paragraph 149.

30. Ibid., paragraph 149.

31. On the tone and content of the apology, see the two articles in *De Ware Tijd*, 17 July 2006, by Ivan Cairo—"Staat biedt excuus aan voor Moiwanaslachting. Regering wast handen in onschuld" and "Moiwana'86 blijft uitvoering vonnis volgen."

32. "Order of the President of the Inter-American Court of Human Rights of 18 December 2009. Case of the *Moiwana Village v. Suriname*. Monitoring Compliance with Judgment." Document available at http://www.forestpeoples.org/documents/ s_c_america/suriname_iachr_order_re_moiwana_dec09_eng.pdf.

33. S. James Anaya and Claudio Grossman, "The Case of *Awas Tingni v. Nicaragua*: A New Step in the International Law of Indigenous Peoples," *Arizona Journal of International and Comparative Law* 19(1):1–15, 2002.

34. The *Aloeboetoe* findings may well have assisted the Court in this judgment.

Trees

1. Various versions circulate of the Chinese arrival, including that it was Saramaka children who first saw and reported them moving through the forest, that the Suriname soldiers showed up only later (after Saramakas had begun stealing equipment from the Chinese), that it was a company called Ji Shen rather than one called Tacoba that made the initial incursion. But everyone agrees on the impact and consequences.

2. These statistics come from http://www.fas.usda.gov/ffpd/wood-circulars/ dec2000tp/solid_wood.pdf and http://www.treehugger.com/files/2007/04/shipping _contai_2.php.

3. By 2001, Chinese and other Asian companies controlled 90 percent of the world's $10 billion trade in tropical hardwood (Mark Jaffe, "Asian Companies Raid the Rain Forest in Weakly Regulated Countries," *Knight Ridder Tribune Business News*, 20 May 2001). For a moving account of the effects of multinational logging on local peoples in Borneo, see Anna Lowenhaupt Tsing, *Friction: An Ethnography of Global Connection* (Princeton: Princeton University Press, 2004).

4. China International Marine Containers (Group) Co. Ltd., "Announcement of Annual Results for the Year Ended 31 December 2001," 15. Available at http://www.cimc.com/UpFiles/Report/303.doc.

5. CIMC Annual Report 1998. The information in the remainder of this paragraph also comes from that source.

6. In early 1998, the Forest Peoples Programme noted that "Tacoba is also known to have relations with the former military dictator, Desi Bouterse, himself active in the timber business as a third-party buyer and other members of Suriname's ruling party, the National Democratic Party. Suriname recently opened an embassy in China and has been seeking expanded trade and aid relations. Tacoba seems to be the first major Chinese investment in Suriname." ("Suriname: Saramacca Maroons Say No to Multinational Logging," 20 April 1998).

7. Some reports claim that Ji Shen Wood Industries is the same CIMC subsidiary as Jin Lin Wood Industries and that it ceased, rather than began, operations in Saramaka territory in 2002. In any case, other subsidiaries, Lumprex and Fine Style (which operated toward Matawai territory) did begin operations in 2002. (See VSG and Forest Peoples Programme, "Free, Prior, and Informed Consent: Two Cases from Suriname," 2006, 7)

8. Forest Peoples Programme, "Logging and Tribal Rights in Suriname," 17 December 2001. See also Colchester, *Forest Politics*, 56–61, and the 1999 CELOS concessions map submitted as Annex F3 to Petition Submitted to the Inter-American Commission on Human Rights, Organization of American States, by *De Vereniging van Saramakaanse Gezagdragers* (The Association of Saramaka Authorities) on behalf of the Saramaka People, *Lôs* and Communities of the Upper Suriname River, Against Republic of Suriname, October 2001.

9. According to the 1999 CELOS concessions map, Barito Pacific had applied for a concession that dwarfed MUSA's and included the bulk of Matawai, Saramaka, and Ndyuka territory. (It is widely believed that Barito Pacific actually owns MUSA.)

10. Iwan Brave, "Goud, coke, en malaria," *De Groene Amsterdammer*, 1 April 1998.

11. Victor Minotti, director of environmental programs at the International Forum on Globalization, cited in Jaffe, "Asian Companies."

12. Brave, "Goud," Colchester, *Forest Politics*, 61–67.

13. Jaffe, "Asian Companies."

14. Brave, "Goud." Another authority said that in 1995 the Foundation for Forestry Management had "just four professional foresters and about ten secondary level forest rangers. . . . With only two jeeps and a couple of motorised canoes the service is now too strapped for cash to venture into the forests" (Colchester, *Forest Politics*, 54).

15. Jaffe, "Asian Companies."

16. Brave, "Goud."

17. J. Hardner and R. Rice, "Economic Opportunities for Forest Resource Use," in Pitou van Dijck (ed.), *Suriname, the Economy: Prospects for Sustainable Development*, Kingston, Jamaica: Ian Randle Publishers, 2001, 247–271, 263.

18. IACHR, OAS, Case No. 12.338, *Twelve Saramaka Communities (Suriname), Supplemental Submission Providing Updated Information and Requests*, 23 January 2003, 4.

19. Brave, "Goud." In 1998, Suriname raised the export tax from 7 Suriname guilders (less than US1 cent) per log to 5 percent of the export value (about US$ 4)—but the cost of concession rights was held steady at only 25 to 100 Suriname guilders (between US1 and 5 cents) per hectare (Kambel, *Resource Conflicts*, 111).

20. Jaffe, "Asian Companies."

21. Based on a study by the Inter-American Development Bank, cited in Jaffe, "Asian Companies."

22. Jaffe, "Asian Companies."

23. "China Wants Closer Trade Relations with Suriname," *De Ware Tijd*, 26 March 2002, cited in IACHR, OAS, Case No. 12.338, *Twelve Saramaka Communities (Suriname), Additional Observations on the Merits Made Pursuant to Article 38(1) of the Rules of Procedure of the IACHR*, 15 May 2002, paragraph 17.

24. Forest Peoples Programme, "Suriname: Saramacca Maroons Say No to Multinational Logging," 20 April 1998. Hugo Jabini told me a different version—that Captain Zepêni and his villagers first noticed the fouling of their creeks with diesel fuel from the earthmoving machines near their garden camps along the Pókigoón-Afobaka highway and that it was MUSA rather than Tacoba who was doing the damage; indeed, he told me the name of the Saramaka man from a middle river village who had first shown MUSA their way around the area of forest near Duwáta (personal communication, 21 September 2009, Amsterdam). This may not be a contradiction, since it was common for one company (such as MUSA) to work for a time in the concession of another (such as Tacoba).

25. Statement of a Saramaka man who now wishes to be anonymous, taken on 21 April 2002, in IACHR, OAS, Case No. 12.338, *Twelve Saramaka Communities (Suriname), Additional Observations on the Merits Made Pursuant to Article 38(1) of the Rules of Procedure of the IACHR*, 15 May 2002, Annex A.

26. "Conservation International Not Authorized to Expand Protected Areas," *De Ware Tijd*, 28 November 2002, cited in IACHR, OAS, Case No. 12.338, *Twelve Saramaka Communities (Suriname), Supplemental Submission Providing Updated Information and Requests*, 23 January 2003, 3.

27. Statement of Captain César Adjako, taken on 21 April 2002 (original in Saramaccan), in IACHR, OAS, Case No. 12.338, *Twelve Saramaka Communities (Suriname), Additional Observations on the Merits Made Pursuant to Article 38(1) of the Rules of Procedure of the IACHR*, 15 May 2002, paragraph 14.

28. "The Military guards important objectives in the interior," *De Ware Tijd*, 12 September 2002, cited in IACHR, OAS, Case No. 12.338, *Twelve Saramaka Communities*

(Suriname), Supplemental Submission Providing Updated Information and Requests, 23 January 2003, 4.

29. IACHR, OAS, Case No. 12.338, *Twelve Saramaka Communities (Suriname), Additional Observations on the Merits Made Pursuant to Article 38(1) of the Rules of Procedure of the IACHR,* 15 May 2002, paragraph 18. There was similar speculation at the time that China's ability to underbid other investors on an oil pipeline-building project in Sudan depended on its ability to export prison laborers—see http://engforum.pravda.ru/archive/index.php/t-206536.html.

30. Peter Poole, who may have taken the photograph of the logging road in the Ji Shen concession, writes of "incompetence" in building such roads: "They used bulldozers both to build and maintain the roads for which they should have used graders. Hence numerous roadside excavations like those in the image" (email of 01/18/2010).

31. See Price, *First-Time*, 74–88.

Resistance Redux

Initial Protests

1. The organization is sometimes referred to as Wanhati—"one heart."

2. Forest Peoples Programme, "Logging and Tribal Rights in Suriname," December 2001, 17.

3. MacKay had visited Suriname for the first time in 1995, on behalf of the World Council of Indigenous Peoples, and learned of logging and mining problems. During his second visit, in November 1996, Hugo Jabini approached him to describe Saramaka concerns and soon after invited him to the March 1997 meeting in Pikísééi.

4. Poole soon came to Suriname and provided the VSG with eight weeks of training and visited again in 1998 and 1999. The final version of the map was presented to Saramaka villages up and down the river and, in October 2002, to officials in Paramaribo. Various NGOs provided funding for the mapping—Novib/Oxfam Netherlands, the Rainforest Foundation U.S., and the German Fund to Protect the Rainforest "Oro Verde."

5. Hugo Jabini told me this story in 2009. He said that for a few days before the soccer players saw the Chinese, people in the village had heard machines far off in the forest, but it was only when the men showed up that they realized what was happening.

6. *De Ware Tijd,* "Inhabitants of the Stuwmeergebied Alarmed about Illegal Logging," 1 August 1997, cited in IACHR, "Pleadings, Motions and Evidence of the Victims' Representatives in the Case of *12 Saramaka Clans* (Case 12.338) *Against the Republic of Suriname,*" 3 November 2006, Annex 3.4.

7. Ibid.

8. I have seen a copy of Gaamá Songó's 1995 request for a 127,000 hectare logging concession in the name of Sorejo Mining N.V. (Sorejo being an abbreviation of Songó, Rene Pansa, and Johann Pansa, the latter two being close associates of the *gaamá*). The concession stretched from just to the west of the Saramaka villages beginning at the

lake and going all the way upstream close to the confluence of the Gaánlío and Pikílío and then westward over to the border with Matawai territory. Stanley Rensch was to be manager of this concession.

9. Hugo Jabini told me of these "seven" meetings—in Saramaccan discourse, "seven" means simply "many" (personal communication, 21 September 2009).

10. "Saramaccaners Make Fist in Battle for Recognition of Land Rights," *De West*, 26 March 1998, cited in IACHR, "Pleadings, Motions and Evidence of the Victims' Representatives in the Case of *12 Saramaka Clans* (Case 12.338) *Against the Republic of Suriname*," 3 November 2006, Annex 3.5.

11. Copies were sent to members of the National Assembly, various cabinet ministers, the Netherlands Embassy, various NGOs, international organizations, and human rights associations.

12. Petition submitted to the Inter-American Commission on Human Rights, Organisation of American States, by *De Vereniging van Saramakaanse Gezagdragers* (The Association of Saramaka Authorities) on behalf of the Saramaka People, *Lôs* and Communities of the Upper Suriname River, Against Republic of Suriname.

13. "Websites Encourage Terrorism in Suriname," *De Ware Tijd*, 25 July 2001, cited in IACHR, OAS, Case No. 12.338, *Twelve Saramaka Communities (Suriname), Additional Observations on the Merits Made Pursuant to Article 38(1) of the Rules of Procedure of the IACHR*, 15 May 2002, paragraph 26.

14. Cited in Forest Peoples Programme, "Press Release," 20 August 2002.

15. Around this time, the IACHR also noted that it had, on two separate occasions (21 November 2000 and 8 August 2001), requested that the State provide information concerning the allegations raised in the Saramakas' original petition but that "so far there has been no reply." (VSG et al., **"Failure of the Republic of Suriname to Recognize, Guarantee and Respect the Rights of Indigenous and Tribal Peoples to Lands, Territories and Resources, to Cultural Integrity and to Be Free from Racial Discrimination,"** Formal Communication [to the United Nations Special Rapporteur on the Situation of Human Rights and Fundamental Freedoms of Indigenous Peoples] Made Pursuant to Commission on Human Rights Resolution 2001/57, June 2002, paragraph 84.)

16. See, for example, "Formal Petition Made Pursuant to Article 22 of the 1987 Constitution of the Republic of Suriname," 15 January 2003, included in IACHR, OAS, Case No. 12.338, *Twelve Saramaka Communities (Suriname), Supplemental Submission Providing Updated Information and Requests*, 23 January 2003, Annex 1.

17. This document, "Report of Dr. Richard Price in Support of Provisional Measures," is annexed to the VSG's *Request for the Application of Provisional Measures by the Inter-American Court of Human Rights*, 15 October 2003. During this period, a new threat to Saramaka territory reared its head—a 2003 deal between the government and Alcoa, worth US$70 million, to expand the 1960s dam and lake, raising the water level by up to 2 meters to increase hydroelectric production so that Alcoa could expand its alumina refinery at Paranam. As the VSG informed the IACHR in several submissions

in 2003, six Saramaka villages at the southern edge of the lake would stand to be flooded if this plan were realized. The VSG repeatedly petitioned that this situation be included in the precautionary measures that had been previously issued.

18. During this period, our writings on Saramakas in Suriname included my largely historical *Alabi's World*, and our joint *Two Evenings in Saramaka* (which benefited from late-1980s fieldwork in Kourou), *Maroon Arts* (Boston: Beacon Press, 1999), and *The Root of Roots: Or, How Afro-American Anthropology Got Its Start* (Chicago: Prickly Paradigm Press, 2003). We also wrote books on Saramakas and other Maroons in French Guiana, such as the jointly authored *Equatoria, Enigma Variations: A Novel* (Cambridge: Harvard University Press, 1995), and *Les Marrons* (Châteauneuf-le-Rouge: Vents d'ailleurs, 2003), as well as my *Travels with Tooy*.

19. Much of this section is taken directly from Price, *Travels with Tooy*, 237–244.

20. A Ndyuka acquaintance of Gaamá Agbagó claims that the chief told him of this preference as early as the 1970s (André R. M. Pakosie, "Een analyse van het huidige conflict om het gaamanschap bij de Saamaka," *Siboga* 15[1][2005]:17–27).

21. See Price, *First-Time*, 45, 160, passim.

22. An amateur video of Ozeni's enstoolment, which I saw in 2009, shows the handsome shotgun that Pésé sent as a gift at Songó's funeral being bestowed on "Gaamá" Ozeni.

23. In an email from July 2006, anthropologist Bonno Thoden van Velzen reported that, according to Ndyuka friends, the five men who made up the delegation returned home feeling unappreciated and "abused" by the Saramakas, who paid them little heed and did not treat them with due respect.

24. This is a First-Time "play" whose name derives from the Yorubaland cult of Nanã Burukú. J. Lorand Matory calls Nanã Burukú "the goddess of death" (*Black Atlantic Religion: Tradition, Transnationalism and Matriarchy in the Afro-Brazilian Candomblé*, Princeton: Princeton University Press, 2005, 98), while Pierre Verger characterizes her as a "very ancient goddess" who shows people "how to act with calm, benevolence, dignity, and gentleness" (*Orixás: Deuses Iorubás na África e no Novo Mundo*, Salvador: Corrupio, 1981, 236–41; see also his *Notes sur le culte des Orisa et Vodun à Bahia, la Baie de tous les Saints, au Brésil et à l'ancienne Côte des Esclaves en Afrique* [Dakar: IFAN, 1957, 271–90]).

25. An article in *De Ware Tijd* on 2 August 2005 describes how in a "great council meeting" held the previous day at Brokopondo, the Saramaka officials from all clans met with the Suriname government minister for regional development and declared Otjútju (Belfón Abóikóni) to be the new *gaamá*. The minister said that he would be officially recognized by the national government without delay. A follow-up article on 3 August reported that the leaders of Dángogó were still not accepting this decision, saying that Otjútju might be *gaamá* as far as cityfolk were concerned, but not for "real Saramakas." However, it seemed clear that Otjútju had won at last. And then on 29 October, *De Ware Tijd* reported that Otjútju would be received that day in the presidential palace and officially recognized by President Ronald Venetiaan as Saramaka *gaamá*, and on 31 October

the newspaper published his photo wearing his new *gaamá's* uniform, presented by the president.

The Depredations Continue

1. VSG et al., "Failure of the Republic of Suriname to Recognize, Guarantee and Respect the Rights of Indigenous and Tribal Peoples to Lands, Territories and Resources, to Cultural Integrity and to Be Free from Racial Discrimination," Formal Communication (to the United Nations Special Rapporteur on the Situation of Human Rights and Fundamental Freedoms of Indigenous Peoples) Made Pursuant to Commission on Human Rights Resolution 2001/57, June 2002.

2. Reports from 2009 describe continuing and massive discrimination in educational (and other) opportunities; see CERD, "Concluding observations of the Committee on the Elimination of Racial Discrimination, Suriname, Seventy-fourth session, 16 February–6 March 2009, CERD/C/SUR/CO/12, 3 March 2009" and The Association of Indigenous Village Leaders in Suriname, The Association of Saramaka Authorities, and The Forest Peoples Programme, "A Report on the Situation of Indigenous and Tribal Peoples in Suriname and Comments on Suriname's 11th and 12th Periodic Reports (CERD/C/SUR/12)," submitted to the Committee on the Elimination of Racial Discrimination at its 74th session (16 February–6 March 2009), both available at http://www.forestpeoples.org/documents/s_c_america/bases/suriname.shtml.

3. I have been told that these funds included compensation to various individuals who had, only weeks before, received logging concessions in what was to become the reserve, and that one of these was Bouterse's buddy Etienne Boerenveen—by then freed on good behavior from his twelve-year drug trafficking conviction in a U.S. Federal Penitentiary and promoted to the rank of colonel in the Suriname army.

4. See Price, *First-Time*, 77–79. I have been told by Saramakas that this sacred pool has recently been irreparably desecrated—filled up with slag from the Gros Rosebel gold mine run by Cambior/Golden Star/Iamgold.

5. Price, *First-Time*, 83–85, which includes a map. This is the area desecrated by Chinese logging roads in 2002.

6. Price, *First-Time*, 92–95.

7. Price, *First-Time*, 98–99; Price, *Travels with Tooy*, 115.

8. Price, *First-Time*, 135–137. For additional details, see Price, *Travels with Tooy*, 257–258.

9. Price, *First-Time*, 167–171; Price, *Travels with Tooy*, 107–109.

10. Price, *Travels with Tooy*, 150–157.

11. Conservation International claimed that the initial impetus (and permission) for the expansion actually came from Gaamá Songó (see, for example, the story in Alanna Mitchell, "The Man with a Plan to Save the Planet," Part 3, *Globe and Mail*, 6 June 2001). Indeed, CI's president, Russell Mittermeier, did obtain Gaamá Songó's signature on a letter (in English!), which he then presented to the government in support of his efforts to expand the reserve. But according to Saramaka law, it is the *lós*, not the *gaamá*, who

have authority over land and territory, so such an agreement by the *gaamá* would have no legal backing in Saramaka terms. The map of the proposed Conservation International expansion includes, in addition to Lángu, the Upper Pikílío—an area of the greatest sacredness to the Matjáu clan that traditionally holds the *gaamá*ship. I am unaware that Matjáus, other than perhaps the late Gaamá Songó (who had by that time suffered a stroke), ever even knew of these plans until they were made public. In any case, there was no consultation with Saramaka authorities other than, perhaps, the *gaamá*.

12. Resolution on the Expansion of the Central Suriname Nature Reserve Adopted at the *Gaan Kuútu* of 23 November 2002, Pikin Slee Village. This document also noted, among other things, that the Saramakas viewed "*with concern* the activities of Conservation International in relation to the Suriname Bioprospecting Initiative, which has been operating in our territory without our full knowledge and consent for many years and which is attempting to use the traditional knowledge of the Saramaka people without prior consultation and agreement with all of the traditional authorities of the Saramaka people." For more on the multiple problems of the SBI, see VSG and Forest Peoples Programme, "Free, Prior, and Informed Consent: Two Cases from Suriname," 2006.

13. See, for example, the letter of "7 Captains and a number of other village authorities" from the Lángu region to the director of Conservation International, 9 February 2003, in IACHR, Case No. 12.338, *Twelve Saramaka Communities (Suriname)*, Response [by the VGA] to Submission of Suriname and Additional Information, 18 March 2003.

14. VSG Letter, 22 August 2003.

15. Ibid.

16. Ibid.

17. VGS, *Request for the Application of Provisional Measures by the Inter-American Court of Human Rights*, 15 October 2003.

18. Andrew Westoll, *The Riverbones: Stumbling After Eden in the Jungles of Suriname*, Toronto, Emblem Editions, 2008, 12–13.

19. VSG et al., "Failure of the Republic of Suriname to Recognize, Guarantee and Respect the Rights of Indigenous and Tribal Peoples to Lands, Territories and Resources, to Cultural Integrity and to Be Free from Racial Discrimination," Formal Communication [to the United Nations Special Rapporteur on the Situation of Human Rights and Fundamental Freedoms of Indigenous Peoples] Made Pursuant to Commission on Human Rights Resolution 2001/57, June 2002. See CERD's reports of 12 March 2004, 18 August 2005.

20. CERD/C/64/CO/9/Rev. 2, 12 March 2004.

21. Forest Peoples Programme, "Press Release," 16 March 2004.

22. VSG et al., "Request [to CERD] for Follow-Up and Urgent Action Concerning the Situation of Indigenous and Tribal Peoples in Suriname," 8 July 2005.

23. CERD/C/SUR/CO/12, 3 March 2009.

24. OAS, IACHR, Application in the Case of *12 Saramaka Clans* (Case 12.338) *Against the Republic of Suriname*, 23 June 2006.

Judgment Day

Pre-Hearing Pleadings

1. "Pleadings, Motions and Evidence of the Victims' Representatives in the Case of *12 Saramaka Clans* (Case 12.338) *Against the Republic of Suriname*," submitted to the Inter-American Court of Human Rights, November 3, 2006.

2. It is both humbling and gratifying that the documentation for this section rests almost exclusively on the anthropological/historical materials in R. Price *First-Time, To Slay the Hydra, Alabi's World*, my testimony in *Aloeboetoe*, and my several submissions to the IACHR.

3. The reasons for these divergences are varied and complex. Some would seem to be differences of strategy (how ready is the Court to deal with issues of tribal peoples' self-determination?), some are differences regarding the germaneness of an issue to the case (is determining the validity of the 1762 treaty necessary to the case at hand [not really], even though Saramakas care greatly about it?), some may stem simply from the Commission's not having attended with sufficient care to the petitioners' arguments (about the Article 3 violation, for example, or in deciding whether to include the evidence about the effects of the dam in the "fact" section or the "legal arguments" section) when it wrote its Article 50 Application to the Court).

4. "Pleadings," paragraph 199.

5. Ibid., paragraph 198.

6. Ibid., paragraph 159.

7. Ibid., paragraph 160.

8. Ibid., paragraph 170.

9. "Official Response of the State of Suriname in Case No. 12.338, *Twelve Saramaka Clans vs. Suriname*, Submitted to the Inter-American Court of Human Rights," 12 January 2007.

10. Ibid., paragraph 79.

11. Ibid., paragraph 100.

12. Ibid., paragraphs 78–102.

13. Ibid., paragraph 105.

14. Ibid., paragraph 106.

15. Ibid., paragraph 205.

16. Ibid., paragraphs 290–292.

17. Ibid., paragraph 118.

18. Ibid., paragraph 218.

19. Ibid., paragraph 20.

20. Ibid., paragraph 283.

21. Ibid., paragraph 294.

22. Ibid.

23. "Observations of the Victims' Representatives in Response to the Preliminary Objections Presented by the Republic of Suriname," submitted to the Inter-American Court of Human Rights 1 March 2007.

24. Ibid., paragraph 17.

25. Ibid., paragraph 145.

The Hearing

1. Wazen's passport apparently spells his name *Wanze*, which is the way news media usually spell it, but his name is *Wazen*, pronounced "wah-ZEN."

2. They were accompanied, as well, by Ine Apapoe, a Ndyuka student at the university in Paramaribo, who helped with travel logistics.

3. At the very last minute, David Padilla cancelled, due to his wife's emergency hospitalization—she eventually recovered.

4. Elizabeth has worked for the IACHR since just before the *Aloeboetoe* hearing in 1992, when I met her for the first time in Costa Rica, and she served as the lead attorney for the Commission in *Moiwana v. Suriname*—so she has considerable experience with the Court.

5. In 2004, the Court changed its rules so that plaintiffs (victims) could be represented by their own attorneys rather than depending solely on the Commission.

6. This speech is translated from a recording I made at the meeting.

7. For the first portion of the hearing, I follow the written transcript, which includes Sally's glosses of Wazen's and César's testimony—though I sometimes add or change a word or two from the audio recording of the hearing. Later in the hearing, particularly during the second day, I rely more heavily on the audio recording.

8. In fact, since the end of the civil war in the early 1990s, about 50 percent of the 55,000 Saramakas have moved outside Saramaka territory, at least on a temporary basis—about 15 percent reside in and around Paramaribo, visiting their home villages from time to time; 30 percent live in French Guiana, often without residence papers—many going back and forth frequently to their villages in Suriname; and at least 5 percent live elsewhere, mainly the Netherlands but also in the United States.

9. He could easily have elaborated, discussing, for example, out-migration from Saramaka territory, the fact that Saramakas now run more than a dozen lodges for tourists (mostly Dutch) near their villages, that the U.S. Peace Corps has had a presence in Saramaka villages since 1995, that evangelical missionaries of various brands have arrived in significant numbers, and that cell phones have become ubiquitous for communication with family and friends around the globe.

10. Lim a Po, arguably Suriname's most distinguished attorney, has had a career closely tied to mining interests in Suriname. After serving as managing director of Billiton Maatschappij Suriname (part of Royal Dutch Shell's mining arm, Billiton International Metals), and later for Billiton in the Hague, he moved to London as Group Legal Counsel for Billiton Plc (the largest mining company in the world after it merged with BHP), with worldwide responsibilities, retiring from Shell in 2000 (Fred Y. Phillips 2008. "The Godfathers: Characteristics and Roles of Central Individuals in the Transformation of Techno-Regions." *Journal of CENTRUM Cathedra* 1 (2): 74–89.

11. This answer seems like a smokescreen. Just as some of the power from the dam is transformed for domestic use on the coast, why couldn't it be similarly transformed for Saramakas and others who live near the dam, either by building a new transformer or by routing power from the existing stations back toward the dam? As Fergus MacKay has said to me, "There may be no national power grid, but there are pylons all the way along the Afobaka road."

The Judgment

1. The full text of the judgment is available at www.forestpeoples.org/documents/ s_c_america/suriname_iachr_saramaka_judgment_nov07_eng.pdf. The ad hoc justice from Suriname, Alwin Baarh, who had participated in the hearing, subsequently informed the Court that, for reasons of *force majeure*, he could not participate in the deliberation of the Judgment itself.

2. I have no idea why the Commission did not consider the many pages of expert affidavits and arguments submitted to them by the representatives of the Saramakas during all those years when they were considering the case and then include them in both their factual and legal arguments to the Court.

3. For a detailed analysis of the Court's judgment and its significance for Suriname, see Fergus MacKay, editor, *Saramaka: De strijd om het bos*. Amsterdam: KIT Publishers, 2010.

4. Kambel and MacKay. *The Rights*. p. 178.

5. It might be argued the word "development," as used here, is forward-looking (rather than tied to backward-looking "tradition") in the sense that it could relate to resources that would be needed for future development.

6. In the Court's 2008 Interpretive Judgment, the justices added (Paragraph 37):

> The Court emphasized in the Judgment that the phrase "survival as a tribal people" must be understood as the ability of the Saramaka to "preserve, protect and guarantee the special relationship that [they] have with their territory," so that "they may continue living their traditional way of life, and that their distinct cultural identity, social structure, economic system, customs, beliefs and traditions are respected, guaranteed and protected." That is, the term survival in this context signifies much more than physical survival.

7. In this Interpretive Judgment (Paragraph 41), the Court also reduced the large-scale project requirement by requiring that cumulative impacts be assessed and taken into account.

8. Interpretive Judgment (Paragraph 49). Clearly, the details of how this applies in practice will need to be worked out in future cases.

9. One commentator noted, correctly in my view, that "the level of compensation appears low, in regard to what experts described as 'severe and traumatic' damage, as

among 'the worst planned, most damaging and wasteful logging possible'" (Marcos A. Orellana. *Saramaka People v. Suriname. American Journal of International Law.* 2008. 102: 841–847.). Expert witness Robert Goodland had testified that the value of the timber removed from Saramaka territory between 1999 and 2006 was in excess of US$1 million (Inter-American Court of Human Rights, Case of *Twelve Saramaka Clans v. Suriname,* Affidavit of Dr. Robert Goodland, Expert Witness, Submitted by the Victims' Representatives, 2 May 2007).

10. That is, the Court concluded,

> The State's failure to do so has resulted in a violation, to the detriment of the members of the Saramaka people, of the right to the recognition of their juridical personality pursuant to Article 3 of the Convention in relation to their right to property under Article 21 of such instrument and their right to judicial protection under Article 25 thereof, as well as in relation to the general obligation of States to adopt such legislative or other measures as may be necessary to give effect to those rights and to respect and ensure their free and full exercise without discrimination, pursuant to Articles 2 and 1(1) of the Convention.

and, furthermore,

> The State violated, to the detriment of the members of the Saramaka people, the right to judicial protection, as recognized in Article 25 of the American Convention on Human Rights, in conjunction with the obligations to respect and guarantee the rights established under Articles 21 and 1(1) thereof.

11. Ivan Cairo. "Staat voert vonnis Inter-Amerikaans mensenrechtenhof uit. Gesprekken grondenrechtenvraagstuk gaan voort." *De Ware Tijd,* 9 January 2008.

12. That document is available at http://www.forestpeoples.org/documents/s_c _america/suriname_iachr_saramaka_judgment_aug08_eng.pdf.

American Dreams

Developments on the Ground

1. On the difficulties that states around the world have had in complying with court rulings that require the demarcation of indigenous (or tribal) peoples' lands, see Andrew Erueti, "The Demarcation of Indigenous Peoples' Traditional Lands: Comparing Domestic Principles of Demarcation with Emerging Principles of International Law," *Arizona Journal of International and Comparative Law* (2006) 23(3):543–612.

2. Letter of Minister of Regional Development Michel Felisi to the Dutch ministry of foreign affairs, with the subject line "Reporting on the implementation of the judgment of the Inter-American Court of Human Rights in the case of *The Twelve Saramaka*

Lôs v. the State of Suriname," dated 16 February 2009. This page-and-a-half-long document was apparently submitted to the Court on 6 August 2009, as an official report.

3. "Comments of the Victims' Representatives on the First Report of the Illustrious State of Suriname in the Case of the Saramaka People (Ser C No. 172 and Ser C No. 185)," 12 September 2009.

4. See, for example, the letters of Gaamá Belfón Abóikóni and Wazen Eduards to President Venetiaan, 13 March 2008, and of Wazen Eduards and Hugo Jabini to Minister Felisi, 25 October 2008, both included as Annex A to "Comments of the Victims' Representatives."

5. Selected speeches from the land rights conference are included, in English translation, as Annex C to "Comments of the Victims' Representatives."

6. Documentation of the request, its acceptance, and the endorsement by CERD may be found in "Comments of the Victims' Representatives."

7. Daan de Hulster, "Vereniging Saramaccaanse Gezagdragers: 'Tijd dringt voor uitvoering Samaaka-vonnis,'" *De Ware Tijd*, 16 November 2009—see also http://abeng-central.wordpress.com/2009/11/16/saramaccans/.

8. These postings will appear on the *Rainforest Warriors* page of http://www.richandsally.net. For documents relevant to these cases, see also http://www.forestpeoples.org/documents/s_c_america/bases/suriname.shtml.

9. See Fenny Zandgrond, "Verharde Afobakaweg officieel geopend: 'Marrons moeten harder aanpakken,'" *De Ware Tijd*, 24 November 2009.

10. "IAMGOLD Delivers on 2009 Guidance," 21 January 2010; see http://www.iamgold.com/news_details.asp?id=3868.

11. In recent years, Bristol-Myers has screened and tested 788 extracts prepared from 394 plants gathered through the SBPI for potential use in developing drugs to combat cancer and AIDS (see http://www.conservation.org/web/fieldact/C-C_PROG/Econ/biopros.htm). As of 1999, work on more than 5,000 extracts had led to the "isolation of bioactive alkaloids, terpenoids, and polyketides as cytotoxic agents" (Kingston et al., "The Suriname International Cooperative Biodiversity Group Program: Lessons from the First Five Years," *Pharmaceutical Biology* 37(1):22–34 [1999]).

12. Eliézer Pross, "Transmigratie inheemsen Para dreigt," *De Ware Tijd*, 11 June 2010.

13. Republic of Suriname, Forest Carbon Partnership Facility (FCPF) Readiness Preparation Proposal (R-PP), 24 August 2009.

14. "Sara Creek Gold Enters into Option Agreement," Reuters, 13 October 2009.

15. Detailed information about this project is available at http://www.nsi-ins.ca/english/research/progress/23.asp. Over the years, the project has been off-again, on-again, as first BHP/Billiton and more recently Alcoa seem to have pulled out. But the Suriname government, which has promoted the project since the 1970s, is currently seeking other partners.

16. Cited in VSG et al., "Request for Additional Follow-Up and Urgent Action Concerning the Situation of Indigenous and Tribal Peoples in Suriname," letter to

United Nations Committee on the Elimination of Racial Discrimination, 6 June 2006.

17. VSG et al., "Request for Additional Follow-Up."

18. See, for example, Marjo de Theije and Marieke Heemskerk, "Moving Frontiers in the Amazon: Brazilian Small-Scale Gold Miners in Suriname," *European Review of Latin American and Caribbean Studies* (2009) 87:5–25.

19. See http://www.cidh.oas.org/annualrep/2007eng/Suriname198.07eng.htm.

20. Republic of Suriname, Forest Carbon Partnership Facility (FCPF) Readiness Preparation Proposal (R-PP), 24 August 2009.

Broader Implications

1. See "Permanent Forum Hails General Assembly Adoption of Indigenous Rights Declaration. Pledges to Make It 'a Living Document,' as Seventh Session Concludes," U.N. Department of Public Information, 2 May 2008. Available at: http://www.un.org/News/Press/docs/2008/hr4953.doc.htm.

2. Lisl Brunner, "The Rise of Peoples' Rights in the Americas: The *Saramaka People* Decision of the Inter-American Court of Human Rights," *Chinese JIL* (2008) 7, paragraph IV.11.

3. Dinah L. Shelton, "Human Rights and the Environment," *Yearbook of International Environmental Law 2007*, Oxford University Press, 2008, 163–172 (qtd. pp. 168–69). For other legal comments on the case, see, for example, James Harrison, "International Law: Significant Environmental Cases 2007–08," *Journal of Environmental Law* (2008) 20:475–81; Marcos A. Orellana, "*Saramaka People v. Suriname*," *American Journal of International Law* (2008) 102:841–47.

4. That article defines tribal peoples as "peoples in independent countries whose social, cultural, and economic conditions distinguish them from other sections of the national community, and whose status is regulated wholly or partially by their own customs or traditions or by special laws or regulations." The ILO's concept of tribal peoples was developed largely for the Asian context, in particular to address alleged difficulties in Asia of establishing aboriginality, an integral component of the definition of "indigenous peoples." In the Americas, it would seem to apply mainly to Maroons such as those in Suriname and French Guiana, who can demonstrate significant sociocultural difference from surrounding populations. Nonetheless, Brazil, Colombia, and Ecuador each apply ILO 169 in certain respects to some Afro-descendant groups.

5. MacKay, *Saramaka*, 27–28.

6. Rolleiv Solholm, "Guyana and Norway to Protect Rain Forest," NRK (Norwegian Broadcasting Corporation), 12 November 2009. On May 26, 2010, Norway signed a similar agreement with Indonesia worth US$1 billion—see http://www.redd-monitor.org/2010/05/27/norway-and-indonesia-sign-us1-billion-forest-deal/.

7. "Suriname zoekt multilaterale boscompensatie," *De Ware Tijd*, 12 November 2009.

8. For a pessimistic assessment of the potentials of REDD, from an indigenous peoples' perspective, see Rebecca Sommer, "UNFCCC, COP15: Indigenous Delegates at Climate

Conference 'REDD Not Fixable Nor Reformable—Don't Greenwash REDD,'" available at http://www.huntingtonnews.net/columns/091210-sommer-columnsredd.html.

9. And Suriname's public relations strategy seems to be paying off as well. According to the *San Francisco Chronicle*, "Ethical Traveler, a Berkeley nonprofit advocacy group that advises travelers on how to use 'economic power to strengthen human rights and protect the environment,'" has included Suriname in its exclusive list for 2010, citing its "unspoiled rainforest biodiversity and sincere efforts toward ecotourism and environmental protection"—Spud Hilton, "Developing World's 10 Best Ethical Destinations," *San Francisco Chronicle*, Sunday, 3 January 2010.

10. See *Report of the Office of the United Nations High Commissioner for Human Rights on the relationship between climate change and human rights*. U.N. Doc. A/HRC/10/61, 15 January 2009, paragraph 53 (explaining the relevance of the UNDRIP and a range of other international instruments to indigenous peoples and climate change issues).

11. For example, the Committee on the Elimination of Racial Discrimination has examined one case of a proposed climate mitigation measure and expressed deep concern about the threat it constitutes to the rights of indigenous peoples to own their lands and enjoy their culture (*Concluding observations of the Committee on the Elimination of Racial Discrimination: Indonesia*. U.N. Doc. CERD/C/IDN/CO/3, paragraph 17).

12. The VSG and the Association of Indigenous Village Leaders in Suriname are actively trying to change this situation and, in 2009, submitted letters to relevant government ministries as well as to the World Bank protesting that Suriname's negotiations with the Bank and other agencies concerning FCPF were conducted without consulting them and were in violation of the Court's 2007 judgment. (Suriname's FCPF application, they pointed out, assumed that the State owned all forests and was written almost as if the 2007 judgment had never occurred.)

13. Although the Saramaka analogy, particularly through the use of citations from my *First-Time*, has been invoked in Brazilian legal cases involving *remanescentes de quilombos* (putative descendants of historical maroon communities), I remain concerned, intellectually and morally, about what is, ultimately, an altruistically motivated anthropological sleight-of-hand—see Richard Price, "Scrapping Maroon History: Brazil's Promise, Suriname's Shame," *New West Indian Guide* (1998) 72: 233–255. In my own testimony before the Court, both in *Aloeboetoe* and the present case, I insisted on the Saramakas' unique historical and spiritual relationship to their territory, and these arguments clearly influenced the judgments. Whether similar arguments can hold in these other cases remains to be seen.

14. I recognize the complexity and political delicacy of determining what it means for a community to be considered as having a "tribal" identity. While it is a relatively easy case to make for the Saramakas (or other Suriname Maroons), to make the case for indigenous peoples who no longer have their own language or other diacritics of cultural difference is more complex. Cases involving apparently "assimilated" peoples who

self-identify as indigenous (whether Native Americans or other indigenous peoples worldwide) have, however, shown that cultural difference is only one criterion for the designation of "tribal" and for the protection of related rights.

15. In fact, anthropology and human rights law have experienced tensions ever since Melville Herskovits's controversial memo written on behalf of the American Anthropological Association to Eleanor Roosevelt, chair of the United Nations Commission on Human Rights, which argued for "the right of men to live in terms of their own traditions." The Universal Declaration of Human Rights proclaimed a series of universal values (concerning, for example, racial, gender, and religious equality) that Herskovits, a staunch cultural relativist and anti-imperialist, did not believe were appropriate to impose cross-culturally. Anthropologists in the mid-1940s, looking over their shoulders at Nazism, were divided on these issues. (See, for discussion, Jerry Gershenhorn, *Melville J. Herskovits and the Racial Politics of Knowledge*, Lincoln: University of Nebraska Press, 2004, 207–214.) For more general discussion of the tension between human rights discourse and cultural relativism, see, for example, Jane K. Cowan, Marie-Bénédicte Dembour, and Richard A. Wilson (eds.), *Culture and Rights: Anthropological Perspectives*, Cambridge, Cambridge University Press, 2001, and Lynda S. Bell, Andrew J. Nathan, and Ilan Peleg (eds), *Negotiating Culture and Human Rights*, New York: Columbia University Press, 2001.

16. Sally Price has pointed to the 2007 speech made by President Nicolas Sarkozy of France at the University of Dakar, where he explained what he saw as the difference between European civilization and that of his listeners, as a prime example of such discourse—"The tragedy of Africa is that the African (*l'homme africain*) has not sufficiently entered into History. The African peasant, who has for centuries been living according to the seasons and whose ideal in life is to remain in harmony with nature, knows only the eternal renewal of a temporal rhythm that depends on an endless repetition of the same acts and the same words. In such a vision where everything is always repeating, there is no place for the human adventure and no place for the idea of progress"—see her "Return to the Quai Branly," *Museum Anthropology* (2010) 33:11–20 (qtd. p. 17).

17. "Introduction: Inventing Traditions," in Eric Hobsbawm and Terence Ranger, *The Invention of Tradition*, Cambridge: Cambridge University Press, 1983, 1–14 (qtd. p. 1).

18. Eric R. Wolf, *Europe and the People Without History*, Berkeley: University of California Press, 1982, 6–7.

19. Ibid., 12–13.

20. Michel-Rolph Trouillot, "Anthropology and the Savage Slot: The Poetics and Politics of Otherness," in Richard Fox, ed., *Recapturing Anthropology: Working in the Present*, Santa Fe: SAR Press, 1991, 17–44.

21. Ibid., 39.

22. One can, of course, make this worldwide category more intellectually defensible by emphasizing colonialism and other historical and present-day similarities of unequal

power—that is, these peoples' similar structural position within nation-states, rather than any cultural similarities or proclivities that they are alleged to share.

Postface

1. See, for references, "Developments on the Ground," above.

2. Vinije Haabo, "The Future," in Thomas Meijer zu Schlochtern and Christopher Cozier (eds.), *Paramaribo Span*, Amsterdam, KIT Publishers, 2010, p. 76.

3. See Pitou van Dijck, "The IIRSA Guyana Shield Hub: The Case of Suriname," 2010. Available at: http://www.cedla.uva.nl/30_research/PDF_files_research/suriname_project/IIRSA.pdf.

References Cited

I list here all books and articles cited in the endnotes. References to documents—those of the United Nations, IACHR, OAS, and so forth—that are cited in the endnotes are not repeated here.

Anaya, S. James, and Claudio Grossman. 2002. The Case of *Awas Tingni v. Nicaragua*: A New Step in the International Law of Indigenous Peoples. *Arizona Journal of International and Comparative Law* 19(1):1–15.

Antkowiak, Thomas M. 2007. *Moiwana Village v. Suriname*: A Portal into Recent Jurisprudential Developments of the Inter-American Court of Human Rights. *Berkeley Journal of International Law* 25(2):101–115.

Bajak, Frank. 2009. Indian political awakening stirs Latin America. Associated Press, 1 November.

Bell, Lynda S., Andrew J. Nathan, and Ilan Peleg (eds.). 2001. *Negotiating Culture and Human Rights*. New York: Columbia University Press.

Bilby, Kenneth M. 1990. The Remaking of the Aluku: Culture, Politics, and Maroon Ethnicity in French South America. Unpublished Ph.D. dissertation. Baltimore: Johns Hopkins University.

———. 1997. Swearing by the Past, Swearing to the Future: Sacred Oaths, Alliances, and Treaties among the Guianese and Jamaican Maroons. *Ethnohistory* 44:655–689.

Binder, David. 1988. Diplomacy and Public Relations: Image Maker Aids New Democracy. *New York Times*, 25 January.

Bourgarel, Sophie. 1988. Migration sur le Maroni: Le cas des réfugiés surinamiens en Guyane. Mémoire de Maîtrise. Montpellier, France: Université Paul Valéry.

Brana-Shute, Gary. 1979. *On the Corner: Male Social Life in a Paramaribo Creole Neighborhood*. Assen, The Netherlands: Van Gorcum.

———. 1993. An Inside-Out Insurgency: The Tukuyana Amazones of Suriname, in Paul Sutton and Anthony Payne (eds.), *Size and Survival: The Politics of Security in the Caribbean and the Pacific*. London: Frank Cass, pp. 54–69.

Brave, Iwan. 1998. Goud, coke, en malaria. *De Groene Amsterdammer*, 1 April.

Brunner, Lisl. 2008. The Rise of Peoples' Rights in the Americas: The *Saramaka People* Decision of the Inter-American Court of Human Rights. *Chinese JIL* 7.

Cairo, Ivan. 2006. Staat biedt excuus aan voor Moiwanaslachting. Regering wast handen in onschuld. *De Ware Tijd*, 17 July.

———. 2006. Moiwana'86 blijft uitvoering vonnis volgen. *De Ware Tijd*, 17 July.

———. 2008. Staat voert vonnis Inter-Amerikaans mensenrechtenhof uit. Gesprekken grondenrechtenvraagstuk gaan voort. *De Ware Tijd*, 9 January.

Cerquone, Joseph. 1987. *Flight from Suriname: Refugees in French Guiana*. Washington, D.C.: U.S. Committee for Refugees.

Chin, Henk E. and Hans Buddingh'. 1987. *Surinam: Politics, Economics and Society*. London: Frances Pinter.

Colchester, Marcus. 1995. *Forest Politics in Suriname*. Utrecht, The Netherlands: International Books.

Conservation International. 2009. Suriname Launches a Bold Plan for a Green Future. Press release, 3 November.

Cowan, Jane K., Marie-Bénédicte Dembour and Richard A. Wilson (eds.). 2001. *Culture and Rights: Anthropological Perspectives*. Cambridge, U.K.: Cambridge University Press.

Dew, Edward. 1978. *The Difficult Flowering of Surinam: Ethnicity and Politics in a Plural Society*. The Hague, The Netherlands: Martinus Nijhoff.

Dijck, Pitou van. 2010. The IIRSA Guyana Shield Hub: The Case of Suriname. Available at http://www.cedla.uva.nl/30_research/PDF_files_research/suriname_project/IIRSA.pdf. Forthcoming in printed form.

Erueti, Andrew. 2006. The Demarcation of Indigenous Peoples' Traditional Lands: Comparing Domestic Principles of Demarcation with Emerging Principles of International Law. *Arizona Journal of International and Comparative Law* 23(3):543–612.

Farah, Douglas. 1998. Drug Corruption Over the Top: High-Level Suriname Officials Linked to Trafficking. *Washington Post*, 17 February, A 10.

Forest Peoples Programme. 1998. Suriname: Saramacca Maroons Say No to Multinational Logging. Press release, 20 April.

———. 2001. Logging and Tribal Rights in Suriname. Press release, 17 December.

Fox-Decent, Evan. 2009. Indigenous Peoples and Human Dignity, in Frédéric Mégret and Florian Hoffmann (eds.), *Protecting Dignity: An Agenda for Human Rights. Research Project on Human Dignity. "Dignity: A Special Focus on Vulnerable Groups,"* McGill Centre for Human Rights and Legal Pluralism, June, pp. 34–46.

Franszoon, Adiante. 1987. Crisis in the Backlands. *Hemisphere* 1, 2:36–38.

Gershenhorn, Jerry. 2004. *Melville J. Herskovits and the Racial Politics of Knowledge*. Lincoln: University of Nebraska Press.

Haabo, Vinije. 2010. The Future, in Thomas Meijer zu Schlochtern and Christopher Cozier (eds.), *Paramaribo Span*. Amsterdam: KIT Publishers, p. 76.

Hardner, J. and R. Rice. 2001. Economic Opportunities for Forest Resource Use, in Pitou van Dijck (ed.), *Suriname, the Economy: Prospects for Sustainable Development*. Kingston, Jamaica: Ian Randle Publishers, pp. 247–271.

Harrison, James. 2008. International Law—Significant Environmental Cases 2007–08. *Journal of Environmental Law* 20:475–481.

Hilton, Spud. 2010. Developing World's 10 Best Ethical Destinations. *San Francisco Chronicle*, 3 January.

Hobsbawm, Eric. 1983. Introduction: Inventing Traditions, in Eric Hobsbawm and Terence Ranger, *The Invention of Tradition*. Cambridge, U.K.: Cambridge University Press, pp. 1–14.

Hoop, Carlo. 1991. *Verdronken land, Verdwenen dorpen: De transmigratie van Saramaccaners in Suriname 1958–1964*. Alkmaar, The Netherlands: Uitgeverij Bewustzijn.

Hulster, Daan de. 2009. Vereniging Saramaccaanse Gezagdragers: 'Tijd dringt voor uitvoering Samaaka-vonnis.' *De Ware Tijd*, 16 November.

Jaffe, Mark. 2001. Asian Companies Raid the Rain Forest in Weakly Regulated Countries. *Knight Ridder Tribune Business News*, 20 May.

Jolivet, Marie-José. 1982. *La question créole: essai de sociologie sur la Guyane française*. Paris: ORSTOM.

Kambel, Ellen-Rose. 2002. *Resource Conflicts, Gender and Indigenous Rights in Suriname: Local, National and Global Perspectives*. Leiden, The Netherlands: Proefschrift Universiteit Leiden.

———. 2007. Land, Development, and Indigenous Rights in Suriname: The Role of International Human Rights Law, in Jean Besson and Janet Henshall Momsen (eds.), *Caribbean Land and Development Revisited*. Gordonsville, Va.: Palgrave Macmillan, pp. 69–80.

Kambel, Ellen-Rose and Fergus MacKay. 1999. *The Rights of Indigenous Peoples and Maroons in Suriname*. Copenhagen: IWGIA.

Kingston, D. G. I., et al. 1999. The Suriname International Cooperative Biodiversity Group Program: Lessons From the First Five Years. *Pharmaceutical Biology* 37(1):22–34.

Lamur, Carlo. *The American Takeover: Industrial Emergence and Alcoa's Expansion in Guyana and Suriname 1914–1921*. Dordrecht, The Netherlands: Foris.

Landveld, Erney R. A. O. 1989. *Ganzë: het dorp dat het meer verdronk*. Utrecht, The Netherlands: Drukkerij Nout B.V.

MacKay, Fergus (ed.). 2006. *Moiwana zoekt gerechtigheid: De strijd van een Marrondorp tegen de staat Suriname*. Amsterdam: KIT Publishers.

———. 2010. *Saramaka: De strijd om het bos*. Amsterdam: KIT Publishers.

Matory, J. Lorand. 2005. *Black Atlantic Religion: Tradition, Transnationalism and Matriarchy in the Afro-Brazilian Candomblé*. Princeton: Princeton University Press.

Meel, Peter. 1990. Money Talks, Morals Vex: The Netherlands and the Decolonization of Suriname, 1975–1990. *European Review of Latin American and Caribbean Studies* 48: 75–98.

Mintz, Sidney W. and Richard Price. 1992. *The Birth of African-American Culture*. Boston: Beacon Press.

Moiwana'86. n.d. [ca. 1990]. *Memre Moiwana*. Paramaribo, Suriname.

———. 1992. *Mensenrechten 1991 Suriname*. Paramaribo, Suriname.

————. n.d. [ca. 1992]. *In Memoriam Herman Eddy Gooding: Viribus Audax, manmoedig door innerlijke kracht.* Paramaribo, Suriname.

Munneke, Harold F. 1991. Customary Law and National Legal System in the Dutch-speaking Caribbean, With Special Reference to Suriname. *European Review of Latin American and Caribbean Studies* 51:91–99.

Nassy, David de Ishak Cohen. 1788. *Essai historique sur la colonie de Surinam.* Paramaribo, Suriname.

Nowak, Manfred. 1989. *Suriname: An International Alert Report.* London: International Alert.

Oostindie, Gert. 1992. The Dutch Caribbean in the 1990s: Decolonization or Recolonization? *Caribbean Affairs* 5:103–119.

Orellana, Marcos A. 2008. Saramaka People v. Suriname. *American Journal of International Law* 102:841–847.

Padilla, David J. 1995. Reparations in *Aloeboetoe v. Suriname. Human Rights Quarterly* 17:541–555.

Pakosie, André R. M. 2005. Een analyse van het huidige conflict om het gaamanschap bij de Saamaka. *Siboga* 15(1):17–27.

Phillips, Fred Y. 2008. The Godfathers: Characteristics and Roles of Central Individuals in the Transformation of Techno-Regions. *Journal of CENTRUM Cathedra* 1(2):74–89.

Polimé, T. S. and H. U. E. Thoden van Velzen. 1988. *Vluchtelingen, opstandelingen en andere Bosnegers van Oost-Suriname, 1986–1988.* Utrecht, The Netherlands: Instituut voor Culturele Antropologie.

Price, Richard. 1983. *First-Time: The Historical Vision of an Afro-American People.* Baltimore: Johns Hopkins University Press. (2nd ed., Chicago, University of Chicago Press, 2002.)

————. 1983. *To Slay the Hydra: Dutch Colonial Perspectives on the Saramaka Wars.* Ann Arbor, Mich.: Karoma.

————. 1990. *Alabi's World.* Baltimore: Johns Hopkins University Press.

————. 1995. Executing Ethnicity: The Killings in Suriname. *Cultural Anthropology* 10:437–471.

————. 1998. Scrapping Maroon History: Brazil's Promise, Suriname's Shame. *New West Indian Guide* 72:233–255.

————. 2008. *Travels with Tooy: History, Memory, and the African American Imagination.* Chicago: University of Chicago Press.

Price, Richard and Sally Price. 1977. *Music from Saramaka.* Washington, D.C.: Smithsonian Folkways 4225 (CD).

————. 1991. *Two Evenings in Saramaka.* Chicago: University of Chicago Press.

————. 1992. *Equatoria.* New York: Routledge.

————. 1995. *Enigma Variations: A Novel.* Cambridge, Mass.: Harvard University Press.

————. 1995. *On the Mall: Presenting Maroon Tradition-Bearers at the 1992 FAF.* Bloomington: The Folklore Institute, Indiana University.

———. 2003. *Les Marrons*. Châteauneuf-le-Rouge, France: Vents d'ailleurs.

———. 2003. *The Root of Roots: Or, How Afro-American Anthropology Got Its Start*. Chicago: Prickly Paradigm Press.

Price, Sally. 1984. *Co-Wives and Calabashes*. Ann Arbor: University of Michigan Press. (2nd ed., 1993.)

———. 2010. "Return to the Quai Branly," *Museum Anthropology* 33:11–20.

Price, Sally and Richard Price. 1980. *Afro-American Arts of the Suriname Rain Forest*. Berkeley: University of California Press.

———. 1999. *Maroon Arts: Cultural Vitality in the African Diaspora*. Boston: Beacon Press.

Pross, Eliézer. 2010. "Transmigratie inheemsen, Para dreigt," *De Ware Tijd*, 11 June.

Quintus Bosz, A. J. A. 1954. *Drie eeuwen grondpolitiek in Suriname*. Assen, The Netherlands: Van Gorcum.

———. 1965. "De rechten van de bosnegers op de ontruimde gronden in het stuwmeergebied." *Surinaams Juristenblad*: 14–21.

Redfield, Peter. 2000. *Space in the Tropics: From Convicts to Rockets in French Guiana*. Berkeley: University of California Press.

Scholtens, Ben. *Bosnegers en overheid in Suriname: De ontwikkeling van de politieke verhouding 1651–1992*. Paramaribo, Suriname: Afdeling Cultuurstudies/Minov.

Shelton, Dinah L. 2008. Human Rights and the Environment. *Yearbook of International Environmental Law 2007*, Oxford University Press, pp. 163–172.

Solholm, Rolleiv. 2009. Guyana and Norway to Protect Rain Forest. NRK (Norwegian Broadcasting Corporation), 12 November.

Stedman, John Gabriel. 1988. *Narrative of a Five Years Expedition Against the Revolted Negroes of Surinam*, newly transcribed from the original 1790 manuscript, with an introduction and notes by Richard Price and Sally Price. Baltimore: Johns Hopkins University Press.

Suriname: An International Alert Report. 1988. London: International Alert.

Suriname: Violations of Human Rights. 1987. London: Amnesty International.

Suriname zoekt multilaterale boscompensatie. 2009. *De Ware Tijd*, 12 November.

Theije, Marjo de and Marieke Heemskerk. 2009. Moving Frontiers in the Amazon: Brazilian Small-Scale Gold Miners in Suriname. *European Review of Latin American and Caribbean Studies* 87:5–25.

Thoden van Velzen, H. U. E. 1990. The Maroon Insurgency: Anthropological Reflections on the Civil War in Suriname, in Gary Brana-Shute (ed.), *Resistance and Rebellion in Suriname: Old and New*. Williamsburg, Va., College of William and Mary, pp. 159–88.

———. 1988. "Ten geleide" and "Militaire patstelling beheerst Suriname," in T. S. Polimé and H. U. E. Thoden van Velzen, *Vluchtelingen, opstandelingen en andere Bosnegers van Oost-Suriname, 1986–1988*, Utrecht, The Netherlands, Instituut voor Culturele Antropologie, pp. 7–9, 14–25.

Thoden van Velzen, H. U. E. and W. van Wetering. 2004. *In the Shadow of the Oracle: Religion as Politics in a Suriname Maroon Society*. Long Grove, Ill.: Waveland.

Trouillot, Michel-Rolph. 1991. Anthropology and the Savage Slot: The Poetics and Politics of Otherness, in Richard Fox (ed.), *Recapturing Anthropology: Working in the Present*. Santa Fe, N.Mex.: SAR Press, pp. 17–44.

Tsing, Anna Lowenhaupt. 2004. *Friction: An Ethnography of Global Connection*. Princeton: Princeton University Press.

Verger, Pierre. 1957. *Notes sur le culte des Orisa et Vodun à Bahia, la Baie de tous les Saints, au Brésil et à l'ancienne Côte des Esclaves en Afrique*. Dakar, Senegal: IFAN.

———. 1981. *Orixás: Deuses Iorubás na África e no Novo Mundo*. Salvador, Brazil: Corrupio.

Vrede, I. 2001. Facing Violence Against Women in Indigenous Communities. The Case of Maroon Communities in Brokopondo District, Suriname. *Symposium 2001* "Gender violence, health and rights in the Americas" Cancun, Mexico, 4–7 June. Available at: http://www.paho.org/english/hdp/hdw/Suriname.pdf.

Walsh, John with Robert Gannon. 1967. *Time Is Short and the Water Rises*. New York: E. P. Dutton.

van Westerloo, Gerard and Willem Diepraam. 1975. *Frimangron*. Amsterdam: De Arbeiderspers.

Westoll, Andrew. 2008. *The Riverbones: Stumbling After Eden in the Jungles of Suriname*. Toronto: Emblem Editions.

Wolf, Eric R. 1982. *Europe and the People Without History*. Berkeley: University of California Press.

Zandgrond, Fenny. 2009. Verharde Afobakaweg officieel geopend: "Marrons moeten harder aanpakken." *De Ware Tijd*, 24 November.

Zwamborn, Marcel. 1992. Suriname, in *Human Rights in Developing Countries*. Utrecht, The Netherlands: Studie- en Informatiecentrum Mensenrechten, Rijksuniversiteit te Utrecht, pp. 1–30.

Illustration Credits

Archives Départementales de la Guyane: p. 46. Martha Cooper: pp. 123, 124. Toon Fey: p. 102. Vicente Franco (Goldman Environmental Prize): p. 116. Antonia Graeber: p. 36. Marieke Heemskerk: pp. 134, 135. Inter-American Court of Human Rights: p. 70. Will Parrinello (Goldman Environmental Prize): pp. 105, 119. Richard Price: pp. 22, 23, 24, 44, 63, 159. Sally Price: pp. 20, 89, 155, 157, 159, 160, 164, 182. Richard or Sally Price: pp. 19, 93. Jason Rothe: p. 31. Wilhelmina van Wetering: p. 21.

From Books

pp. 4, 5: John Gabriel Stedman, *Narrative of a Five Years Expedition Against the Revolted Negroes of Surinam*, newly transcribed from the original 1790 manuscript, with an introduction and notes by Richard Price and Sally Price, (Baltimore: Johns Hopkins University Press, 1988), pp. 105, 403.

p. 17: Willem van de Poll, *Suriname: Een fotoreportage van land en volk* (The Hague: W. van Hoeve, 1959).

p. 30: John Walsh, with Robert Gannon, *Time Is Short and the Water Rises* (New York: E. P. Dutton, 1967), p. 30.

p. 32: O. J. R. Jozefzoon, *De Saramaccaanse wereld* (Paramaribo: Varekamp, 1959), p. 28.

Photographer Unknown

p. 126: Print courtesy Moesoela Amiemba.

p. 108: Photo may be by Peter Poole, but he is unsure—the image, dated 2000, is attributed to him at http://treesnotgunns.org/fileadmin/materials/old_growth/trees_not_gunns/Legal_Forest_Destruction_-_February_2006.pdf.

Acknowledgments

My forty-four-year relationship with hundreds, if not thousands, of Sarama-kas has incurred debts far too numerous to list here. May this book take its place among my other efforts to give them something in return.

A tension between my roles as full-time scholar and part-time activist has colored these pages in subtle ways. And the realities of ongoing and potential future litigation concerning Suriname has imposed more specific constraints on the way I have told this story, rendering it less colorful than I would otherwise have wished.

Fergus MacKay has been of incomparable assistance in helping me understand legal issues, in giving me access to documents, and in restraining my prose, and I am deeply grateful to him. Nonetheless, I alone bear all responsibility for the contents of this book, including all opinions expressed and any remaining errors of fact.

I would like to thank Gilles Colleu for help with a number of photographic images, and all the photographers and organizations listed in the credits, who generously allowed their images to be used in this book. I also thank Meredith Mahoney for drafting the two maps and Peter Poole for providing a scan of the Saramakas' map.

I am grateful to Ken Bilby, John Collins, Leah Price, and Niko Price who kindly read a draft of the book and offered a number of helpful comments. Sally Price has accompanied me, as always, on every single step of this adventure... 'Nough said.